Law and Employment

GW00976124

Contracts

Olga Aikin, LL.B. FIPD, graduated with a first-class honours degree in Law from the London School of Economics, qualified as a barrister and is a Sloan Fellow of the London Business School, where she taught for several years. She was a Council Member of ACAS from 1982 to 1985, Legal Adviser to the Industrial Society and was a member of the IPM National Committee for Employee Relations from 1986 to 1992. She writes regularly for *Personnel Management* and other legal and management journals.

Olga Aikin is the Senior Partner in the Aikin Driver Partnership, which specialises in the provision of advice on matters relating to employment law. Other publications include *Employment Welfare and Safety at Work* (with Judith Reid, Penguin, 1971) and *Legal Problems of Employment* (with Sonia Pearson, Industrial Society, 2nd edition, 1990).

Law and Employment series

General editor: Olga Aikin

The law relating to employment can seem labyrinthine – but with today's escalating number of legal claims, managers ignore it at their peril.

Managers must be able to construct sound yet flexible and progressive employment policies built on firm legal foundations. This important series will enable them to meet the challenge. It forms a superbly practical and, above all, accessible source of reference on employment practice and the law.

The IPD specially commissioned Olga Aikin – one of the UK's foremost authorities on employment law, a qualified barrister and well-known legal writer – to steer the project. Individual titles have been written by leading legal experts and human resource practitioners. Together they provide a unique combination of up-to-date legal guidance with in-depth advice on current employment issues.

Other titles in the series include:

Discipline
Philip James and David Lewis

Discrimination
2nd edition
Linda Clarke

Industrial Tribunals
2nd edition
Roger Greenhalgh

Stress and Employer Liability
Jill Earnshaw and Cary Cooper

The Institute of Personnel and Development is the leading publisher of books and reports for personnel and training professionals and students and for all those concerned with the effective management and development of people at work. For full details of all our titles please telephone the Publishing Department on 0181 263 3387.

Law and Employment series

Contracts

Olga Aikin

INSTITUTE OF PERSONNEL AND DEVELOPMENT

For my husband, Michael Driver

First published 1992
Second edition 1997

Typesetting by The Comp-Room, Aylesbury
and printed in Great Britain by
Short Run Press Ltd, Exeter

British Library Cataloguing in Publication Data

A catalogue record for this book is available from the British Library

ISBN 0-85292-672-3

INSTITUTE OF PERSONNEL
AND DEVELOPMENT

IPD House, Camp Road, London SW19 4UX
Tel: 0181 971 9000   Fax: 0181 263 3333
Registered office as above. Registered Charity No. 1038333
A company limited by guarantee. Registered in England No. 2931892

Contents

Contents

List of tables

General editor's foreword

This series is essentially a user's guide to employment law and good employment practice. The objective is to provide managers, trade unionists and the employees themselves with a basic understanding of the legal rules and basic principles which affect the employment relationship. There is no intention of turning everyone into a lawyer, but today a little knowledge of employment law is far from dangerous and a fair amount can be a positive advantage.

In the past 30 years we have moved away from a situation in which the law relating to employment could be ignored, in which legal actions were few and far between, into one in which the number of legal claims is increasing and in which the law is becoming far more complex. But this does not mean that it is a matter for lawyers, or, even when lawyers are essential, that the decisions have to be left to them alone. Lawyers and consultants can only advise. Business decisions have to be made by managers; employees have to decide whether there is an advantage in suing. The law is rarely 100 per cent certain and the ultimate decision has to be made by the client.

The law is not enough. The purpose of the law is to set minima and devise means of dealing with the fall-back situation when the parties cannot reach a solution. Good employment relations demand far more than mere compliance with legal requirements. They require an understanding of the nature of the relationship between employer and employee and how the manager manages it.

This series is concerned not only with the practical application of the law but also with the problems and issues which arise before, during and after employment. For this reason it starts with the practical situation and explains the law relating to it, the pitfalls and advantages, and suggests approaches which may be helpful.

The authors are all experts in their fields and combine legal knowledge with practical expertise.

Olga Aikin

List of abbreviations

AC	Appeal Cases
ACAS	Advisory, Conciliation and Abitration Service
All ER	All England Law Reports
CA	Court of Appeal
CBNS	Common Bench New Series
Ch(D)	Chancery (Division)
CS(OH)	Court of Session (Outer House)
Ct Sess	Court of Session
EAT	Employment Appeal Tribunal
ECJ	European Court of Justice
EP(C)A	Employment Protection (Consolidation) Act 1978
EU	European Union
HL	House of Lords
ICR	Industrial Cases Reports
IDS	Incomes Data Services
IRL(I)B	Industrial Relations Legal (Information) Bulletin
IRLR	Industrial Relations Law Reports
IT	Industrial Tribunal
ITR	Industrial Tribunal Reports
KB	King's Bench
LIFO	Last in, first out
NHS	National Health Service
NIHC	Norther Ireland High Court
PAYE	Pay As You Earn
PC	Privy Council
QB(D)	Queen's Bench (Division)
RPC	Restrictive Practices Court
SSP	Statutory Sick Pay
TLR	Times Law Reports
TULR(C)A	Trade Union and Labour Relations (Consolidation) Act 1992
TURERA	Trade Union Reform and Employment Rights Act (1993)
WLR	Weekly Law Reports

Acknowledgements

This book is the culmination of long and dedicated training given to me by many clients. It was their explanation of their particular needs and requirements which led me to look beyond the law and to realise that the most important part of drafting any contract was not producing the right words in elegant form but identifying a satisfactory compromise between the conflicting desires of the two parties. No amount of elegant words are an adequate substitute for an ill-thought-out deal. Of course all errors remain my own responsibility, but I should like, publicly, to thank all those who have contributed to my education.

I should also like to thank the IPD, and in particular Anne Cordwent, Judith Dennett and Matthew Reisz, without whose encouragement the book would never have been completed. I sorely tested their patience yet they constantly treated me with kindness.

Further thanks are due to Dawn Woodward, who not only became expert at deciphering my scrawl but also became quite interested in the contents, and to Gareth ValentineGriffiths, who managed to create time for me to write. As always, my thanks to my husband whose support was invaluable and who survived the shortfall in output from the kitchen.

This series has been produced for instruction and information. Whilst every care has been taken in the preparation of the books, they should not be used to provide precedents for drawing up contracts or policies. All terms should be carefully considered in the light of the prevailing law and the needs of the organisation. When in doubt, it is recommended that professional legal advice is sought. Please note also that all references to 'he' and 'his' should be taken as applying to both men and women.

1
The objectives

Traditionally in the United Kingdom far less attention has been paid to the formalities of employment contracts than to those of commercial contracts. There is a good reason for this. Contracts tend to be well documented and detailed only when there is a risk of legal action, and for many years the legal remedies available to most employees were so meagre that few bothered to enforce their legal rights, leaving both employment contracts and employment law underdeveloped.

The main remedy available to employees at common law is to sue for damages for breach of contract. The most common breach is failure to give proper notice to terminate the contract. The contract can always be ended by giving proper notice, and no reason has to be provided. If there is serious breach of contract going to the root of the contract the contract can be terminated summarily, without notice. Damages will be the equivalent of the employee's contractual remuneration package for the period of notice. Prior to the introduction of statutory minimum periods of notice in 1963, notice was short for most employees – even perhaps as short as a shift of 20 minutes, so there was little incentive to take legal action.

But circumstances have changed, and indeed are still changing. First, employment protection rights introduced in the 1960s and 1970s are based on contract terms. For example:

- An employee is redundant if fewer people are needed at his place of work (Employment Rights Act 1996, s. 139(1)) and this place is determined by his contract.
- A woman returning from maternity leave returns to 'the job in which she was employed under the original contract of employment' (Employment Rights Act 1996, s. 79(2)).
- Constructive dismissal is dependent upon serious breach of a contract term by the employer (Employment Rights Act 1996, s. 95(1)(c)).

So the contract terms have considerable impact on statutory employment rights, and constant reference of those rights to the tribunals has resulted in a review and development of basic contractual rights. The total number of cases referred to the ACAS conciliation officers in 1995 was 84,564, and this figure does not include redundancy claims.[1] Many of the claims were settled or withdrawn, but the number of claims is increasing every year and illustrates the growing willingness of employees to litigate. Even the cases that were settled or withdrawn necessitated management attention and so incurred costs.

Secondly, contract terms have improved, with better salary and benefits being provided and with the contractual notice frequently exceeding the statutory minimum period. This has encouraged claims for damages. One drawback to these claims used to be that, although claims for £5,000 or less could be brought in the lower civil courts (the county courts in England and Wales, sheriff's courts in Scotland), larger claims had to be commenced in the High Court or the Court of Session, involving greater cost and delay. But the upper limit of the lower courts was raised to £50,000, and this is likely to encourage breach of contract claims. In 1994 the tribunals were given additional jurisdiction in breach of contract (now Industrial Tribunals Act 1996 s. 3(2)). This is proving to be a popular ground for complaint to the tribunal with ACAS dealing with 15,371 breach of contract referrals in 1995.[2] One major attraction of breach of contract claims is that they require no qualifying period of service.

No doubt it is this prospect of legal claims in both courts and tribunals which has caused employers to pay more attention to contract terms. Perhaps the revelation to dismissed employees of the extent to which their termination payments are based on their contract terms has made them also appreciate their importance.

But a well-drafted contract offers far more than grounds for legal action and defences to claims. It is the basis of the employment relationship, and it can provide positive benefits as well as be the source of claim or defence in the breakdown situation.

It is the contract which provides the legal framework of the employment relationship. The contract is in essence the expression of the aspirations of the parties. It should be approached by both parties in the same way as any other negotiation. Each should have identified the terms which are essential to them, those which are desirable, and those which are of lesser interest. Many employers do so – but fewer employees give it sufficient attention. Yet unless the employee also understands the terms and their implication he may enter into a contract which will be unsatisfactory for him and may lead to his departure and a search for new employment.

The contract, if it is to be effective, needs to be balanced. The employer gains as little from a contract which is too beneficial to him and too detrimental to the employee as he does from one which gives everything to the employee and nothing to the employer. Rather the terms should amount to an acceptable compromise between the aspirations of both parties from which both parties can benefit.

The terms will also express the risks each is willing to take. The employee who signs a contract containing a worldwide relocation clause accepts the risk of being moved at short notice to a far-flung corner of the world. The employer whose contract has a term fixing hours as 9.00 a.m. to 5.00 p.m. without mandatory overtime accepts the risk that staff will not work overtime to meet unexpected demand.

Although, especially where industrial relations are good, parties normally accommodate each other's extra-contractual requirements, the contract terms set out the fall-back position. If this is clear, legal disputes can be avoided, because the parties can easily see where they stand, and they, or their representatives, can easily identify their respective rights and duties.

A well considered contract can also make arrangements for flexibility. As, once the terms are agreed, neither party can change them without the consent of the other, flexibility is very difficult to achieve unless it is provided for in the contract itself.

Finally, the employer is under a duty by virtue of the Employment Rights Act 1996, s. 1, to give each employee written particulars of certain key terms in his contract. This can be fulfilled by the contract itself.

Key points

The contract can

- avoid legal claims
- provide a legal framework for the employment relationship
- set out the aspirations and risks of the parties
- identify the fall-back position
- provide for flexibility
- meet certain legal requirements.

References

1 ACAS Annual Report, 1995.
2 ACAS Annual Report, 1995.

Part I
The mechanics

2
Introduction

Contracts are normally described as legally binding agreements. They must be distinguished from agreements which have no binding effect.

The modern rules for making contracts were developed during the nineteenth century and are based on the twin concepts of *laissez-faire* and the equality of man. It is assumed that the contract is a bargain reached after two equal parties have negotiated the individual terms. In the area of employment this was quite unlikely to have been the case in the nineteenth century and in many instances is untrue today. But, generally speaking, little attention is paid to the fact that the parties may have unequal bargaining power, that bargaining may be non-existent or that the bargaining may be between union and employer, with the employee having no role at all. However, one or two judges are beginning to question the suitability of these old concepts in today's conditions and to impose a duty on employers to draw their employees' attention to certain terms which have not been individually negotiated. Thus in *Scally v. Southern Health and Social Services Board (1991)*[1] the House of Lords decided that the employer should have drawn employees' attention to a term in the superannuation scheme which, for a few years, permitted employees to buy additional years of pension at advantageous rates.

Employment contracts, like most other contracts, do not have to be made in any particular form, although, once made, certain key terms ('written particulars') have to be notified to the employee in writing. Obviously it is advisable to put as much as possible into writing so that the terms are certain.

Contracts and agreements

Although contracts are frequently referred to as agreements, the fact that the parties are in agreement does not prove that a contract exists. A contract exists only when it can be proved that there is;

- an offer
- acceptance
- consideration (causa in Scotland)
- intention to create legal relations.

So it is possible to have a contract when the parties are not in agreement because, perhaps, the employer was not aware that he had made an offer, or there may be an actual agreement but no offer and acceptance can be identified. The latter situation is unlikely to cause problems so long as both parties wish the contract to exist. The former, occasionally, does.

Offer

An offer is usually described as an expression of willingness to be legally bound. Offers must be distinguished from 'invitations to treat'. An invitation to treat is a statement which is intended to get people excited about or interested in the prospect of entering into a contract when the person making it lacks the intention of being legally bound. It is not the actual intention of the individual which concerns the court but his intention as perceived from his actions. Ultimately the courts will decide whether or not a person intended to be bound. The courts normally hold that job advertisements, job information and application forms are invitations to treat. However, the employer may at some subsequent point incorporate the advert in the offer – for example, by offering employment on the terms as set out in the advertisement or the job information. Or the advert may be a guide to the employer's intentions.

When the offer is made all the key terms must be identifiable. Either they may be expressed or there must be some indication of where they can be found. So the offer may refer to pension schemes, staff handbooks or collective agreements or other documents. They do not have to be set out, but it must be possible to identify them. This is illustrated by *Loftus v. Roberts (1902)*.[2] A man was employed at a 'West End salary to be mutually arranged'. No salary was ever agreed and from the term itself it was not possible to say what the sum should be. Because a key term was missing the court held that there was no contract. If the parties had added in some mechanism, such as arbitration, which would have produced a decision in the event of their failure to agree, then the wage would have been ascertainable and there would have been a valid contract. Such key or skeletal terms can be fleshed out later with implied terms. It is not possible to list the key terms. 'Wage' is one and 'the work' must surely be another.

Offers do not last for ever and are subject to a time limit. This may be specified in the offer itself, otherwise the offer remains open for a reasonable time. A 'reasonable time' is difficult to define, and it is obviously better for the offer to set the time for acceptance. The offer may be withdrawn at any time before acceptance, but withdrawal is effective only when received by the candidate.

Sometimes offers are conditional on the receipt of references, passing an examination, obtaining release from an existing contract, etc. These are not valid offers until the condition has been fulfilled, and only then can they be accepted and a valid contract come into existence. Any purported acceptance before the fulfilment of the condition is ineffective until suitable references, etc., have been received.

References cause particular problems. If the employer simply specifies that the reference must be 'satisfactory' it is not entirely clear whether it is to be assessed on the basis of some general objective standard or by the subjective standard set by the prospective employer. It may well be the latter. In *Wishart v. National Association of Citizens Advice Bureaux (1990)*[3] the employer required 'satisfactory references'. The references supplied did not meet the employer's standard but the employee considered they were satisfactory. Wishart sought a mandatory injunction to force the employer to employ him. This the Court of Appeal refused, as such orders are rarely given. But two of the judges said that they thought the employer's standard would apply, though there was a strong argument in favour of the objective standard. So they sat on the fence. The employer can avoid the problem by requiring the reference to be 'satisfactory to us', which will ensure that the employer's standard will apply.[4]

Acceptance

Acceptance must be complete and unequivocal. A positive act is required. Doing nothing does not amount to acceptance.

Acceptance must not be conditional. It must amount to 'yes' and not 'yes, but'. There must be no conditions attached to it. If a condition is attached, then it is not acceptance but a counter-offer. So if a candidate were to write, 'I am delighted to accept your offer but I want the notice period to be six months, not three,' he is still bargaining, he is not accepting. And technically he is making a counter-offer. This has the effect of removing the offer of employment on three months' notice and that offer is no longer available for him to accept unless it is renewed by the employer.

Acceptance must be within the specified time. If no time is specified, then it must be within a reasonable time.

Usually the person accepting is required to notify the person making the offer before the acceptance is complete. Theoretically, it is possible to waive the requirement of notification for acceptance. In an employment situation, however, this is highly unlikely and would be completely undesirable. It is essential for an employer to know whether a prospective employee has accepted the offer or not.

Unless the offer provides otherwise, the applicant may inform the employee of his acceptance in any normal manner, including by post. Acceptance by post is complete when the letter is put in the post box, not when it is received. To avoid problems, many organisations require acceptance to be notified to a particular person by the end of normal working hours on a set date. If acceptance has not been received by then the offer terminates. It does not, however, prevent the employer contacting the applicant to check whether he does indeed wish to accept the offer.

Consideration

The law in England and Wales views contracts as bargains. Although the bargain does not have to be fair, each party must get something of value out of it. This is known as consideration. Consideration may be a detriment suffered by the other party or a benefit received from that party. Each party must give and receive consideration.

Consideration may consist of an act or a promise. Normally the consideration consists of an exchange of promises: the employee promises to be ready, able and willing to perform work in accordance with the contract in return for a promise to pay wages. But occasionally wages may be due only if the work is actually completed – a promise to pay in return for actual work. In one old case a sailor was to be paid 30 guineas if he completed a voyage from Jamaica to England. He died just before the voyage was complete. His estate was not entitled to any money because payment was due only when there had been complete performance of the task.[5] This type of arrangement is very rare.

The concept of causa used in Scotland is wider. It includes moral obligations.

Intention to create legal relations

This is another element which is designed to distinguish legally binding contracts from mere agreements. In commercial and employment contracts the necessary intention is presumed. If, therefore, the parties wish their employment agreement to have no legal effect they must make express provision to that effect in the agreement. Such agreements are known as 'gentlemen's agreements' because it was assumed that a gentleman's word was his bond and no legal enforceability was necessary.

There are, however, three areas in which intention is relevant. The first is where an individual may be performing work out of the kindness of his heart and without expectation of payment. This uncertainty can arise where relatives or friends help in small businesses or when people work for charities. In such instances it should be made clear whether there is employment or not.

The second is the unpaid volunteer or honorary contract. Although it has often been assumed that these are gentlemen's agreements because of lack of pay, this is not necessarily so. The volunteer may be obtaining key experience to enter a course or obtain other employment. In these cases there could well be an enforceable contract unless the terms provide otherwise.

The third area is that of collective agreements. Since *Young v. Canadian Northern Railway Company (1931)*[6] the courts have held that collective agreements are not intended to be legally binding unless the terms so provide. This is now enshrined in statute (Trade Union and Labour Relations (Consolidation) Act 1992, s. 79).

Flawed contracts

A contract may contain all these essential elements but nonetheless be flawed. Where the flaw is serious the contract is void; less serious flaws render it voidable. A void contract is a complete nullity, one that has never existed, so money and goods obtained under such a contract have to be returned. Voidable contracts can be set aside by the court at the request of the parties.

The commonest flaws are mistake and illegality both of which render the contract void; and misrepresentation, fraud, duress and undue influence, which make the contract voidable.

Mistake

To have the effect of making the contract void the mistake must be a serious mistake of fact going to the root of the contract: it must be a fundamental mistake. Such a mistake is difficult to prove. In *Bell v. Lever Bros (1932)*[7] the employer paid the employee £30,000 as a settlement to terminate a contract. Had he known that the employee had invested in competitors contrary to the contract terms he could have terminated the contract summarily without payment. The employer's mistake, though expensive, was not fundamental. He had got what he had bargained for, termination, although, had he known all the facts, he could have achieved his object more cheaply. In *Bell* the employee did not deliberately conceal any facts from the employer. The employer's hand is strengthened if his mistake is induced by his employee's fraud. In *Sybron Corporation v. Rochem (1983)*[8] managers concealed the fact that they were siphoning off work from their employer to their own companies. This was fraudulent, and so the employer was able to rely on his mistake to void pension schemes entered into during the period of fraud.

The most common mistakes are to offer a wage higher than the one intended or to offer employment at a higher grade. In order to constitute an operative mistake the error must be obvious. Generally mistakes like these are not operative mistakes, and the employer must negotiate himself out of the situation. The mistake will be operative if it is an obvious one – for example, offering a wage of £200,000 instead of £20,000 or the position of managing director instead of secretary to the managing director. But placing an employee too high on a wage band is unlikely to be an operative mistake.

Illegality

The concept of illegality is an extremely difficult one. Contracts which are illegal are not enforced by the courts. They are said to be void, but this is not strictly true. If a contract were void then the position would be as if the contract had never existed, and all money, etc., would have to be returned. Illegal contracts are quite simply not enforced by the courts. Money is not returned. The loss lies where it falls. So an employee does not have to return wages paid to him, but cannot claim unpaid wages. Nor can he sue for breach of contract or claim unfair dismissal or redundancy benefit.

Deciding whether a contract is tainted with illegality is not easy. Contracts to perform unlawful acts such as crimes or serious civil wrongs are illegal. Contracts are illegal if they are contrary to statute. The courts may also declare a contract to be illegal because it is contrary to public policy, which has not been defined and is adjusted by the courts to take into account current *mores*. What amounts to public policy is determined by the court and not by the government. In *Allen v. Thorn Electrical Industries (1968)*,[9] it was decided that a contract to pay a wage increase was not contrary to public policy even though the government believed it was contrary to the national interest and it was contrary to the government's policy of imposing wage restraint. This difficulty was avoided in a later pay freeze by making the freeze retrospective by legislation to the date of the White Paper declaring the intention of imposing restraint.

The illegality may occur in two ways. The contract may be illegal on the face of it, clearly involving the performance of an unlawful act, or the illegality may arise only in the way the party or parties decide to perform it. In *Coral Leisure v. Barnett (1977)*[10] it was alleged that the employment contract involved illegal performance because the employee was required to provide women for a casino's clients. That would have made the contract illegal. But every unlawful act committed during the performance of a contract does not render a contract illegal. A driver who exceeds the speed limit is unlikely to render his contract void by his unlawful act. Unless it is actually proscribed by statute the court will decide whether the unlawful act taints the contract with illegality.

For the contract to be totally unenforceable the parties must be equally guilty, *in pari delicto*. If one party is innocent that party will normally be permitted to enforce the contract.

These rules are well illustrated by cases concerning one of the common illegalities affecting employment contracts, namely tax evasion. Tax evasion is illegal and renders the contract void. In *Newland v. Simons & Willer (Hairdressers) (1981)*[11] a young assistant did not know that it was unlawful to be paid wages only partly with a wage slip showing tax and National Insurance deducted from the written sum, the remainder coming as cash without reductions from the till. She was innocent and could enforce the employment contract and claim unfair dismissal. On the other hand in *Hyland v. Barker (1985)*[12] an employee received unlawful tax-free expenses for a period of working away from home. Because he knew this was illegal his contract was void for the period of the illegality. This amounted to an interruption of his continuity of employment, so that when he was made redundant he lacked sufficient continuity of employment after the interruption to be entitled to claim redundancy benefit.

Misrepresentation

Contracts which are voidable can be set aside by the courts at the request of one of the parties so long as:

- no one outside the contract has acquired any interest in the contract (this is unlikely in employment contracts)
- there has been no approval since the misrepresentation came to light
- there has been no delay in seeking redress.

Where the representation was made negligently and/or fraudulently the representer may also be sued for damages.

A representation is innocent where the representer is unaware of its falsity. A representation is negligent when the representer, although unaware of its falsity, should have known it was not correct. A fraudulent misrepresentation is one which is made knowingly or recklessly, without regard to whether it is true or false. Damages may be obtained where loss results from negligent or fraudulent misrepresentation but not for innocent misrepresentation. Under the Misrepresentation Act 1967 representations made to induce a person to enter into a contract are presumed to be negligent, and so, to avoid damages, the representer has to prove his innocence.

Usually the misrepresentation is made by the employee. He may make positive claims of qualification he does not possess or of positions he has not held, as in *Johnson v. Tesco Stores (1977)*,[13] where a trainee manager declared he had for six years been in the service of a company which had never employed him. Or it may consist of failure to disclose information, as in *O'Brien v. Prudential Assurance (1979)*,[14] where the employee withheld information concerning a mental breakdown. The information must affect the decision to employ, and the candidates must be aware that it should be disclosed. If the form itself provides that 'any mis-statement or failure to provide the information requested will render this contract and any subsequent contract void' the applicant should be fully aware of the consequences. In practice employers do not usually apply to the courts in such cases to have the contract set aside. They dismiss the employee instead. Where the misrepresentation is relevant to selection the dismissal will be fair. *Johnson* and *O'Brien* were both dismissal cases.

Although most misrepresentations tend to be made by the employee, some may occur as a consequence of the employer's actions. One such case was *McNally v. Welltrade International (1978)*,[15] where a candidate was assured, despite his own doubts, that his experience was relevant to a job abroad in a refinery. He accepted the position, only to be dismissed a few weeks later because he lacked oil industry experience. The recruiter had been negligent in giving his assurance and was held liable for his negligent misstatement, McNally being awarded £1,965.26 damages. It is worth noting that, although it is unusual to sue the employee for negligence, it is an employee (in this case the recruiting employee) who is actually negligent. The employer is vicariously liable for an employee's negligence if it occurs in the course of his employment. This is in addition to the employee's liability, not as substitution for it. Both are liable, although the plaintiff does not receive double compensation.

Duress and undue influence

These rarely occur in relation to employment contracts. Duress arises when one person forces another to enter into a contract by using threats, and undue influence arises when excessive influence deprives a contracting party of his free will. Such contracts can be avoided by the party who suffered the duress or undue influence.

Key points

- Make it clear when an offer is being made.
- Specify time and manner of acceptance.
- Avoid promises which are made outside the contract.
- Check offer document for mistakes.

References

1 4 All ER 563, IRLR 522 HL.
2 18 TLR 532 CA.
3 ICR 794, TLR 489 CA.
4 Since *Spring v. Guardian Assurance plc* (1994) IRLR 460 HL it is now clear that employers are liable for negligent references not only to the recipient but also to the employee. Lord Woolf also stated that there might be a legal duty to provide a reference because the employer was a member of a body requiring references to be given (in this case LAUTRO), or because references were normally required to obtain that particular type of job.
5 *Cutter v. Powell (1795)* 6 Term. Rep. 320.
6 AC 83 HL.
7 AC 161 HL.
8 IRLR 253.
9 1 QB 487.
10 IRLR 204 EAT.
11 IRLR 359.
12 IRLR 403 EAT.
13 IRLR 103 IT.
14 IRLR 140 EAT.
15 IRLR 497 QB.

3

The manner of making contracts

There is no prescribed form for making employment contracts. They may be written, oral, or even made by conduct.

Conduct

Contracts made entirely by conduct on the part of both parties are very rare but theoretically possible. It is not uncommon, however, for the contract to be made partially by conduct. Offers made through conduct may be distinctly unusual, but acceptance by conduct is not. Acceptance by conduct can occur when an offer is made, the applicant does not notify his acceptance to the employer, but starts work under that contract. His working is an act of acceptance. Or there may be acceptance by conduct of a variation in the contract terms when an employer proposes new shift hours and the employee does not formally accept the variation but works the new hours. Conduct is not an advisable mode of entering into agreements. It can be ambiguous. The intention of the person concerned is not always clear, and whenever possible contracts should be made in a more formal manner.

Oral contracts

Although oral contracts are valid contracts there is always the problem of proof. The recollections of the parties may not be identical or may be hazy. Memory is not always reliable. Where there is a dispute over oral agreements the court or tribunal will decide whose version is the correct one. This will be more difficult if the dispute arises some considerable time after the event. In *Lassey v. Salterville Nursing Home (1988)*[1] the tribunal had to decide whether, at an interview which had taken place some two and a half years earlier, the employer had given an oral binding undertaking to Miss Lassey that he would upgrade the facilities and improve the standard of nursing care provided at his nursing home. The burden of proving that the promise was made lay upon Miss Lassey but it was not a heavy burden. Whether a statement has been made or not depends on the balance of probabilities; it does not have to be proved beyond all reasonable doubt. So once Miss Lassey had put her version

16

forward the burden of proof shifted to Dr Salterville and the tribunal had to decide which version they thought was the right one. The tribunal, and on appeal the EAT, decided in Miss Lassey's favour. Some two and a half years after the event an oral promise was proved to have been made.

The belief of many managers – and some employees too – that oral terms cannot be proved is based on false foundations. For the sake of certainty, if a term is worth agreeing, it is worth recording it in writing. Preferably it should be put in the contract itself. If it is not put into the contract a 'contemporaneous note' should be made. A contemporaneous note is any note made close to the event. Notes written up immediately after the interview would suffice. Contemporaneous notes are not conclusive proof of their content, but they are admitted as evidence. And employees who receive an oral undertaking would be well advised to write a confirming letter or at least to make a contemporaneous note.

Written terms

This is by far the most satisfactory form of contract. The terms are the easiest to prove and the least likely to be uncertain. However, it is unusual for a document to set out every term in writing. It is far more common for part to be set out in writing and the rest to be found in other documents incorporated into the contract.

Incorporated terms

The reference in a contractual document such as an offer of employment to another document – perhaps a collective agreement, staff handbook or pension scheme – will incorporate the relevant part of that other document contract.

This is an extremely useful way of avoiding lengthy contracts – but it does have its drawbacks. There may be a conflict between the terms set out in the offer and those in the agreement, etc. Also it is not always clear whether all or only parts of the agreement handbook or scheme are to be incorporated into the employment contract; and if only parts are to be incorporated, which parts are they?

Incorporating collective agreements
Collective agreements themselves are presumed not to be legally binding between the parties to them, i.e. the union and the employer. This was the position at common law and it has been given statutory authority by the Trade Union and Labour Relations (Consolidation) Act 1992, s. 179, which provides that collective agreements are presumed not to be legally binding. If the parties want the agreement to be binding they can rebut

this presumption by putting the terms in writing and expressly stating that they have legal effect. Most collective agreements include a contrary provision stating they are not to have legal effect, even though this is not strictly necessary.

In *Marley v. Forward Trust Group (1986)*[2], the Court of Appeal was faced with an interesting problem. The employer and employee both accepted that a collective agreement on redundancy had been incorporated into the contract of employment. The collective agreement contained an express term to the effect that it was not intended to be legally binding. Did this only apply as between the union and the employer or did it mean that even when the agreement was incorporated into the employment contract it had no legal effect and so gave no redundancy rights to the employee? The court held that once it had been incorporated into the employment contract it was the perceived intention of the employer and employee that mattered and not the intention of the union and employer. The employer and union might have intended the agreement to have no legal effect between themselves, but the employer and employee could, and in the view of the court did, intend the agreement to be binding as part of the employment contract. So the provision that the collective agreement was of no legal effect was relevant only in relation to the enforcement of the collective agreement; it had no effect in relation to the contract between the employer and employee. The parties to the employment contract were found to have intended the redundancy agreement to be an enforceable part of the employment contract.

So, legally, there are two quite separate agreements – the collective agreement and the employment contract. This becomes very clear when the employer wants to change the terms in the contract which have been incorporated from the collective agreement. Changing or getting rid of the collective agreement will not necessarily change or remove the employment term. The term in the employment contract has to be changed as well. In *Robertson v. British Gas Corporation (1983)*,[3] British Gas had employed staff under an incentive terms scheme, to be calculated in accordance with the rules agreed in collective agreements with the union. Contrary to the wishes of the men and union, the employer wanted to dispense with the scheme. So British Gas gave notice to terminate the collective agreement. This removed the collective provision but had no effect on the terms incorporated into the employment contracts. They remained firmly in place until the employment contract was changed in accordance with the rules for changing employment contracts.

One partial way around such an impasse is to ensure that future collective agreements are automatically incorporated into the contract. If an employee is engaged on 'the terms set out in the agreement with the union', only the terms of the union agreement then in effect are incorporated. Compare this with *Callison v. Ford (1969)*.[4] Callison's contract provided that it was 'subject to the terms of agreements made from time to time between the company and the trade unions'. A collective agreement completely changed both job classification and pay. Callison said they had no right to regrade him, but the tribunal held that his terms automatically changed when the new collective agreement became operative.

For employers who negotiate employment terms collectively the advantages of expressly incorporating collective agreements and using phrases like, 'such as may be agreed from time to time' is obvious. The current and future collective agreements can be incorporated into every employee's contract. Their consent is not required. They need not be union members.

But what is a collective agreement? The union may approve or accept the employer's action, but that does not make a collective agreement. In *Tucker v. British Leyland Motor Corporation (1978)*[5] the union did not object to the employer's transferring, contrary to the contract terms, several days of the employees' annual leave to fill the slot between Christmas and New Year and so enable the plant to shut down. Future collective agreements were incorporated into the contract. But this, held the court, was not a collective agreement. There is a difference between a management decision reached after union consultation and a collective agreement.

A collective agreement can be incorporated only when it is complete. In *Ford v. AEU (1969)*[6] the court held that the agreement came into effect only when it had been formally signed by all the unions and the employer. On the other hand, in *York City & District Travel v. Smith (1990)*[7] the EAT decided the agreement was effected when it was agreed and before it was signed. The time of effectiveness will be the time the parties treat it as effective – when the formalities were complete in *Ford* and upon agreement in *York City*.

Not all incorporation arrangements are clear and precise. In such instances the outcome of any legal dispute is difficult to predict. This is sadly illustrated by the two cases of *Alexander v. Standard Telephones & Cables (1990)*[8] and *Alexander v. Standard Telephones & Cables No. 2 (1991)*[9]. Alexander claimed that a collective agreement on redundancy was incorporated into his contract and that one of the terms of the redundancy agreement was that the employer would select for redundancy on the basis of 'last in, first out' (LIFO). On this occasion the employer had selected the staff he wished to retain and dismissed the others. Alexander was chosen for dismissal, although had LIFO been followed he would not have been selected for redundancy. Alexander sought an injunction to prevent the employer dismissing him; in effect to compel the employer to retain him.

Injunctions are granted at the discretion of the court and not as of right, and mandatory injunctions to compel performance of an employment contract are rarely given because the court has no means of monitoring and ensuring the performance of personal duties. So mandatory injunctions are not granted if money would be an adequate remedy. Even where it would not be adequate they will not be granted if the employer refuses to accept the injunction – unless the court is satisfied that the employer could have sufficient trust in the employee that the contract would be properly performed. In the first case the court decided that an injunction was not justified but suggested that Alexander should consider an action for damages for breach of contract. So he brought one. The case was heard by a different judge and Alexander lost.

In the second case the judge took a careful look to see whether the contract had been incorporated into the contract, and he required clear incorporation. He held that if the collective agreement had been referred to in a contractual document it would have been incorporated. The only contractual document in relation to the contract of employment was the offer letter, which did not refer at all to the redundancy agreement, or indeed to collective agreements of any kind. The only reference to collective agreements was in the written particulars of employment given to Alexander by Standard Telephones & Cables in pursuance of their duty to notify existing employees in writing of certain key contract terms under the Employment Protection (Consolidation) Act 1978, s. 1 (now the Employment Rights Act 1996).

The terms which must be notified are specified in section 1 (see below) but the employer is free to add information on additional terms. Redundancy rights are not one of the specified terms. Written particulars are not contractual documents. The contract terms are fixed when the employment offer is accepted but the employer is given three months after the commencement of employment to provide written particulars. So written particulars are no more than evidence of what the employer thinks these terms are, and either party can apply to a tribunal for correction of the particulars. However, in the absence of a written term they are regarded as very good evidence.

The reference in the written particulars was not to the redundancy agreement in particular but a general reference at the beginning of the particulars to the effect that:

> The basic terms and conditions of your employment with this company are in accordance with and subject to the relevant provisions of the agreements made between the parties to the Joint Industrial Council for the Cablemaking Industry (national agreements); the collective agreements between the company at plant level and the trade unions or organisations of workers concerned (plant agreements). . .

The judge decided that this reference related only to any terms set out in the particulars in question, e.g. the specified terms plus any added by the employer. As the particulars did not contain a provision on redundancy, the redundancy agreement had not been incorporated into the contract. It must be said that the judge could well have reached the opposite conclusion, and the moral of the case is that unless the incorporation is very clear the parties render themselves hostages to fortune, or rather to the sometimes unpredictable decisions of the court or tribunal.

The effect of *Alexander No. 2* has been somewhat ameliorated by the incorporation of the EU Directive on the Employer's Obligation to Inform Employees of the Conditions applicable to the Contract of Employment or the Employment Relationship into UK law. This added to written particulars the requirement to inform the employee of any applicable collective agreement[10]. Any agreements so mentioned are likely to be incorporated. A general reference such as 'any agreements which may be made from time to time with the union' will incorporate every collective agreement. Where this is not desired, either the reference must be specific, e.g. 'the agreement made on 1 January 1996 and any amendments deletions or additions thereto', or the reference must be to specific terms, e.g. 'your wages/hours/holidays . . . will be subject to such collective agreements as may be made from time to time with the union'.

But the difficulties do not end with incorporation. Not every provision in the collective agreement may be suitable for incorporation, nor may the intention (as perceived by court or the tribunal, not the actual intention) be to incorporate each and every term. Inevitably the final decision will rest with the court or tribunal. In *Robertson v. British Gas*, *Marley v. Forward Trust* and *Alexander No. 1* the decisions favoured the incorporation of any term which gave rights to individuals or which dealt with procedures involving individuals, but not procedures which related to the employer and the union. Thus any consultation and negotiation with the union would be excluded, but consultation with the individual, on pay, hours, redundancy benefit and selection methods, would be incorporated into the employment contract.

Yet another problem is the possible conflict between the terms in the contract and those of the incorporated collective agreement. A classic example of this is *Marley v. Forward Trust*. Marley had a mobility clause in his contract. At a later date a collective agreement on redundancy was incorporated and subsequently amended. The agreement provided that, if a person was transferred as a result of redundancy, he would have a six-month trial period in the new job. If he then rejected the position he would be entitled to his redundancy payment as set out in the agreement. The office in which Marley worked was closed down and he was transferred to London. After six months he said the job was unsuitable and claimed redundancy. Forward Trust denied that he was redundant. They said he had been moved under his mobility clause, not under the redundancy agreement. The Court of Appeal remitted the case to the industrial tribunal, to decide which of the two conflicting terms in his contract applied: the personal one making him generally mobile or the later one requiring limited mobility but applying only to redundancy. The parties then settled the claim, so no actual decision was reached. But the case shows that where clauses conflict the parties have left themselves at the mercy of the courts.

Conflicts of this kind are almost inevitable whenever contracts consist of an amalgam of individual terms and incorporated documents. The solution is to decide in advance which clauses shall prevail. There are various possible approaches:

- There can be a general provision in the contract such as: 'should there be any conflict between the provisions of this contract/document/letter and any other document incorporated into this contract, then the terms of this contract/document/letter shall prevail'.
- Or the provision may relate to a specific provision, e.g. location, hours or bonus rather than the totality of the terms.
- Or there can be a provision in the incorporated document. So Forward Trust could have put into the collective agreement a term to the effect that 'this will not affect any other power which the company may have to relocate you'. Unfortunately for them they had made such a provision, i.e. 'This agreement shall not apply in situations where the company is promoting or transferring staff in accordance with established procedures and the terms of individual contracts' in the first redundancy collective agreement, but it was omitted from the amended agreement.

Finally, but by no means least, there is the requirement to draw the employee's attention to certain provisions in incorporated documents of which the employee might otherwise be unaware. This was the decision of the House of Lords in *Scally v. Southern Health and Social Services Board (1991)*.[11] In this case doctors were unaware of a provision in the pension scheme, incorporated into their contracts, which allowed them to purchase extra years of pension benefit at advantageous rates. They came to know of it only when the rates were far less beneficial. The Lords held that there was an implied contractual duty to bring to the notice of the employee those terms which:

- were not negotiated with the individual employee, but which resulted from negotiation with a representative body or were otherwise incorporated by reference
- gave a valuable right to the employee which was contingent upon their taking some action to avail themselves of it
- the employee could not reasonably have been expected to be aware of without them being drawn to their attention.

An earlier commercial case, that of *Interfoto Picture Library v. Stiletto Visual Programmes (1988)*[12] had already held that an onerous term in the contract itself had to be brought to the attention of the other party before it became enforceable. In the case in question it was a provision for drastically increasing hire charges if the hired goods were retained beyond the hire period. This ruling applies to employment contracts also. Therefore if clauses are incorporated into the contract which require action by the employee or which are unduly onerous they must be brought to the employee's attention. Exactly how this is to be done is not clear. Interfoto favoured a red pointing hand on the document itself. The Lords suggested a short explanatory leaflet. Such a leaflet was available in *Scally* but had not been distributed to the doctors involved. But it must be borne in mind that these are recent cases and there can be no certainty until we have more examples.

Identifying onerous and beneficial terms is not easy. Benefits available on maternity, training, relocation, etc., might be unknown. Deductions, provisions or relocation terms might be onerous.

In *Scally* the Lords pointed out that the contractual duty of the employer related only to benefits provided by the employer and not to those provided by third parties. Insurance-based pension schemes and those run by trustees are not covered by the ruling in *Scally*.

Incorporating staff handbooks
This is very similar to the incorporation of collective agreements. The need to:

- identify the agreement
- include future issues by using 'such as may be issued from time to time' or a similar phrase
- identify the date when the new issue becomes effective
- deal with conflicts between the contract and the incorporated terms
- bring onerous and beneficial terms to the employee's notice

are all the same.

But there is one respect in which the handbook may cause more problems than the collective agreement, and that is in distinguishing the contractual from the non-contractual elements. Handbooks tend to cover a large number of topics, from the clearly contractual to the purely informative. At either end of the spectrum the position is clear. As far as the uncertain middle is concerned, once again it will be a matter for the court or tribunal. In *Secretary of State for Employment v. ASLEF (No. 2) (1972)*[13] the court was faced with a rule book of 280 pages containing 239 rules. Every employee had signed a form saying that he would abide by the rules. But not all these rules were 'terms of the contract. Some are only instructions to a man as how he is to do his work.' Buckley J. thought the overtime procedures were contractual, but not the instructions as to how the work was to be done. (For more details on this see 'Job description' below, pp. 41 and 56.)

One way of approaching the problem is to collect together all the employment contractual documents and the incorporated documents, analyse them as to whether they are contractual or non-contractual, and then ensure that the wording is clear enough to leave no room for doubt. For the purposes of analysis the following categories may be useful. They are not legal categories, and are not legal rules, but they have been based on decided cases. Indeed, it may be impossible to draw a line between them, as one category will merge into the next.

Real terms and conditions. These are the provisions which you would expect to find in a contract and to be legally binding. They will include work, wage, hours, location, holidays, sick pay, pension, etc. They are provisions which can be changed only if the contract makes arrangements for changes (see Chapter 8, pp. 56–71).

Optional or variable discretionary terms. Optional terms are legally enforceable, but the employer is free to remove them or vary them at any time. In *Cadoux v. Central Regional Council (1986),*[14] a case which involved the construction of a complicated network of incorporated agreements, the court held that a non-contributory pension scheme was not *ex gratia* but a term in the contract. But the term could be unilaterally varied or withdrawn by the employer. The Central Regional Council were lucky in getting a favourable decision. They had not used words indicating that the term was variable or discretionary.

In a more recent case, *Baynham & ors* v. *Philips Electronics (UK) Ltd & ors (1995)*[15] the court refused to find a term discretionary even though it was included in a section of the contract headed 'Additional Discretionary Benefits'. In 1974 the employer had introduced group membership of PPP health insurance for all staff above a certain grade, making it clear that staff who retired would continue to benefit from the scheme along with their families. The first information sheet on the scheme reiterated this, as well as making it clear that PPP had the right to make changes to the limits on benefits, the payments made by the company and the notional subscriptions of each employee for tax purposes. In the standard terms of employment the scheme fell in the section headed 'Additional Discretionary Benefits'. In 1982 the employer withdrew the most expensive hospitals from the scheme without any objection from the employees. In 1985 the company introduced an excess payment of £25 and again there were no objections. The scheme was still too costly, so pensioners were told they would have to move to an inferior scheme providing fewer benefits. The court held that the employees had been promised health cover at the same rate as at their retirement for the rest of their lives. Putting the benefit under 'discretionary' benefits was not enough to make it discretionary – the actual term itself was the critical factor. The court concluded that the term was not discretionary. PPP could change the terms, the employer could not. In addition, once employment had ended the employees' accrued rights crystallised and could not be changed, even if changes could have been made during employment.

Employers introducing discretionary benefits would be unwise to follow the council's example. A clear indication of the discretionary nature of the term should be given, e.g. 'the employer may at any time alter or remove . . .' There may be a procedure such as consultation to be complied with first and/or written notification or a period of notice.

This type of provision is suited to benefits which are dependent on favourable tax laws, the availability of funds or, as with private medical care, where the employer may wish to change the provider or the coverage.

Ex gratia provisions. *Ex gratia* provisions are not legally binding. No legal action can be brought in relation to them. In *Petrie v. MacFisheries (1940)*[16] sick pay was allowed for up to 21 days a year, but it was provided that 'These allowances are purely "Act of Grace" on the company's part and cannot be claimed as a right.' Petrie could not sue for unpaid sick pay, nor, today, would he be able to claim that non-payment was a breach of contract and so tantamount to constructive dismissal.

There is a vital difference between discretionary and *ex gratia* terms. The former are legally enforceable whilst they remain in the contract; the latter are not. *Ex gratia* provisions are often used to deal with extra leave, payments during absence and some other fringe benefits.

Information and policies. Handbooks in particular contain much information about the organisation, about promotion prospects, sports facilities, etc., as well as about various procedures for dealing with sickness, redundancy, maternity, grievances, discipline, etc. They will also include policies on health and safety, recruitment, retirement, equality, etc.

It is unlikely that the general organisation information will be legally binding. Policies also should not be binding in the sense that they form part of the contract. It is the duty of the employer to ensure that the policy is a good one, and therefore he must be free to change it. That is not to say that consultation is inappropriate, nor that an employee can ignore the policy with impunity. Policies work best when the workforce support them and it will be misconduct to fail to comply with a policy. There may even be an express term requiring compliance with any policies which may be issued from time to time, thus making breach of a policy breach of contract. The employer is entitled to give the employee lawful instructions as to how the contractual duties are to be performed. An instruction to comply with the organisation's policies and procedures will be a lawful instruction, and failure to do so may justify dismissal.

If a procedure, especially a grievance or disciplinary procedure, is set out in an incorporated handbook it is likely to be contractual unless steps are taken to provide otherwise. A disadvantage of including procedures is the added compensation payable in the event of a breach. It has been evident since *Polkey v. A. E. Dayton Services (1987)*:[17] any dismissal without the employer having followed a reasonable procedure will be unfair unless to follow the procedure would have been 'pointless'. But compensation will be reduced where the employee contributed to his dismissal, for example by his misconduct.[18] Yet if the procedure is in breach of contract the employee will receive damages to cover contractual loss during the period it would have taken to follow the procedure and the period of notice. In calculating damages for breach of contract there is no reduction for contribution. So an employee dismissed for misconduct following an unsound procedure could lose 50 per cent or even more of his unfair dismissal compensation – but there would be no reduction in his damages.

This applies to failure to follow the grievance procedure, any redundancy policies and procedures, and any other procedure which has been incorporated into the contract.

The decision whether to make a policy or a procedure contractual or not lies with the employer. It is sometimes thought that grievance and disciplinary procedures which have to be notified to the employee in writing under the Employment Protection (Consolidation) Act 1978, s. 1, have to be contractual. Section 1 does not provide this (see below, 'Written particulars', p. 35).

Some topics may be dealt with under several headings. Sick pay may be contractual for a fixed period and thereafter discretionary or *ex gratia*. The receipt of sick pay may be subject to compliance with a procedure, etc.

Express terms inserted by statute

These are very rare. Mostly, statutory provisions exist outside the contract, and the employee can choose to enforce the statutory or contractual term if there is one. But some statutes replace the contractual term with the statutory one. The statutory provision is then enforced as a term in the contract. This is how Wage Regulation Orders made by wages councils under the Wages Act 1986 were enforced. They replaced any lesser provision in the employment contract.

Terms outside the contract

The parties may enter into further contracts relating to employment. These are dependent on the main employment contract; they are known as collateral warranties. They often arise during the recruitment process or when an employee is being persuaded to vary the contract terms.

A good example is *Gill v. Cape Contracts (1985)*.[19] Men gave up work in Northern Ireland to work on Sullom Voe oil terminal. The contracts of employment they accepted provided for one month's notice. The men said they had been told during the interview that the job would last at least six months. In the event they did not start work because of industrial action by Scottish workers who objected to them. The question was: were they entitled to damages for the period of notice, i.e. one month, or for six months? The court held that the men had two contracts, an employment contract giving them one month's notice and a collateral warranty giving them a guarantee of six months' work if they accepted the offer of employment. This collateral warranty had been broken, and they were entitled to damages based on loss of employment for six months.

There is a collateral warranty whenever the employer makes a representation to the employee knowing and intending the employee to act upon it. The intention is not the actual intention the employer may have had in mind but the intention as it is perceived by the court from the employer's actions. The court concluded in *Gill* that the employer certainly intended to offer six months' work. Employees who already had secure employment in Northern Ireland would be seeking just such an assurance.

Lassey v. Salterville Nursing Home (above, p. 16) is another example of a collateral warranty. The question of proof is discussed in the comments on that case.

Key points

Conduct

- Should be used as the basis of a contract only as a last resort.

Oral terms

- Confirm them in writing or make a contemporaneous note.

Written terms

- As many terms as possible should be clearly set out in writing.
- Give a copy to the other party or make sure a copy is accessible to the other party.

Collective agreements

- An incorporating provision should be included in the contractual document.
- A phrase such as 'as agreed from time to time' should be used if future collective agreements are to be incorporated automatically.
- Collective agreements must be distinguished from management decisions reached after consultation with the union.
- If all collective agreements are not to be incorporated, then those to be incorporated must be identified.
- The date when the collective agreement becomes effective should be understood.
- The particular parts of the agreement to be incorporated should be identifiable.
- A provision should exist to deal with conflict between the contract terms and the collective agreement.
- Attention should be drawn to onerous or beneficial clauses of which the employee might otherwise be unaware.

Staff handbooks

- Incorporation should be specified in a contractual document.
- A phrase such as 'as issued from time to time' should be used if future handbooks are to be incorporated.
- If not all the provisions are to be incorporated, this should be clear.
- The date of issue should be clear.
- A provision should exist to deal with conflicting terms.
- Attention should be drawn to onerous or beneficial clauses of which the employee might otherwise be unaware.

Other documents

- Incorporation must be expressed in a contractual document.
- Provision must be made to deal with conflicting terms.
- Attention must be drawn to onerous or beneficial terms of which the employee may be unaware.

Terms outside the contract

- Check for the existence of such terms.
- Such promises should be noted wherever possible.

References

1 Noted in (1988) *IDS Brief* 376.
2 IRLR 369 CA.
3 IRLR 302 CA.
4 ITR 74 IT.
5 IRLR 493 Cty Ct.
6 1 WLR 339, 2 All ER 481 QB.
7 IRLR 213 EAT.
8 IRLR 55.
9 IRLR 287.
10 ERA s. 1
11 4 All ER 563, IRLR 522.
12 1 All ER 348 CA.
13 2 All ER 949 CA.
14 IRLR 131 Ct Sess.
15 *IDS Brief* 551 QBD.
16 1 KB 258.
17 IRLR 503 HL.
18 Employment Protection (Consolidation) Act 1978, s. 74(6).
19 IRLR 499 NIHC.

4
Implied terms

Where the parties do not themselves set the terms, either directly or by incorporation, a term may be implied into the contract. Terms are implied into contracts far less frequently than is generally supposed.

Firstly, where there is an express term there cannot be an implied term. Implied terms fill in gaps left by the express terms. The only way an express term can be removed or changed is by varying the contract. This can be done in the same way as a contract is made, orally, in writing, or by conduct. But conduct must be viewed with great care when looking at variation of the terms because conduct is frequently ambiguous. This is well illustrated by *Hedger v. Davy & Co. (1974)*.[1] In past years Hedger had worked extra hours over the Christmas period, whereas his contract required only 45 hours per week. This year he refused to work an extra 74 hours. It was held that his previous conduct had not resulted in a change to his terms of employment. His dismissal for refusing to work overtime was unfair.

There are two main approaches to the implication of terms into contracts. The first seeks to identify the intention of the parties to the contract. It asks, 'What would the parties have said if the question had been put to them?' Sometimes it is obvious that the parties intended a particular provision to be in the contract.

This is illustrated by the case of *Ali v. Christian Salvesen Food Services Ltd (1996)*.[2] Christian Salvesen had changed to annual hours. These were 1,842 a year, based on a notional 40-hour week. Overtime was to be paid only when an employee had completed his annual hours for that year. Ali was made redundant part way through a year and without having completed his annual hours. He claimed under the Wages Act 1986 overtime pay for each week in which he had exceeded 40 hours. The EAT implied a term into the contract to the effect that employees were entitled to overtime in such circumstances. They decided that, had the point been put to the employer and the union during negotiations, this is what they would have agreed. They also felt that a term was needed to fill a gap in the contract. But the Court of Appeal overturned this. They held there was no evidence that the parties intended to provide for this eventuality in the contract.

Frequently there can be no answer, and then the second approach has to be used. The second approach is based on the necessity of a term to give business efficacy to the contract. The key question is 'Must there be a term to make the contract workable?' If the answer is 'yes', then a term is implied. In some instances the courts have been required to imply a term for so long that the form of the implied term is presumed. So in relation to the payment of wages in the absence of work it is presumed that the full wage will be paid for the total period of worklessness unless the provision of work is beyond the control of the employer. But in relation to sick pay there is no presumed term, although in *Howman & Sons v. Blythe (1983)*[3] the judge did think the time was approaching when a presumption of some payment should be made.

It is important to note that a term is not implied because it would be reasonable to imply it. The courts will not make a reasonable contract for the parties. However, once it has been decided that a term must be implied, the content of that term must be reasonable.

This clearly gives the courts and tribunals considerable scope in relation to implied terms, and the lack of a universal approach is unhelpful. The guidance of Stephenson LJ in *Mears v. Safecar Security (1982)*[4] – 'consider the facts and circumstances of the relationship between employer and employee concerned, including the particular contract of employment since it was made in order to imply and determine the missing term' – takes us no further forward.

When analysing an existing situation to see whether there are any implied terms the following procedure may prove helpful. It must be emphasised that it is not a set of legal rules, although it is based on several legal decisions, particularly *Orman v. Saville Sportswear (1960)*[5] and *Howman & Sons v. Blythe (1983)*.[6]

Is it necessary to have a term to give business efficacy to the contract? If the answer is 'yes' the court or tribunal will imply a reasonable term. Reasonableness can be based in descending order on:

- *The presumed agreement of the parties.* If there is a term which would have been assented to by both parties, that will be implied.
- *The conduct of the parties.* Thus, if regular hours have actually been worked, these may be implied. In *Mears* the employee had been off sick before but had not asked for sick pay then, so it was implied that there was no sick pay.
- *The custom in the workplace.* This may well be based on collective agreements which, although not incorporated into the contract, have been put into practice and become the norm. This, and the custom of the industry or of the locality (below), are sometimes referred to as the 'normative' effects of collective agreements. They are implied not because there is an agreement but because the collective agreement has become standard practice.
- *Custom in the industry or locality.* There are fewer of these since the demise of national collective bargaining.

- *Implied by the courts.* In some instances, such as sick pay, the courts simply have to decide on the facts before them. In others there is an actual presumption which will apply unless it is rebutted by a term express or implied. For example, in *Devonald v. Rosser & Sons (1906)*[7] it was decided that the employer had to pay full wages to his employees even when there was no work for them unless the provision of work was beyond his control – or the contract provided otherwise. The duty to pay is a rebuttable presumption.

The strict proof required before a term will be implied has made it virtually impossible to imply a term incorporating future collective agreements, or even an existing recognition agreement.

There is some confusion as to whether collective agreements can be incorporated into a contract by way of custom. The first case was *Young v. Canadian Northern Railway Co (1931)*[8] in which the Privy Council decided that an employee could not rely on the redundancy provisions in a collective agreement simply because the company's practice was to apply collective agreements. The company's actions were ambiguous. The agreements could be followed as a matter of policy rather than contract. This view was followed in *Faithful v. Admiralty (1964)* in which it was held that a custom of applying collective agreements spanning 40 years did not support a term that all future collective agreements were incorporated. It only showed that the employer had accepted the advice rendered to him via the agreement; it did not mean he had to bind himself to accept all future advice.

But tribunals have occasionally taken a less stringent view, as *Arthur H Wilton Ltd v. Peebles (1994)*.[9] There was no written contract or written particulars. When employment commenced the employer paid the collectively agreed national wage. Over the next 20 years the employer had paid collectively agreed rates. But, having agreed a date for the application of the 1993 increase, he then pleaded financial difficulties and did not pay, trying to delay its introduction. The tribunal had 'no difficulty' incorporating the collective agreement, but did not refer to the earlier cases. It may be that they were influenced by the employer's conduct, which does give the impression that he thought it was contractual. Collective agreements that the employer proposes to adopt are treated as offers to the employees. In this case there would have been ample evidence on which to find an offer and acceptance, and thus a legally binding agreement, without having to resort to implied incorporation of collective agreements. As it is, the EAT leave the implied incorporation of collective agreements in a state of considerable confusion.

Recognition agreements are not really appropriate to incorporation. In *Gallagher v. Post Office (1970)*[10] Brightman J held that it was not necessary, on grounds of business efficacy, to imply the incorporation of a recognition agreement.

Key points

- Whenever possible, terms should be express and in writing.
- Terms are not implied where there is an existing express term.
- Generally a term is implied only when business necessity requires it.
- At common law, some terms are implied unless a contract term – express or implied – provides otherwise.

Summary: identifying the contract terms

Note. This is for guidance only. Although it is based on cases, the courts and tribunals do not follow the detailed sub-headings.

- Find the express contract terms. These may be:

  Oral.
  Written.
  Incorporated.
  Included by statute.
  Additional terms outside the contract – collateral warranties.

Written particulars may provide evidence of the agreed terms.

- Where there is no express term there may be an implied term where the parties obviously intended such a term or business efficacy requires one. This term may be based on:

  The conduct of the parties.
  Custom in the workplace.
  Custom in the locality or industry.
  Implication at common law.
  Implication by the tribunal to complete the written particulars.

- Compare these contract terms, both express and implied, with any relevant statutory employment protection rights. Offer the employee a choice between the contractual and the statutory provisions, whichever is more favourable.

References

1 IRLR 138 IT.

2 CA, noted in *IDS Brief* 579.
3 IRLR 139 QB.
4 IRLR 183 CA.
5 All ER 105 QB.
6 As 3 above.
7 2 KB 728 CA.
8 AC 83 PC.
9 IRLR 510 EAT.
10 2 All ER 712.

5
Written particulars

In many instances the only document the employee may have setting out his employment terms is a statement of the particulars of his employment. This was introduced in the Contracts of Employment Act 1963 when it was realised that some employees were ignorant of their terms and consequently unable to check, for example, any complicated overtime, bonus or other payments. At first the idea met with considerable employer resistance but now the benefit of terms recorded in writing is recognised by employers as well as employees. The EU Directive on Written Information 1991 has had an important impact on written particulars, introducing greater detail and formality as well as additional topics of information. The combined UK and EU requirements for written particulars are now to be found in the Employment Rights Act 1996 ss. 1–7.

These written particulars are not the contract itself. The contract terms are fixed when the contract is made, normally when the employee accepts an offer of employment. The written particulars are simply the employer's view, in writing, of those specific terms which he is required to provide to the employee. They are legally nothing more than evidence of the employer's version of those terms, and are not absolute proof of the terms. But they are very good proof. Employees should check them, and if the employer will not correct an error they should apply for correction to the tribunal, not let the matter lie, because as evidence of the terms set out in it the statement is very potent. It should be treated by both parties with as much respect as the contract itself.

It is, or course, open to the employer to convert the written particulars of employment into the contract, by, for example, obtaining the employee's signature to the particulars as the terms of his contract. But a signature acknowledging receipt of the terms will not make them contractual.

If the employer has already provided the information to the employee in writing, for example in a full contract of employment or offer letter, there is no need for the employer to issue written particulars; indeed the duplication could lead to confusion, especially if the contract and particulars are not identical. Where the contract or offer does not provide the full information written particulars will be necessary.

Written particulars have to be provided to all employees who have completed one month's employment regardless of hours worked. They must be given to the employee by the end of second month of employment and the information must be correct at the seventh day before it is given. If the employment terminates before the two months is completed the employer must still give the employee his written particulars by the two-month date.

Certain information must be set out in one document: the principal statement. No one is quite certain as to what a 'document' is. For example, is a loose-leaf file a document? Does all the information in one envelope or given at the same time constitute one document? To be safe, there should be a clear link between them, such as pagination or annexation, or the attachment of appendices or schedules. The other information can be delivered in 'instalments' (a delightful concept of written particulars as a part-work).

The following information has to be in the principal statement:

- the names of the employer and employee
- the date when employment began
- the date on which the employee's period of continuous employment began (including any employment with a previous employer which has to be taken into account)
- the scale or rate of remuneration or method of calculating remuneration
- the intervals at which remuneration is paid (that is weekly, monthly or at specified intervals)
- any terms and conditions relating to hours of work (including any terms and conditions relating to normal working hours)
- entitlement to holidays including public holidays and any entitlement to accrued holiday pay on contract termination
- the title of the job that the employee is employed to do or a brief description of his work
- either the place of work, or where the employee is required or permitted to work at various places, an indication of that and the address of the employer.

The information that may be delivered in instalments is:

- terms and conditions, if any, relating to incapacity for work due to sickness or injury, including any provision for sick pay
- terms and conditions relating to pensions and pension schemes unless the pension or scheme is established by statute and that statute requires a body or authority to provide the information
- if applicable, a statement that the employment is contracted-out employment for pension purposes, and whether a contracting-out certificate under the Pension Schemes Act 1993 is in force

- if the employment is not intended to be permanent the expected length of the contract or, if fixed term, the termination date
- any collective agreements that directly affect the terms and conditions of employment including, where the employer is not a party, the persons by whom they were made
- where the employer and any associated employers together employ 20 or more persons there must be a note
  1 specifying any disciplinary rules applicable to the employee
  2 specifying the person to whom the employee should apply if dissatisfied with any disciplinary decision taken against him
  3 specifying the person to whom he should refer any grievance relating to his employment
  4 specifying any further steps consequent on these actions

  Note – this does not apply to rules, discipline, grievances or procedures relating to health and safety at work

There is a special provision concerning persons working abroad. If the employee is to work abroad for at least one month he must be provided with information on

- the period he is to work outside the UK
- the currency of his remuneration while outside the UK
- any additional remuneration or benefits payable to him while outside the UK
- any terms and conditions relating to his return to the UK.

If he is to leave the UK before the two-month period has elapsed he must be given the information before he leaves.

A new requirement introduced by the Directive is that the information has to be set out in the particulars with only limited power to refer the employee to other documents. It is possible to refer to another document in respect of sick pay, pension entitlement, disciplinary and grievance procedures. In relation to notice the employer may choose to refer to the law (statutory minimum notice is in the Employment Rights Act 1996 s. 86) or to a collective agreement. (It is recommended that this particular option should be ignored. It is better to inform the employee direct of the notice provisions rather than sending him off to find them out.) Where the employer does refer to another document or collective agreement, that document or agreement must be one that he has reasonable opportunity of reading in the course of his employment or that is made reasonably accessible to him in some other way. It must be doubted whether a document in the personnel manager's office, which he can see upon request, meets these requirements. There is, after all, a built-in disincentive to asking.

If there is a change to the written particulars the employee must be informed of the change by a written statement at the earliest opportunity and in any event within one month of its being made. The updating provision is often misunderstood by employers, who erroneously believe that it gives them the power to change the terms in the particulars merely by giving one month's notice. Far from it. The provision relates to changes which have been validly made, not to the making of the change itself.

These new written particulars raise important questions for the employer. One obvious one is how he will produce the particulars. There is no single right answer to this. Some employers put all the details in the contract or offer letter. Others put the personal parts – job title, wage, commencement date etc. – in the offer and append the standard items – notice, holidays, sick pay etc. – in a schedule. Another option is to produce a full set of particulars. Some make the offer letter the principal statement, with the additional information being supplied later and separately. A final option might be to use all or part of the staff handbook, inserting a page of personal details.

As the purpose of the written particulars is communication, they have at times been used to convey information which is not contractual but which is relevant to employment. Thus under the Industrial Relations Act 1971, s. 5, the employer had to include an explanation of the employee's statutory right not to join a union. And now under section 1(4) there must be a note of the grievance and disciplinary procedures. The directive contains more topics which may not be contractual. Sick pay, some of the remuneration package, and many collective agreements may affect the relationship but not be contractual. This can pose a problem. The courts and tribunals tend to assume that, if a provision is described in the particulars and is not clearly identified as discretionary, then it is contractual.

So the way in which these non-contractual provisions are notified is important. If they are simply listed without distinction alongside the other terms, that in itself will indicate that the employer considers them contractual unless the provision itself makes it clear that they are not part of the contract. Where it is intended keep the non-contractual elements out of the contract it is better to make the intention quite clear. It can be done by:

- an express statement in the provision
- separating the written particulars into two parts, for example:

Part A

(Details of contractual provisions required under the Employment Protection (Consolidation) Act 1978, section 1.)

Part B

The organisation is also required to provide you with information on the grievance and disciplinary procedures and other benefits and procedures currently operated by the organisation. These do not from part of your contract and may change from time to time.

Employers who have not already made the disciplinary and grievance procedure contractual may wish to consider carefully whether they should do so. If the procedure is contractual, the employee will be entitled to bring a breach of contract claim (up to £25,000 damages in the tribunal, £50,000 in the County Court or Sheriff's Court and unlimited in the High Court or Court of Session) regardless of service as well as an unfair dismissal claim if he has two years' continuity of employment.

The discretionary nature of any sick pay benefits, bonuses etc. should also be made clear.

If the written particulars are to be the only or main document setting out terms and conditions the employer may wish to include additional items such as confidentiality and restraint clauses, training provisions, deductions from wages, and guarantee pay. If additional items are included they will be treated as contractual unless the employer clearly indicates otherwise.

What should the employer do if he has no employment term under one of these sections? S. 2 requires the employer to say that there are no employment particulars under that head. So the employer who does not recognise unions may find it appropriate to say that there are no collective agreements affecting the employment, and one who does not provide sick pay to state that there is no sick pay.

Although employers employing fewer than 20 persons (together with persons employed by associated employers) do not have to notify their staff of the procedures, they would be well advised to do so. Such employers are still bound by the requirement to follow a fair procedure when dismissing staff, and an essential element of fairness is that the employee should know what is happening. Without a written procedure this requirement may be difficult to fulfil.

If the information is incorrect the employer can always issue new particulars.

If an employer does not provide the written information, or the employer or the employee believes the information given to be incorrect, the remedy is to apply to an industrial tribunal for the information to be corrected or supplied.

In *Eagland v. British Telecom (1990)*[1] the Employment Appeal Tribunal stated that the tribunal was not concerned with the fairness of the terms, only with their accurate communication. If no terms have been communicated, then the tribunal must ascertain them and supply the information to the employee. The EAT divided the types of particulars into (1) mandatory particulars and (2) those which need be itemised only if the benefit concerned is provided by the employer. If mandatory terms are omitted from the particulars the tribunal, after hearing evidence, must set out the terms (i.e. using the second approach to implied terms, above, p. 30). When a non-mandatory term has been omitted the tribunal can insert a term only if it is convinced that the parties would have agreed to it had the question been put to them (using the first approach to implied terms, above, p. 30). The mandatory items are those which section 1 specifies as having to be given to the employee. The mandatory items are:

- names of the employer and employee
- commencement date and continuity
- rate of remuneration and periodicity of payment
- notice
- job title
- length of temporary employment and fixed-term contracts
- place of work
- if required to work outside the UK, the period outside the UK and currency of his remuneration.

The two categories set out in *Eagland* are based on the wording of section 1. They do not entirely accord with the terms which the courts will imply into a contract. It is quite likely that, on the basis of past conduct, the court would imply terms relating to hours in order to give business efficacy to the contract. It is always possible that the EAT may have confused a term which provides that there is no benefit, e.g. no sick pay, with the absence of any term on that topic, e.g. no term relating to sick pay. There is a vital difference between the two. To avoid any confusion, where it is the intention of the employer not to provide a common benefit such as sick pay it is better to state that there is no sick pay. Then it is not possible for court or tribunal to imply a term. To make no provision leaves the contract open to the possibility of an implied term.

To reiterate, the written particulars of major items relating to employment are often referred to as the 'contract of employment'. They are not the contract. That is made by the individual employer and employee when the employment offer is accepted. The written particulars can come into being at any time during the first three months of employment, and that could be a considerable time after the contract was made. But, although they are not the contract, the particulars are good evidence of the contract terms, at least as the terms are seen by the employer. However, recent cases have emphasised that both employer and employee are free to show that the statement is wrong.

Where there is a conflict between the offer letter, which is contractual, and the written particulars, which are only evidence, then the offer letter prevails unless it can be shown that meanwhile the contract has been varied (*Robertson v. British Gas (1983)*).[2]

The content of the provisions to be included in the particulars will be discussed in Part III. Some require careful thought before they are added to the existing terms.

Under the directive the place of work will have to be notified, or, if there is none, that the employee is employed at various places and the registered place of employment or, where appropriate, the domicile of the employer. This is new and to be welcomed. It will avoid many of the problems in determining whether there is redundancy and whether the employee is mobile. (See 'Location', p. 142.) But mobility requirements need to be considered.

As regards describing the work, the directive suggests several options: title, grade, the nature or category of work, or a brief specification or description of the work. The danger here is the temptation to put the job description into the particulars. The particulars are evidence that the provision is contractual. This means that, if the job description were included as part of the information, then in order to change the job description the employer would have to follow the tortuous route required for changing contract terms. Failure to do so would result in constructive dismissal. The change might, of course, be justified on the grounds of business need, but it would put the organisation to needless concern.

If the job description is kept outside the contract it amounts to lawful instructions. Employers are entitled to give lawful instructions as to the performance of the work and to change the instructions when it appears appropriate to them. The employee has no right of refusal to comply, and should he refuse he will be in breach of contract. This was made clear in *Cresswell v. Board of Inland Revenue (1984)*.[3] So it may be better to use a job title or grade and not be tempted to expand into job specifications or job descriptions.

If the contract is a temporary contract the employee must be informed of its expected duration. Temporary contracts under EU law include:

- fixed-term contracts, whatever their length
- task or money-based contracts (those which end not on a predetermined date but when the work is done, or when the money runs out, or when some other agreed event occurs)
- any other contract which is not of indefinite duration. So casual and temporary workers will have to be given an estimate of the length of the contract.

This has a positive advantage, as it is likely to be fair to dismiss for such a reason if it is notified to the employee (*Lee v. Nottinghamshire County Council* below), although the employee may still be made redundant.

We have not completely incorporated the Directive into UK law. The Directive's requirement to inform the employee of his entitlement to paid leave or a formula for its allocation covers more than holidays, which are the only requirement under written particulars. It may include sick leave, training leave, compassionate leave, maternity and family leave, jury service, etc.

The information on wages might also be more extensive. The Directive does not refer to remuneration but to the initial basic amount of the wages. 'Initial basic amount of the wage, other component elements and frequency of payment of remuneration', depending on the definition given to 'remuneration', could include some fringe benefits. Again, if these are discretionary it is essential that the fact is pointed out.

But the Directive's greatest innovation must be the provision relating to collective agreements. This provision needs very careful wording where there are collective agreements but they are not incorporated into the contract. (See 'Collective agreements' above, p. 17.)

An extremely useful addition concerns the terms on which an employee is transferred to a non-member state whose laws govern the relationship or contract. If the transfer is for more than one month the employee must be given details of some of his rights on transfer and return. They must be given them before departure. This is totally new. It is a start towards looking at provisions for persons working abroad. The provision on repatriation could be very important if given a wide purposive interpretation. It could then cover entitlement to the same or a similar job, compensation for redundancy, whether contractual benefits accrued during the period abroad, whether the employee was seconded or not, etc. The provision does not apply to transfer to member states, because they will be covered by the directive whilst they are within the EU.

As an interim measure, where employment was in existence when the Directive was incorporated into UK law in August 1994, the employer was not bound to issue new written particulars unless they were requested by the employee. However, any changes have to be notified in accordance with the new rules.

Key points

- Provide all staff, regardless of their hours, with written information.
- Ensure that every employee has the information by the end of the second month.
- Have a procedure to ensure that employees leaving before completion

of two months' employment receive their written particulars.

- Have a procedure to ensure that employees working abroad for more than one month are provided with a relevant statement.
- Deal with every item in the written particulars (otherwise a term may be implied by the tribunal).
- Make it clear whether the item is contractual, discretionary, there is no benefit or there is no term.
- If procedures are not to be incorporated, make this clear.
- If not every collective agreement is to be incorporated, make this clear.
- Have a procedure for updating in the aftermath of changes.
- If a reference is made to other documents or laws, ensure that they are reasonably accessible to the employee.
- Make provision for the solution of possible conflicts between the contract terms and written particulars.
- Make arrangements for updating.

References

1 IRLR 403 EAT.
2 IRLR 302 CA.
3 IRLR 190 Ch.

6

Interpreting the terms

There are no hard-and-fast rules to be applied. It is for the court or tribunal to make up its own mind as to the meaning of the term. But there are certain discernible approaches.

First, if the words are clear they will be applied – even if the outcome is foolish. The courts are there not to ensure that the parties have a fair bargain but to apply whatever bargain the parties have concluded. If words are used they are assigned a meaning wherever possible.

One employer found to his cost that by including the words 'permanent and pensionable position' in the contract he had made it extraordinarily difficult to dismiss the employee. He had restricted his common law right to terminate the contract. As a general rule an employer has the right at common law to terminate a contract by giving contractual notice (now subject to statutory minimum periods) or, in the absence of a contractual term, by giving a reasonable period of notice. But the right to terminate in this way may be restricted by the contract terms.

This was held to be the effect of the words 'permanent and pensionable position' in a contract in *McClelland v. Northern Ireland General Health Services Board (1957)*.[1] Mrs McClelland had been appointed to a permanent and pensionable position. She could be dismissed for gross misconduct, inefficiency or if her continued employment was not merited. Except in the case of gross misconduct, she had to be given a month's notice. She was made redundant because she had married, and was given six months' notice. The Lords held that 'permanent and pensionable' meant that 'apart from misconduct or inability to perform the duties of [her] office, the employment would continue for an indefinite period'. So Mrs McClelland could be dismissed only for the reasons set out in the contract, and these included neither redundancy nor marriage. The board had no right to dismiss her.

Another example is *Hooper v. British Railways Board (1988)*.[2] The board had entered into a collective agreement with the union on sick pay, and it was incorporated into individual contracts. Where an employee's doctor certified the employee was fit to work, but British Rail's doctor found that he was not fit to work, British Rail agreed to pay the employee's basic pay until either British Rail's doctor decided he was fit to work or he was offered suitable non-contractual work or, implicitly, he retired. Hooper's own doctor decided that he was fit to work but

Hooper suffered from a stress-related illness and British Rail's doctor considered his future employment prospects to be poor. So Hooper was dismissed. Both the tribunal and the EAT thought British Rail had acted fairly. But the Court of Appeal said that British Rail were in breach of contract. It might be reasonable to dismiss, and the term preventing dismissal might be foolish, and the term might well not express British Rail's actual intention, but the words were clear and they had to be applied.

Where words are capable of more than one meaning the tribunal or court decides which meaning is to apply. There is no strict legal rule, but the courts tend to apply one of the following approaches:

- *Contra proferentem*, i.e. taking the interpretation which is least favourable to the person putting the term forward to gain a benefit. Usually it is the employer, relying on a clause to give him power to relocate, change shifts, etc.
- Interpreting the term against the person who put that clause in the contract. If a person inserts an ambiguous clause he cannot complain if the other party has taken it to have a different but tenable meaning. The person inserting the clause should have removed the ambiguity.

  This does not mean that the employer always loses if the claim is based on an ambiguous statement, but it does mean the cards may be stacked against him. Contrary to common belief, leaving a provision vague does not help the employer.
- Finally, totally meaningless terms are usually deleted.

One important question is whether interpreting contracts is a matter of fact or of law. This is because issues of fact cannot be taken on appeal from an industrial tribunal to the EAT. Where there is a contract term, and it has to be interpreted, that is a matter of law. But where the term depends on interpreting the evidence – for example, as to the content of an implied term – this is treated as fact, or at least the decision of the tribunal or court of first instance is difficult to overturn. This is because only the court of first instance has access to the evidence.

Key points

- Ensure that the terms say what you mean. If the meaning is clear they will be applied, however unsatisfactory the result.
- Check for ambiguity. Ambiguous terms will be allocated a meaning by the court or tribunal. The meaning may not favour the employer.
- Use express terms wherever possible. Terms implied by the courts may not be what either party intended.

References

1 2 All ER 129 HL.
2 IRLR 517 CA.

7
Remedies and sanctions for breach of contract

Contract disputes which cannot be solved by the parties themselves can come before the courts and tribunals in various ways. There may be:

- a claim for damages in the civil courts or industrial tribunal for breach of any contract term
- an action for an injunction (or, in Scotland, an interdict) to prevent breach of a term
- a dispute over entitlement to terminate the contract without notice for serious breach of the contract terms
- a claim of unfair dismissal under the Employment Rights Act 1996 seeking compensation and/or re-engagement or re-employment
- a claim for redundancy benefit under the Employment Rights Act 1996
- claims relating to various statutory rights under the Employment Rights Act 1996 which are dependent on the contract terms, especially written particulars
- claims for wrongful deductions from wages or wrongful demands for repayment under Employment Rights Act 1996.

Damages for breach of contract

Once such claims had to be brought before the ordinary courts. Claims of up to £50,000 are brought before the lower courts (the county courts in England and Wales, the sheriff's court in Scotland) and larger claims before the High Court, or the Court of Session in Scotland. The time limit for these claims is six years from the date of breach, but only five years from breach in Scotland.

Claims for damages may be brought during the continuance of the contract, although it is unusual for the parties to sue each other whilst the employment relationship subsists. Claims may relate to such matters as unpaid benefits, the provision of insurance or entitlement to relocation allowances. Sometimes the cases are test cases, brought with union support in order to prevent changes in the contract terms.

In August 1994 tribunals were given limited jurisdiction in breach of contract. This jurisdiction does not replace that of the civil courts but exists alongside it. The provisions are set out in the Industrial Tribunals Act 1996 s. 3 and the Industrial Tribunals Extension of Jurisdiction Orders 1994. The jurisdiction is not as wide as that of the ordinary courts. Before a claim can be brought

- the employment must have terminated
- the claim must arise out of the termination or be outstanding on termination
- the claim must be for damages or another sum other than a sum in respect of personal injuries – there cannot be an action for an injunction
- the claim must be brought within three months' of termination
- the maximum damages that can be awarded is £25,000
- the employer may set off money to which he is entitled against the damages (eg a loan that must be repaid) or counterclaim for damages (eg for money obtained by fraud). The set-off or counterclaim must arise out of a contract with the employee. So for the first time the tribunal may order the employee to pay damages to the employer. The employer can set off or counterclaim only if the employee brings a contract claim. The employer cannot do so if the employee seeks only a statutory right.

Disputes over living accommodation, intellectual property, obligations of confidence and restraint of trade are not covered. There is no service qualification of any kind for contract claims.

Breach of contract claims can be settled by the parties. No form is needed but it is sensible to put them in writing. The ACAS conciliation officer is authorised to conciliate.

This means that claims concerning wages in lieu of notice or failure to follow a contractual dismissal procedure can be brought before the tribunals. The right is being used extensively. Employees with less than two years' continuity of employment can now complain to the tribunal, and those with more than two years' can seek £25,000 on top of the £11,300 maximum for unfair dismissal. But the employee will not receive double compensation for his loss.

Action for an injunction or an interdict

Either employer or employee may seek an order to prevent the other breaking a contract term. So in *Cresswell v. Board of Inland Revenue (1984)*[1] the employees sought (unsuccessfully) to prevent the employer introducing computers on the grounds that it would be in breach of their contract. The employer may seek to prevent an employee working for another organisation in breach of the employee's undertakings in the contract.

This remedy too is used by unions in dispute with employers over contract changes. It is helpful in preventing the introduction of change in breach of the contract and forces the employer back to the negotiating table.

But orders are not granted, or are granted only in very rare circumstances, when they would in practice amount to enforcing performance of the contract, or when damages would be an adequate remedy. In *Warner Bros Pictures v. Nelson (1936)*[2] the studio sought to prevent Bette Davis, who was under an exclusive acting contract to them, from working as an actress for any other organisation. The contract did not prevent her from undertaking other types of work, so she was not compelled to work for Warner's and the injunction was granted. In *Wishart v. National Association of Citizens Advice Bureaux (1990)*,[3] a dispute over the satisfactory nature of references, the candidate sought an injunction to restrain the employer from preventing his starting work (in other words, to force them to accept him into employment). The injunction was refused because damages would be an adequate remedy and because it would in effect have amounted to enforcing performance of the contract. There are instances in which mandatory injunctions compelling performance are granted. They will be granted if the employer is willing to accept the order or if there is no doubt that the individual could do his work properly and the court decides that the employer could have confidence in him (*Powell v. Brent London Borough Council (1987)*).[4]

Termination without notice

At common law a contract (other than one for a fixed term or a task) can always be terminated by giving proper notice and following any procedure which may have been included in the contract. Proper notice is the notice expressed in the contract or, in the absence of an express clause, a reasonable period of notice. If this period is less than the statutory minimum under the Employment Rights Act, s. 86, it must be replaced by the statutory period. (See below, 'Notice', p. 222.)

The contract can be terminated without notice, i.e. summarily, only where the other party has broken a vital provision in the contract. This is variously described as breach of a fundamental term, breach of a condition or serious breach going to the root of the contract. It may be a breach causing serious loss or it may appear quite minor but indicate total disregard for the contract terms. It is very similar to gross misconduct in unfair dismissal and, as with gross misconduct, each case has to be decided on its merits. The innocent party must exercise the right to terminate without notice promptly. If there is delay the right is lost.

The terms of the contract may affect the right to dismiss summarily. If a procedure agreement is incorporated in the contract the procedure must be followed. The procedure agreement can, therefore, cut down the employer's right to dismiss with or without notice. This occurred in *Gunton v. London Borough of Richmond upon Thames (1980)*[5] and in *Dietman v. London Borough of Brent (1988)*.[6] Both the authorities failed to follow the contractual dismissal procedure and the subsequent dismissals were found to have been in breach of contract.

Damages for breach of contract are based on the remuneration which the employee would have received had the contract been terminated correctly. It therefore consists of the total remuneration package, not just the wage, for the period of notice, plus – if there is an appropriate procedure which has not been followed – the period of time it would have taken to complete the procedure. Damages of £30,000 or less are not taxable, but, in order to prevent the employee gaining an additional benefit as a result of his dismissal, damages up to this sum are calculated net of PAYE and National Insurance contributions. Thereafter damages are calculated gross, because they are taxed in the hands of the recipient. Other benefits to which the employee may be entitled as a result of the loss of employment will also be deducted. These benefits do not include pension payments, private insurance benefits or payments from charities.[7]

Similar rules, the 'golden handshake' rules, apply to sums paid by way of settlement of claims. The tax details are to be found in the Finance Act 1988.

The employee must mitigate the loss by seeking new sources of income. The duty to mitigate does not require the employee to take the work with the highest salary, only to take reasonable steps to mitigate the loss from his own standpoint. This might involve going into business on his own account and taking a drop in income. If he fails to mitigate, or takes inadequate steps, the court will nonetheless deduct the sum it feels he should have earned in mitigation.

Unfair dismissal claim

This is a statutory right which must be enforced in an industrial tribunal. Unlike the common law rights, not every employee is able to claim unfair dismissal. With the exception of dismissals relating to union membership and activities, only those employees who can show that they have at least two years' continuity of employment can claim unfair dismissal.[8]

The employer can counterclaim only if the employee brings a contract claim. The employer cannot counterclaim if the employee seeks only a statutory right. The continuity rules were simplified when, in *R v. Secretary of State for Employment ex parte the Equal Opportunities Commission (1994)*[9] the Lords decided that the requirement for the employee to work 16 hours a week (eight hours after five years) discriminated against part-timers, who were predominantly female, and could not be justified. The requirement was contrary to the EU Equal Treatment Directive. The hours thresholds were removed for all statutory rights by the Employment Protection (Part-time Employees) Regulations 1995. So the sole qualification for an unfair dismissal claim is two years' continuity.

On the other hand, the meaning of dismissal is far wider than that used at common law. Under the Employment Rights Act 1996, s. 95, it encompasses:

- termination of the contract by the employer, with or without proper notice
- expiry of a fixed-term contract, unless it is renewed on similar terms or there is a valid exclusion clause
- constructive dismissal. This occurs when the employee terminates the contract, with or without notice, because of the employer's serious breach of the contract. A common example is an imposed unilateral variation of the contract terms by the employer which the employee refuses to accept. If the employee terminates the contract, that is constructive dismissal.

The definition excludes genuine resignation, mutual agreement to terminate the contract, expiry of a contract for a particular task, and frustration of the contract.

For a dismissal to be fair the employer must prove his ground for dismissal and show that it was fair to dismiss for that reason. It is assumed that there is no ground for dismissal, and the burden of proof lies on the employer. Once the ground has been proved the question of fairness is decided on the balance of probabilities and takes into account the equity and substantial merits of the case, including the size and administrative resources of the employer.

The acceptable grounds for dismissal are found in the Employment Rights Act 1996, s. 98(2), which provides that a dismissal can be fair if mainly due to one or more of the following:

- The capacity or qualifications of the employee for performing work of the kind he was employed by the employer to do.
- The conduct of the employee.
- The employee was redundant.
- The employee could not continue to work in the position which he

held without contravening (either on his part or on that of his employer) a duty or restriction imposed by or under an enactment.
- Some other substantial reason. This includes such matters as personality clashes and unilateral change of contract terms for business need.

It will not be fair to dismiss, even if the ground is a valid one, unless a proper procedure, complying with ACAS Code of Practice No. 1, *Disciplinary Practice and Procedures in Employment*, has been followed. This was the decision of the House of Lords in *Polkey v. A. E. Dayton Services (1987).*[10]

Compensation for unfair dismissal falls into three categories:

- *a basic award*, which is closely related to the redundancy benefit to which the employee would have been entitled.
- *a compensatory award* to cover expenses incurred and benefits lost as a result of the dismissal. This would include non-contractual as well as contractual benefits, and is wider than damages at common law. But unlike damages the award is subject to a maximum, currently £11,300. The maximum is subject to annual review.
- *additional awards*. These are granted when the employer is offered to re-engage or re-employ the ex-employee but refuses to do so. The tribunal will award between 13 and 16 weeks' pay at their discretion in normal claims but 26 to 52 weeks' pay if the claim was based on sex or race discrimination or on union membership. The week's pay is subject to a limit, currently £210, and is also reviewed annually.[11]

The employee may request an order for re-engagement or reinstatement. Such orders are rare and cannot be enforced. If the employer refuses to comply he is subjected to an extra financial penalty in the form of the additional award.[12]

Claims of unfair dismissal must be made within three months of the effective date of termination of the contract.[13]

Further information on disciplinary dismissals will be found in the companion volume, *Discipline*, in this series.

Redundancy benefit

Redundancy claims are subject to the same qualification requirements as unfair dismissal and must also be brought before an industrial tribunal. Redundancy arises when the employer requires or is likely to require fewer employees to do the work, either because he is ceasing to carry on that particular business or because he requires fewer people to do the work at the place where the employee in question is working.[14]

The amount of benefit is based on a combination of length of continuity of employment, age and weekly wage. The wage is subject to a maximum of £210 (reviewed annually) and the entitlement for each year of continuous service is:

- from age 18 to 21: half a week's pay
- from age 22 to 40: one week's pay
- from age 41 to 64: one and a half weeks' pay.

Entitlement ceases when the employee reaches the normal age of retirement or 65, whichever is the earlier. Once the employee has reached the age of 64 the entitlement is reduced by one-twelfth for every further month worked, entitlement being extinguished at the age of 65.

A maximum of 20 years' service can be taken into account. The highest-paid years are used if service exceeds 20 years.

Claims must be made within six months of the effective date of the termination of the contract.

Redundancy is discussed fully in the companion volume, *Redundancy*, in this series.

Statutory rights

Many statutory rights are dependent on some aspect of the contract. Redundancy is based on the work the employee is required to do and his place of work, both of which are determined by the contract. But perhaps the most obvious connection between statutory rights and the contract is the Employment Rights Act 1996, section 1 of which requires the employer to provide the employee with written particulars of the key contract terms. The correctness of the statement can be disputed before an industrial tribunal. This is fully discussed above, p. 35.

Wages claims

The provisions of the old Wages Act 1986 are now to be found in the Employment Rights Act 1996 Part II. The number of claims relating to wrongful payment of wages continues to rise with ACAS dealing with 21,912 cases in 1995[15] Claims can be made where the employer has not made the payment in the agreed manner or has made deductions or demanded repayments to which he is not entitled. Success or failure depends mainly on the terms of the contract. See below, 'Wages', p. 152.

These claims are all separate, and there is no reason why, given appropriate circumstances, the employee should not bring several. The inter-relationship between different claims based on the same contract term can be seen in *O'Laoire v. Jackel International (1991).*[16] O'Laoire was informed in his offer letter that it was 'envisaged' that he would be made managing director when the current managing director retired in two years' time. When the retirement occurred another person was appointed instead. O'Laoire, having complained, was summarily dismissed. He claimed that his dismissal was unfair. The dismissal was indeed found to be unfair because the employer had failed to follow a proper procedure.

When the tribunal came to calculate his compensatory award they calculated the sum he would have received had he been given his six months' notice, plus any other benefits which he would have received during that period. They assumed that for one of the six months he would have been deputy managing director but that for the remaining five he would have been managing director. They made this decision because they had found that he had received a binding promise to be made managing director in the offer letter and so was contractually entitled to the appointment. They assessed compensation at £100,700 but he could be awarded only the statutory maximum, which at that time was £8,000. Jackel did not appeal. O'Laoire then brought an action in the High Court claiming the remainder of his loss, £92,700, as damages for breach of contract. The Court of Appeal held that the finding that he was contractually entitled to be made managing director was 'palpably wrong'. To say that it was 'envisaged' that he would be made managing director fell short of a binding promise to appoint him.

Unfortunately for Jackel, there is a rule known as 'issue estoppel'. This rule provides that once a decision has been made by one court or tribunal, and the parties have not appealed against it, that decision is binding on every other court and tribunal. So the Court of Appeal was unavoidably bound by the decision of the tribunal that O'Laoire had a contractual right to be appointed managing director. He was therefore entitled to damages for breach of that promise. But the court of Appeal pointed out that compensation for unfair dismissal included compensation for the loss of non-contractual benefits. Of the £100,700 awarded by the tribunal £32,500 was for the loss of non-contractual stock options. Damages can be awarded only for contractual loss, so he was not entitled to the £32,500.

There was one more twist in the tale. Jackel said that O'Laoire could not be compensated twice for the same loss, so, as he had already received £8,000 from the tribunal, that too should be deducted from his damages. The court agreed that there could be no double compensation, but Jackel had to show that double compensation would occur. The tribunal had not specified exactly what head of loss the £8,000 represented. It might be his contractual loss, or the lost stock options, or a part of both. So Jackel could not prove double compensation, and there was no deduction of the £8,000. With hindsight it is easy to see that Jackel should have appealed to the EAT against the finding that there was a contractual agreement to appoint O'Laoire to the position of managing director, although at the time it would not have been so obvious.

References

1 IRLR 190 Ch.
2 3 All ER 160, 1KB 209.
3 IRLR 393 CA.
4 IRLR 466 CA.
5 IRLR 321 CA.
6 IRLR 229 CA.
7 *Hopkins v. Norcros plc* (1994) IRLR 18 CA.
8 At the time of writing, a case claiming that the two-year continuity requirement discriminates against women is awaiting a hearing by the House of Lords (*R v. Secretary of State for Employment ex parte Seymour Smith and Perez*).
9 IRLR 176 HL.
10 IRLR 503 HL.
11 Employment Rights Act 1996, s. 227.
12 Employment Rights Act 1996, s. 117.
13 Employment Rights Act 1996, s. 111.
14 Employment Rights Act 1996, s. 139.
15 ACAS annual report, 1995.
16 IRLR 170 CA.

8
Changing contract terms

The extent to which an employer can unilaterally change working arrangements or the terms of a contract depend entirely on the terms themselves. The employer has no inherent or implied power to change the contract terms, no matter how unreasonable or inconvenient they may be.

But this applies only to contract terms. It does not apply to non-contractual benefit packages, nor to job descriptions unless the job description has been put into the contract. Job descriptions are no more than instructions given by the employer as to which parts of the contractual duties the employee should concentrate on and how those duties are to be performed. For more detail see p. 41.

Although job descriptions are not contractual, they are lawful instructions and so they must be obeyed, and refusal to do so can justify dismissal. This can be seen clearly in *UBAF Bank v. Davies (1978)*.[1] A senior manager, having asked for a job description, refused to accept the responsibilities it imposed on him. This was a serious breach which would ultimately have justified dismissal. In fact his dismissal was unfair because the bank had not clearly specified to him that his refusal would result in dismissal.

Changing the job description to introduce new working methods will not, therefore, amount to a contract variation so long as the new work method is within the parameters of the contract. This is not always easy to decide, but in two cases *Cresswell v. Board of Inland Revenue (1984)*[2] and *McPherson v. London Borough of Lambeth (1988)*.[3] The courts held that computerisation of coding for PAYE and housing benefits respectively did not amount to a work method outside the contract, even though use of computers was not mentioned in the contract.

Some working arrangements lie in the discretion of the employer. Matters such as work space allocation and whether smoking is permitted are examples of these. In *Rogers v. Wicks & Wilson (1988)*[4] the employer, after due notice, imposed a smoking ban. Mr Rogers alleged this was breach of contract but the tribunal found otherwise – smoking came within the category of works rules fixed by management and which management could change.

The employer may also provide non-contractual benefits. Whether the benefit is contractual or not will depend on the contract terms. Where it is not contractual the employer is free to change it – or even remove it.

Policies and procedures may also be outside the contract terms and thus be changeable without fear of legal repercussions. But two points must be emphasised:

1. Whether a term is contractual or not depends on the contract terms. So if an offer letter were to state, 'Your job duties are as set out in the attached job description,' or the employer presents an employee with a job description which the employee agrees and signs as being 'the work which I am required to perform under my contract', the job description may be contractual.

If it is not to be contractual it might be better not to refer to the job description in the offer letter, or to enclose a copy of the current job description 'for information only'. Many job descriptions include a statement specifying that they are guidance as to performance and are not contract terms.

2. Good practice should not be ignored. Employees should be given ample notice of any changes in non-contractual arrangements.

It is possible to change the contract terms. First, flexibility may be built into the contract in four main ways:

- *by a very wide term*, e.g. 'You may be required to work anywhere within the UK,' or 'Your hours of work are such as is necessary to meet the requirements of our organisation.'
- *by a narrow, but changeable, term*, e.g. 'Your place of employment is Century House but we reserve the right to change this to any other establishment, present or future, within the UK,' or 'You will work eight hours in 24, day, night or shift work.'
- *by using discretionary terms*, that is to say, terms which can be altered in content or removed. So in *Cadoux v. Central Regional Council (1986)* (see p. 24) the employer was able to remove discretionary insurance benefits. The courts are now insisting that the term should be clearly identified as a discretionary one. The employer had not done this in *Baynham & ors v. Philips Electronics (UK) Ltd & ors (1995)*.[5] In 1974 the employer had introduced group membership of PPP health insurance for all staff above a certain grade, making it clear that staff who retired would continue to benefit from the scheme along with their families. The first information sheet on the scheme reiterated this, as well as making it clear that PPP had the right to make changes to the limits on benefits, the payments made by the company and the notional subscriptions of each employee for tax purposes. In the standard terms of employment the scheme fell in the section headed 'Additional Discretionary Benefits'. In 1982 the employer withdrew the most expensive hospitals from the scheme without any objection from the employees. In 1985 the company introduced an excess payment of £25 and again there were no objections. The scheme was still too costly, so pensioners were told they would have to move to an

inferior scheme providing fewer benefits. The court held that the employees had been promised health cover at the same rate as at their retirement for the rest of their lives. Putting the benefit under 'discretionary' benefits was not enough to make it discretionary – the actual term itself was the critical factor. The court concluded that the term was not discretionary. PPP could change the terms: the employer could not. In addition, once employment had ended the employees' accrued rights crystallised and could not be changed, even if changes could have been made during employment.

- *by giving notice of the change.* The contract may provide that the employer can change a term by giving an agreed period of notice. This occurred in *Candler v. ICL Systems Services (1996).*[6] ICL had inserted a clause in the contract enabling them to change the terms by giving the same period of notice as that needed to terminate the contract. This was upheld by the EAT.
- Less useful are the *'catch-all' terms*, e.g. 'Such other duties as may be assigned to you.' This is likely to be interpreted restrictively.

The courts and tribunals are tightening up on discretionary clauses, not only by questioning whether they are indeed discretionary but also by looking at the way in which they are exercised. They have imposed considerable restraints by using the implied term of mutual trust and confidence. This requires both parties to behave in a way that allows the other to trust and respect them. For some time it has been clear that the employer who springs a change on the employee at short notice is in breach of this duty. In *United Bank v. Akhtar (1989),*[7] when Akhtar was moved, as his contract permitted, from Leeds to Birmingham, he was told only on the Friday that he would be based and working in Birmingham on the following Monday; the EAT held that such short notice was breach of mutual trust and confidence. But the duty has now been taken further. The employer has to talk to the employee to find if he will face difficulties in accommodating the change, and the actual exercise of the discretion itself is subject to review. So in *Johnstone v. Bloomsbury Health Authority (1991),*[8] although the health authority had a discretion to require the doctor on 40 hours a week to work a further 48 hours a week, making his hours 88 in total, to do so might be a breach of both the implied duty of mutual trust and the implied duty to provide a safe system of work. A similar decision was reached in *St Budeaux Royal British Legion Club v. Cropper (1995).*[9] Cropper had entered into a new contract in 1987 which gave the club power to vary his hours. When the club ran into financial difficulties they reduced his hours from 56 to 51, so reducing his wages by £27 and making it impossible for him to fulfil his duties. He was given six weeks' notice of the change. He resigned and claimed constructive dismissal. The EAT decided that there had been a constructive dismissal and it was unfair. They decided that the implied duty of mutual trust and confidence included the duty not to make it impossible for the employee to do his work, and this overrode the exercise of the employer's discretionary power to change the hours.

In the light of these cases the employer would be well advised to follow a short procedure before exercising a discretionary power:

- Talk to the employee about the change and consider his views.
- If only one or some of a group are subject to the change, justify the choice.
- Give adequate time for the change.
- Use any appropriate discretionary benefits, eg relocation allowance.
- If the employee finds it impossible to make the change, see if there is alternative work available.

Secondly, machinery for change can be included in the contract and this can provide wide scope for variation.

The contract may provide for negotiating arrangements whose outcome is automatically incorporated into the contract without the need for acceptance by the individual employee. Collective agreements are the commonest type of incorporated machinery, but other machinery, not dependent on unions, can be devised. For details on the incorporation of collective agreements see above.

Collective agreements will not automatically be incorporated into employment contracts unless there is a contract term to that effect, e.g. incorporating 'such collective agreements as may be made from time to time with [the trade union]'.

If the collective agreement is not included in the contract, then when one has been concluded the employment contract is not changed, and the employer who insists on the change will be varying the contract unilaterally. This is breach of contract and amounts to constructive dismissal, which the employer must then justify. If the vast majority of the workforce accept the agreement the constructive dismissal will probably be fair, as in *Ellis v. Brighton Co-operative Society (1976)*.[10] Mr Ellis was unwilling to work the longer week agreed with the union (but not incorporated into his contract) and accepted by the majority of the men. His dismissal was fair, even though the longer hours were outside his contract, as it amounted to 'some other substantial reason for dismissal'. This is discussed further below.

Collective agreements may be construed as offers to the employees, as in *Gascol Conversions v. Mercer (1974)*.[11] Note that procedure agreements are rarely incorporated in employment contracts. The Trade Unions and Labour Relations (Consolidation) Act 1992 s. 179 must be complied with before such incorporation can occur (see above, p. 17).

Where future collective agreements are incorporated the terms can be changed only by giving proper notice under the collective agreement or by expressly agreeing the change with the individual employees (*Robertson v. British Gas (1983)*[12]).

The employer may reserve the right to change any contract term but undertake to consult or notify before the change becomes effective. *Humphreys & Glasgow v. Broom and Holt (1989)*[13] is an example of this. The employers had the power to change the contract terms, but first had to consult the employees. They raised the hours from 37 to 40 hours without increasing pay. But they failed to consult, so no variation had occurred.

Another method is to incorporate existing and future staff handbooks. These are not incorporated in the contract automatically, so an express term is required. Handbooks are often a mixture of contractual terms, job descriptions and general information about the organisation, so not every part of the handbook is suitable for incorporation. Where the parts to be incorporated have not been identified by the parties (usually the employer) the court or tribunal will decide which parts are in and which parts are out. In *Secretary of State for Employment v. ASLEF (1972)*,[14] sections in rule books dealing with rotas and overtime were found to be contractual. In *Cadoux v. Central Regional Council (1986)* the employer was able to withdraw insurance cover which was a 'discretionary right' so long as he followed the agreed notification procedure (see above, p. 24). If the contract provides that further terms may be found in such hand-books as may from time to time be issued, then changes may be made by issuing a new handbook.

Ways of keeping the terms flexible

A flexible clause

You are employed to work at St Luke's House but the company reserves the right to relocate you to any other establishment in the London and south-east region on a temporary or permanent basis.

Change made by issuing new handbooks

You will find further terms and conditions in staff handbooks which will be issued from time to time.

Incorporating collective agreements

Your wage will be such as may be agreed from time to time with the union.

A catch-all provision

. . . in addition you will undertake such other duties as your manager may assign to you from time to time.

Often employers, employees and unions believe that contract terms can be changed by custom. Custom can only fill in gaps in the contract. It cannot change agreed terms, unless it can be shown that the parties intended, by their conduct, to change the terms. Conduct alone is usually too ambiguous to have this effect.

The customary performance of non-contractual duties does not make them contractual, nor does it automatically justify dismissal for refusal to perform them. *Hedger v. Davy & Co (1974)*[15] was just such a case. Mr Hedger had regularly worked unpaid non-contractual overtime at Christmas. This year he requested payment. The tribunal held that there was no duty to work overtime. This conclusion could not be drawn from his past conduct. Nor does failure to enforce a right for some time mean that it is lost, though proper warning of a return to enforcement should be given if unfair dismissal claims are to be avoided.

If the custom or conduct totally contradicts the term, and the parties treat the change as contractual, then the contract terms may be changed. But it must be emphasised that conduct is frequently ambiguous and it can be dangerous to rely upon custom as having changed the contract terms.

If there is no provision in the contract itself for making the change, then the consent of the individual employee or employees is needed. The consent of the majority will not do; the consent of every individual is required. This is illustrated by *Miller v. Hamworthy Engineering (1986)*,[16] in which the employer imposed short-time working. Collective agreements were written into the contract but ASTMS would not agree to the terms proposed by the employer, although the other unions, and thus their members, did. Miller himself did not accept the new terms. When the employer imposed short-time work with an accompanying reduction in wages Miller successfully sued for his full wage. The Court of Appeal insisted that the employer had to show an agreed variation of the terms and the employer was unable to do so.

For the change to be effective there must be both an offer and acceptance. The employee is free to accept the new terms but is not bound to reject them. If he does not positively accept, then the terms do not change. Acceptance must be positive and unequivocal. It must also be unconditional. No particular form of acceptance is required, unless the employer has specified one, e.g. 'Sign below if you accept.' So acceptance may be written, oral or even by conduct. 'Conduct' means some positive action. It may mean working the new shift system, or turning up at the new place of work. But doing nothing will rarely amount to acceptance. The problem arises when the change is notified but not put into immediate effect. If the employee does not object but continues working, this will not normally be acceptance. Two recent cases illustrate this. In *Anglia Regional Co-operative Society v.*

O'Donnell (1994)[17] Ms O'Donnell's original place of work did not include Lowestoft. After a series of mergers she received new terms and conditions which included Lowestoft, but she did not sign them. She was later moved to Lowestoft but refused to transfer. It was decided that the employer had no contractual right to transfer her, because she had not accepted the change to her terms. Consent should not easily be assumed to a unilateral change that does not have immediate affect. She was redundant – but Lowestoft was found to be suitable alternative employment. A similar decision was reached in *Aparau v. Iceland Frozen Foods plc (1996)*.[18] Ms Aparau was employed to work in one retail outlet. She was then presented with terms making her mobile between outlets. She did nothing, but continued working. The employer's subsequent attempt to compel her to move was breach of contract: she had not accepted the term.

So an employee who receives an offer to vary his contract has two options. He can continue on the old terms or accept the employer's offer of new ones. If the employee ignores the offer the terms do not change.

But it is possible for the employee to accept the new terms by his conduct. That is what occurred in *Joel v. Cammell Laird (Ship Repairs) (1969)*.[19] Collective agreements were not incorporated into the employment contracts so Cammell Laird put the package agreed with the union to the staff. It included an increase in wages and other benefits as well as mobility between shipbuilding and ship repairing. The men took the wage increase but afterwards some refused to move from shipbuilding to repairing. The tribunal decided that their terms had changed. They were offered a package and could not select just the parts they liked. Taking the higher wage was a positive act of acceptance of the whole package: it was quite unequivocal. So if the employee changes his behaviour to comply with a term in the offer that will be accepted and the terms will have changed. He will not be able to bring any legal action in relation to the variation.

The only time when doing nothing definitely amounts to acceptance is when the contract contains a term making it so. For example, 'You will be notified of any change and if you do not object in writing within 14 days you will be deemed to have accepted the change.' But it will not happen in the absence of an express term.

This assumes that the employee has a choice. Sometimes he has not. He is told that the new terms will apply whether he likes them or not. Such an imposition of new terms contrary to the wishes of the employee is a breach of contract by the employer. It is a serious breach of contract, amounting to repudiation of the contract terms.

Whenever the contract is broken the innocent party is always entitled to damages, but when the breach is serious – i.e., in legal terminology,

amounts to repudiation of his contractual duties by the party in breach –
then the innocent party is entitled in addition to terminate the contract
without notice. This right is frequently used by the employer to dismiss
the employee who has committed gross misconduct, but it applies to all
serious breaches of contract and the employee can use it too.

Of course such a serious breach by the employer will also amount to
constructive dismissal under the Employment Rights Act 1996, s.
95(1)(c), entitling his employee to claim unfair dismissal and, where
appropriate, redundancy.

So the employee has several options open to him in the event of an
imposed unilateral change in his contract terms:

- Terminate the contract without notice. A common law right. The termination must occur promptly after the breach.
- Claim constructive dismissal under the Employment Rights Act 1996,
  s. 95, and bring a claim for unfair dismissal. The employee must show
  there were grounds permitting him to terminate the contract without
  notice at common law as in the first point above. The termination must
  occur promptly after the breach and the claim must be lodged within
  three months of termination.
- Claim constructive dismissal as in the second point above but bring a
  claim for redundancy. The claim must be lodged within six months of
  termination.
- Sue for damages for breach of contract or for performance of the
  contract term. A common law right. The claim must be brought
  within six years of the breach in England and Wales or five years in
  Scotland and within three months before the tribunal.

These are separate claims, and one may be lost without another being
affected. In particular the employee may fail to act promptly and so lose
his right to claim unfair dismissal or redundancy, but the terms of his
contract will not have changed, so he can enforce his rights as Miller
enforced his right to full pay during short-time working.

It is not unusual for the employee to lose an unfair dismissal claim by
not acting with sufficient promptitude. To make it even more difficult for
employees, there is no definition of 'prompt': it will all depend on the
facts. In *Rice v. Bryson Meats (1989)*[20] Ms Rice was faced with a drastic
wage cut, the loss of her company car and a reduction in her job. The
EAT decided this amounted to breach of contract. But, although she
protested initially, she continued in employment for at least 11 weeks,
partially on sick leave, whilst seeking other employment. This was too
long. She had a 'reasonable' time in which to act, but she should have
taken some steps before eleven weeks. She could not claim constructive
dismissal.

Rigby v. Ferodo (1987)[21] is a good illustration of enforcement of the contractual right after loss of the unfair dismissal claim. In that case Ferodo had attempted to impose a variation in Rigby's wages, namely a 10 per cent reduction. Rigby objected, refusing to accept the change, but he did continue to work and took home his reduced wage. It was held that the old terms continued to apply, and his action for the unpaid 10 per cent was upheld. The House of Lords pointed out that Rigby had not claimed repudiation, although, given the seriousness of the breach, he would have been entitled to do so had he acted promptly. By not acting promptly he had lost his unfair dismissal claim, but not the right to his full wage.

In cases where the employee either needs time to think and plan his course of action or is faced with a unilateral variation under which he cannot stick to his original contract he is in a position of some difficulty. But there is a way out.

The way out was used successfully in *Hogg v. Dover College (1990)*.[22] Hogg was head of the history department, but after a severe attack of meningitis he was able to work only part-time. The headmaster assumed he would be able to work only part-time the following year and removed him as department head. Hogg wrote accepting the new terms – but without prejudice to his unfair dismissal claim. In other words, he said that the college had broken the contract. This amounted to repudiation because it was a serious breach. The college, being the guilty party, could not end his contract. He was terminating it as a result of the college's breach. Thus there was constructive dismissal. He then accepted the new contract in mitigation of his loss.

The EAT considered that the facts might also be interpreted as withdrawal of the original contract by the employer. This would amount to the outright dismissal of Hogg. In either case there was a claim for unfair dismissal. There are two interesting points in this case. The first is the way in which Hogg responded quickly to his employer's action by sending a letter of objection, thus preserving any rights he might have. The second is that it is not necessary to leave employment before bringing a claim for unfair dismissal. But, bearing in mind the problems faced by Ms Rice, any employee intending to remain in employment should follow Hogg's example and make his position clear – in writing.

The effect of these rules can be seen in three different situations:

- If an employee is offered new terms, and accepts them, the contract is varied: there is no breach, and no claims can be made. If the employee acts in accordance with the contract terms – for example, by moving to a new location or accepting a higher wage – then he will have accepted the new terms.
- If the employee does nothing (i.e. neither by word nor by conduct

indicates acceptance), then the old terms continue to apply. He will then be able to claim damages for breach and enforce any claim such as a claim for wages (see *Rigby v. Ferodo*). But he must act promptly if he wishes to terminate the contract or claim constructive dismissal.

- Where the imposed new terms are in breach of the original contract the employee can retain his rights both at common law and for unfair dismissal and redundancy if he clearly protests at the time.

If the employee will not agree to the new terms there is only one further option open to the employer, and that is to dismiss the employee and offer employment on the new terms. This removes the old terms, and any continuation of employment will be on the new ones. But whenever there is a dismissal the employer must take steps to avoid three possible claims:

- breach of contract
- unfair dismissal
- redundancy.

Breach of contract can be avoided by giving due notice and following any contractual procedure. Dismissal can be justified where there is a genuine organisational need for the change and in addition the employer can show that he has followed a proper procedure. This is a good defence to a claim for unfair dismissal.

There is no prescribed procedure for organisational need but the following procedure is based on the cases involving organisation need. It may be possible to show that the dismissal is fair without taking every step. But that is a risk.

1. The employer must show a valid business need. He must show that the matter has been fully considered and a proper reasoned decision has been reached. In *Genower v. Ealing, Hammersmith and Hounslow Area Health Authority (1980)*[23] there had been a prosecution of an employee in the authority's purchasing department, and so to avoid future problems it decided to rotate the purchasing functions. Genower was employed to purchase surgical equipment and was transferred to the less skilled provision purchasing. Need had been shown and his dismissal following his refusal to accept the change was held to have been fair.

How vital must the need be? This is not clear. In early cases, e.g. *Moreton*, (7) below, it was a matter of the company's economic survival. In *Wilson v. Underhill House School (1977)*[24] the EAT required a 'genuine reorganisation and not some trumped-up excuse to dress up financial stringency in the form of redundancy'. But in later cases the EAT has merely required the reorganisation to be 'beneficial'. In *Smith v.*

Grampian Regional Council (1991)[25] the need of a local authority to change the terms of employment of staff in a direct labour organisation so that they could submit a competitive tender for contractual services was accepted as a valid business need. It is not necessary to show that the organisation will collapse unless the change is made, but the need must be real. The tribunal will balance the need of the organisation against the effect on the employee.

2. The employer must then produce a draft plan.

3. Since *Williams v. Compair Maxam (1982)*[26] it has been recognised that, if the employer is legally bound to consult representatives in respect of the dismissal, he will comply with the law and do so. If he does not so consult, the dismissal will be unfair. Originally the employer had only to consult the representatives of recognised trade unions when proposing to make employees redundant (Trade Union and Labour Relations (Consolidation) Act 1992 s. 188). Two major changes have extended the duty to consult. First, anticipating the decision of the European Court of Justice in *European Commission v. United Kingdom (1994)*[27] the definition of 'redundancy', for the sole purpose of consultation (entitlement to pay is not affected), was widened. For consultation purposes, 'redundancy' is defined as a 'dismissal for a reason not related to the individual concerned or for a number of reasons all of which are not so related'. (Trade Union and Labour Relations (Consolidation) Act 1992 s. 195(1).)[28] This is wide enough to cover dismissals to achieve re-organisation,[29] or to change terms. Second, to comply with the decision of the ECJ in the same case that the UK was in breach of the Redundancy Directive 1975 by restricting compulsory consultation to representatives of recognised trades unions, the Collective Redundancies and Transfer of Undertakings (Protection of Employment) (Amendment) Regulations 1995 were introduced. These require the employer to consult elected representatives, although, where there is recognition, he may choose instead to consult representatives of recognised unions or, if there is another suitable body which has been elected for a different purpose (eg a company council), he may consult that body. It is therefore essential that the employer consults the relevant representatives and where necessary includes the time for holding elections in the schedule.

Consultation must begin 'in good time'[30] and must be 'with a view to reaching agreement'. This means that in form it will resemble negotiation, but there is no duty actually to reach agreement. The employer must provide the representatives with written information about the number of persons involved, arrangements for dismissals, payments to be made, steps to avoid dismissal, etc.

The consultation must last for a minimum period of time, depending on the number to be dismissed:

- If 20–99 are to be dismissed within a period of 90 days, the consultation must be in good time, and for at least 30 days.
- If 100 or more are to be dismissed within a period of 90 days, the consultation must be in good time, and for at least 90 days.
- There is no need to consult if fewer than 20 are to be dismissed.

The penalty for failure to consult is a protective award. The representatives complain to the tribunal of failure to consult. If this is upheld the tribunal can make an award of up to 30 days' pay where 20–99 employees are involved, and up to 90 days' pay where 100 or more are involved. All the staff covered can claim the award, regardless of service, and the sum is not set against any other payment made to the employee.[31]

4. After the consultation the plan will become a final plan. The staff affected and the steps to be taken will now be identified.

5. It is also essential to consult the individual prior to any dismissal. In *Polkey v. A. E. Dayton Services (1987)*[32] the House of Lords insisted that there had to be a proper procedure for each dismissal and that it should include prior consultation with the individual unless such consultation would be pointless.

6. The offer made to the employee must be reasonable. Reasonable from the standpoint of a reasonable employer, not reasonable for the employee. In *Chubb Fire Security v. Harper (1983)*[33] the EAT pointed out that in dismissal claims the issue was whether the employer had acted as a reasonable employer would act, not whether the act was reasonable from the employee's point of view. Changes in terms are frequently unreasonable in the employee's eyes. In the Chubb case the employer was faced with a diminishing demand for a product, so he reorganised the sales force and the method of remuneration. Chubb considered that, as a result, the employee would earn considerably less. The case was remitted to the tribunal to consider whether the employer's action was reasonable.

But employees' views are taken into account by reasonable employers. In *Evans v. Elemeta Holdings (1982)*[34] a new manager introduced mandatory unpaid overtime on weekdays and four hours' unpaid overtime on Saturdays. The wage was also increased. Evans refused to accept the new terms. Management were unwilling to make an exception for him, saying that the standardisation of the terms was a commercial necessity. Doubt was thrown on this by the EAT. But they found clearly in Evans's favour on the unreasonableness of the term. It was unreasonable to change his contract from one which did not require overtime to one which imposed an unlimited obligation to work overtime.

If the majority of the staff accept the new terms, or the change has been negotiated with the union, it is easier to show the reasonableness of the terms. In *Ellis v. Brighton Co-operative Society (1976)*[35] the union had negotiated an agreement involving longer hours. Union agreements were not automatically incorporated into the employment contracts. Ellis was not a union member, and he rejected the new terms because they might affect his health. The dismissal was held fair. No medical evidence was available to the tribunal. Evidence showing that his health would have been affected might well have changed the decision.

7. The objecting staff should be given full information, the consequences should be explained to them, and they should be allowed time to come to terms with the change. In *Moreton v. Selby Protective Clothing (1974)*[36] the company was justified in changing the work pattern to include working during school holidays. The employer gave plenty of advance notice to enable Mrs Moreton to make arrangements for child care. The dismissal was fair.

8. Dismissal must be with full notice, or wages in lieu, and the new terms should be offered again.

Claims for redundancy will arise where there is relocation outside the contract provisions or where fewer people are needed to do the work the employee was engaged to perform. This will arise where fewer staff are required or the place of employment changes. The procedure above covers the requirements of redundancy procedures. Details of redundancy are explained in *Redundancy*, a companion volume in this series.

If the term changed affects wages it is essential to ensure that the change is a valid one, otherwise the employee may bring a claim for wrongful deduction of wages under the Employment Rights Act 1996 s. 13 (previously the Wages Act 1986). A claim could arise when hours are changed, reducing pay, or the method of calculating bonus or commission is changed etc. Although the claim has to be brought within three months of the breach, if the breach is a continuing one the claim can be brought within three months of the last wrongful payment. This was made clear in *Taylorplan Services Ltd v. Jackson (1996)*.[37] The claim was brought by school cleaners who had transferred from the council to Taylorplan under the Transfer of Undertakings (Protection of Employment) Regulations 1981. Taylorplan had wrongly assumed that the terms of the transferred staff provided for payment only when they were working, and did not include bank holiday and holiday payments. Accordingly they withdrew these payments from the transferred staff. There was some doubt as to whether the claims were in time. The EAT referred the issue back to the tribunal to see if there had been a series of deductions and, if so, to calculate time from the last one.

The Transfer of Undertakings (Protection of Employment) Regulations 1981 puts additional hurdles in the way of an employer seeking to change terms. When an economic entity transfers from one employer to another the staff transfer on their existing terms and conditions.[38] [39] Clearly any imposed change will be breach of contract and constructive dismissal. Regulation 8 makes any dismissal connected with the transfer automatically unfair unless it can be justified for an economic, technical or organisational reasons requiring a change in the nature of the workforce. This is far narrower than business need. There may be a business need to harmonise the terms of the acquired and the existing staff, but it does not involve a change in the nature of the workforce and the change is caught by Regulation 8.[40] *Berriman v. Delabole Slate Ltd (1981)* IRLR 305 CA. In *Wilson v. St Helens Borough Council (1996)*[41] the EAT, in a momentous decision, held that in the absence of an economic, technical or organisational reason requiring a change in the nature of the workforce the employee was legally incapable of agreeing to the change of any term in his contract if the change was detrimental to him. They based their decision on earlier decisions of the ECJ. The only way to achieve such a change, even when buying out rights or offering a different, but equally good, package is to use a compromise agreement or utilise the services of the ACAS conciliation officer. An ineffective change could result in a wages claim a year or two later![42]

Key points

- Do the terms provide for flexibility?
- Is there machinery for change?
- Make an offer to the employee.
- Dismiss and re-engage:

  Show need.
  Draft a plan.
  Consult representatives.
  Finalise the plan.
  Make a reasonable offer to staff; consult individuals.
  Dismiss with notice or wages in lieu.
  Offer new terms.

References

1 IRLR 442 EAT.
2 IRLR 190 Ch.
3 IRLR 470 Ch.
4 Noted in (1988) *IDS Brief* 366.

5   *IDS Brief* 551 QBD.
6   *IDS Brief* 562.
7   IRLR 505 EAT.
8   IRLR 118 CA.
9   *IDS Brief* 552.
10 EAT IRLR 419 EAT.
11 IRLR 155 CA.
12 IRLR 302 CA.
13 Noted in (1989) IRLIB 369 EAT.
14 2 All ER 949 CA.
15 IRLR 138 IT.
16 IRLR 461 CA.
17 *IDS Brief* 16 EAT.
18 IRLR 121 EAT.
19 ITR 206 IT.
20 EAT, noted in *IDS Brief* 407, IRLIB 319.
21 IRLR 516 HL.
22 ICR 39 EAT.
23 IRLR 297 EAT.
24 IRLR 475 EAT.
25 EAT, noted in IRLIB 419.
26 IRLR 83 EAT.
27 IRLR 412 ECJ.
28 Introduced by TURERA 1993 s. 34.
29 *NATFE v. Brooklands College* (1996) IT unreported.
30 It used to be 'at the earliest opportunity', defined in *Hough v. Leyland DAF Ltd (1991)* ICLR 696, IRLR 194 EAT as the time when dismissals were inevitable – in that case when the decision to contract out the service was made.
31 TULR(C)A 1992 ss. 189, 190.
32 IRLR 503 HL.
33 IRLR 311 EAT.
34 IRLR 143 EAT.
35 IRLR 419 EAT.
36 IRLR 269 IT.
37 IRLR 184 EAT.
38 This is a complex legal issue outside the ambit of this book; further information can be found in Harvey, *On Industrial Relations and Employment Law*, or from legal advisers.
39 Regulation 5.
40 *Berriman v. Delabole Slate Ltd (1981)* IRLR 305 CA.
41 IRLR 320 EAT.
42 In *Meade and Baxendale v. British National Fuels* (1996) IRLR 541 EAT, the EAT held that a dismissal just prior to the transfer was effective to terminate the employment and so end the original

employment terms. All that transferred to the new employer was any unfair dismissal liability in respect of that dismissal. The employees were employed on the new employment terms offered to them after the transfer.

Part II
Types of contract

9
Introduction

The choice of the type or form of the contract should not be haphazard, nor should it automatically be identical to that of other similar organisations. It should suit the needs of the organisation itself, and the needs of organisations can differ even when the product or the service they provide is identical.

Whether contracts are permanent or casual, part-time or full-time, will depend on various factors such as:

- the long- or short-term nature of the product or the length of service contracts
- whether there is only a short-term need for a skill
- how secure the financial situation is
- whether the need is for a one-off task
- whether the product or service is provided on a twenty-four-hour basis
- the availability of staff, and so on.

The type of contract may also be influenced by the culture of the organisation. Some organisations encourage long service, rewarding it with incremental pay and other benefits. Others positively seek a high turnover of staff, looking for a constant stream of new ideas. The latter are likely to be in industries or services where the clientele or the business is fickle and dependent on fashion. Such organisations may incline to high rewards but short security.

The organisation structure will also have an impact. The management gurus have long been exhorting organisations to adopt a 'core' structure, engaging a small number of key staff on secure long-term contracts and bringing the others in on fixed-term, casual or temporary contracts as and when they are needed, or putting the work out to sub-contract with the self-employed. It is interesting to note that few organisations have deliberately moved to this core structure, although there has been a growth in part-time and temporary work.

The labour pool itself may influence the type of contract offered. For example, where alternative seasonal work is available, a large pool of women with children may want part-time work.

It would be possible to employ staff to perform the same job on different types of contract, e.g. indefinite, fixed-term, temporary, part-time. But managing a workforce on such diverse terms could prove difficult. Also 'fringe' staff tend to receive less training than the permanent workforce and so, with time, their skill diminishes.

One essential factor which cannot be ignored in selecting the type or form of the contract is the law. Legal rules make many of the perceived benefits of some of these contract forms difficult to achieve. For example, fixed-term contracts are often assumed to terminate on expiry without the employee being able to make any claims upon the employer. But under the Employment Rights Act 1996 the expiry of a fixed-term contract gives rise to possible claims for unfair dismissal and redundancy. These may be excluded by a written term, but without such an exclusion term the benefit of the exclusion is lost. Nor should it be assumed that part-timers are cheaper to employ than full-timers. A series of largely German cases taken before the European Court of Justice have established that a woman part-timer can compare herself with a male full-timer and obtain *pro rata* benefits. (And, of course, vice versa.)

So, despite the wide range of types of contract available, the number of types needs to be manageable, and they should deliver benefits to the organisation.

To ensure that the types and the content of contracts meet the needs of the organisation, they should be identified from the organisation's forward plan. This should identify:

- the work to be done (job analysis)
- the location of the work
- the time span of the work
- the availability of funding
- changes in technology
- methods of production
- expectations of the workforce likely to be available
- existing and trainable skills in the current workforce.

From this it is possible to decide whether, for example:

- the job is long-term
- the job is short-term because of:

   relocation
   new replacement product or service, or
      constantly changing product or service
   new production methods which require new skills
   the need to fill a gap while current staff are trained
   the job is for one task and will end on its completion
   the fact that funding may run out

- the work is regularly available but only for short periods
- the work is available for, or can largely be completed in, only part of the year
- the work can be done by one or more persons part time.

This will indicate whether the contract should be temporary, permanent, fixed-term, for the task, casual or part-time.

The types of contract considered in Part II are only some of the more common ones. There are many variants of them, and new types are constantly being developed.

10
Self-employed or independent contractors

Strictly speaking, this is not an employment contract. But it usually falls within the remit of the personnel department, and it is often considered when work is being offered.

Self-employment is nothing more than a commercial sub-contract or contracting-out, but the contractor is an individual rather than a company or firm. He is an independent contractor. However, individual independent contractors are frequently used as substitutes for employees, performing the same tasks and receiving the same instructions as real employees. The only difference may lie in the manner of payment, or rather of taxation, the employees' pay being subject to Schedule E (PAYE) and that of the independent contractor to Schedule D. It may be difficult for an outsider to separate them from real employees, and legally they probably are employees.

It has always been difficult to separate independent contractors from employees. The original test used by the courts was one of control. Under the test the distinction between employment and the independent contractor was that employment was a contract of service and the employer had the right to control that service, whereas the independent contractor is engaged under a contract for services and the manner of fulfilling the contract is left to the contractor.

With the increasing skills of employees, and the ever more detailed specifications in contractors' contracts, the test had to be modified, and the control element moved towards general control over employment. The new test was set out in the case of *Mersey Docks & Harbour Board v. Coggins & Griffith (Liverpool) (1946).*[1] In that case the Harbour Board hired out a crane and driver to Coggins & Griffith. The hire contract stated clearly that the driver was to be regarded as the employee of Coggins & Griffith. The driver negligently drove the crane into a third party. Clearly his employer was liable in negligence – but who was his employer? It depended on who 'controlled' him. The House of Lords decided that the Harbour Board did. The board set his holiday times, could dismiss him and had general control over his employment.

Denning LJ augmented the test by looking at the extent to which an individual was incorporated into the organisation. In a series of cases of medical negligence he was therefore able to find that skilled staff, including in one instance an NHS consultant, were employees of the hospital, which was therefore vicariously liable for the negligence of the consultant and other medical staff. (*Cassidy v. Ministry of Health (1951)*.[2])

In the 1960s the courts tended to concentrate on whether a person was in business on his own account. They looked at matters such as his ability to set his own work schedule, having to make an investment such as purchasing equipment and being able to control profit. This is illustrated by *Ready Mixed Concrete v. Ministry of Pensions (1968)*.[3] The company had decided to concentrate on making and selling concrete and was no longer going to deliver it. The company offered delivery contracts to its drivers, who then entered into hire-purchase agreements to buy their lorries from the company. These lorries were to be used only for Ready Mixed Concrete work and were painted in RMC colours. In addition the men wore RMC uniforms. But the drivers could set their own routes, decide where to buy fuel and had to provide substitutes while they were away. The Court of Appeal concluded that they had invested on their own account and so were independent contractors. The EAT reached the opposite conclusion in *Withers v. Flackwell Heath Football Supporters' Club (1981)*.[4] In that case a barman was paid a lump sum from which he had to pay any staff he engaged. This gave him control over his profit. But opening hours and prices were controlled by the club.

These cases illustrate the difficulty of ensuring that a contract is for services rather than for service. Each case depends on its own particular facts. Whether or not a person is employed or an independent contractor is a matter of law.

A further complication is that the same test is used by different bodies – the Inland Revenue, the DSS, the courts (health and safety and vicarious liability) and the tribunals. Yet the decision of one is not binding on another, although it may be taken into consideration. It is therefore possible for someone to pay tax under Schedule D as a self-employed person but be considered employed as far as regards health and safety or statutory employment rights claims.

The approach today is to ask the question 'Is he in business on his own account?' and to answer it by reviewing the nature of the relationship. This is sometimes done by separating those factors which indicate employment from those which indicate an independent contract. The factors on each side are not summed; they are weighed, so the greater number of factors will not necessarily carry the day. Not only does each body on the tribunal take into account different factors (the key ones are likely to be the same) but they will also attach different weightings to them. In other words the outcome may be difficult to predict. Finally, the EAT has recently warned against too great a reliance on the 'list' approach, insisting on a return to the question 'Is he in business on his own account?'

The approach of the tribunals is illustrated by *Harris v. Reed*

Employment (1985).[5] Harris was an accountant whose contract provided that he would work for Reed clients and that his hours and work would be fixed by the client. Reed referred to Harris as their employee in their communication with the client and in a document sent to Harris. His tax payment, luncheon vouchers and travel expenses were the same as for other employees, although the actual pay was negotiated for each job. Harris was free to reject jobs he did not like, and Reed were under no obligation to provide him with work. The EAT remitted the case to the tribunal with the following guidance. First, it should consider the nature of the relationship the parties intended to create; then it should consider whether there was anything in the terms of the agreement incompatible with employment. The EAT said that none of the above terms was incompatible with employment, but the tribunal also made it quite clear that there could be no employment contract without 'mutuality'. There had to be reciprocal obligations between the parties. The tribunal thought that, as Reed was under no obligation to provide work and Harris was under no duty to accept it if it were offered, there might be no such mutuality in the relationship. The tribunal finally decided that he was not an employee because of the lack of mutuality.

It is clearly difficult to ensure that a contract is for services and not for service. One useful approach to the problem is to remember that the individual is to be an independent contractor, and to use the organisation's contract for contractors' service contracts as a model rather than as an employment contract. If the agreement will not fit into the service contractor format, that is a very good indication that the contract is after all one of employment.

Certain points are worth watching. They will not necessarily of themselves turn an independent contractor into an employee, but they do give a clear impression of employment:

- the use of the word 'employee' rather than 'contractor'
- payment of a 'wage' rather than a 'fee'
- providing holidays, especially holidays with pay
- payment whilst off sick
- using disciplinary and/or grievance procedures rather than contract management techniques
- the only difference between the employee and contractor is one of payment.

It is also advisable to avoid including terms that are redolent of employment. In *McMeechan v. Secretary of State for Employment and another (1995)*[6] the contract provided that the employee was to 'fulfil the normal common law duties which an employee would owe to an employer', including fidelity, confidentiality and obedience, and that there could be dismissal for not using proper conduct and a grievance procedure. This was sufficient to tip the balance towards employment.

Although the 'list' approach may not be the method favoured by the tribunals, it is easier to operate than the question 'Is he in business?' It is extremely useful so long as it is recognised as nothing more than guidance towards answering the vital question, 'Is he in business on his own account?' The list has two main purposes. It can be used to check existing contracts or it can be used to plan new ones. Most of the issues dealt with in employment contracts have their different equivalents in commercial contracts. For example, questions of performance and disagreements between employer and manager are dealt with under the disciplinary and grievance procedure in employment contracts. In contracts for services there will be provisions for termination and damages for breach of contract, implied if not express, and there will normally be a procedure for managing the contract to deal with performance and any disputes which may arise. Table 1 sets out a list of some of the common factors to be found in each type of contract.

Table 1   List of common factors

Employment	Self-employment/independent contractor
Described as employee	Described as self-employed or contractor or agent
PAYE	Schedule D
Class 1 National Insurance contributions	Class 2 National Insurance contributions
SSP or SMP paid	SSP or SMP not paid
Contractual sick pay	No sick pay
Holiday pay	No holiday pay
Disciplinary procedure	Breach gives principal the right to terminate, find a substitute and claim damages. Liquidated damages clause
Grievance procedure	Project management provisions
Consultative procedure	See above
Basic pay guarantee	Up-front payment, minimum fee
Wage	Fee
Payment similar to that of employed staff	Negotiate own fee
Bonus on profit of the company	
Work method fixed	Fixes own method Can use management techniques to improve profit*
Machinery and equipment provided and/ or maintained by employer	Provides own equipment and machinery or pays cost of use
Supervision as for staff	Specification for the job
Insured as employee	Carries own insurance
Fixed hours	Fixes own hours (subject to site

	provisions)
Long-standing relationship	
Must work for employer*	Free to work elsewhere*
	Must provide a substitute
	Employs own staff
	Custom of the trade*
Integrated into the organisation	Separate business name
	Registered for VAT*

* Currently heavily weighted, but this may change.

If the individual is free to refuse future work (clearly the work accepted under the contract has to be fulfilled) and can negotiate a different fee this will tend to show he is in business on his own account.

It is not possible to state that particular types of work or individuals will or will not be accepted as independent contractors, but the following cases are good examples.

Regular casual catering staff were held not to be employees in *O'Kelly v. Trust House Forte (1983)*[7] and *Ahmet v. Trust House Forte Catering (1983)*.[8] In both instances PAYE was deducted by agreement with the Inland Revenue and benefits such as sick pay and holiday pay were provided. Importance was attached to the fact that each catering event was offered as a separate job and could be refused by the individual. However, similar facts in *Four Seasons (Inn on the Park) v. Hamarat (1985)*[9] resulted in a decision that a regular casual wine waiter was an employee, even though he was not paid a retainer and the hours and days of work varied from week to week. In subsequent cases it seems to have been assumed that such regular casuals were employees.

Freelance casual musicians were independent contractors, according to *Midland Sinfonia Concert Society v. Secretary of State for Social Services*.[10]

In *Market Investigations v. Minister of Social Security (1969)*[11] a market researcher engaged to obtain answers from the public for specific surveys was held to be an employee, even though she set her own hours and was given irregular work.

In *Lee v. Lee's Farming (1961)*[12] a managing director and major shareholder in the company was held to be an employee even though he had control over other employees. Now it is generally concluded that executive directors are employees but that non-executive directors are not. All directors' emoluments are subject to PAYE.

Home workers were frequently thought to be self-employed until this view was changed by a series of cases in the late 1970s and 1980s. In *Nethermere (St Neots) v. Gardiner and Taverna (1984)*[13] two ladies worked at home sewing trouser pockets. The instructions were detailed. They chose how many pockets to sew, and set their own hours. Machinery was supplied by the employer. Their fees were fixed and were not negotiable. The relationship was of long standing. They were employees.

Self-employed sub-contractors are common in the construction industry. The collection of tax was difficult but now the Inland Revenue (Regulations 1990) require tax to be deducted from payment to sub-contractors unless the sub-contractor has obtained an exemption certificate. (Guidance is available from the Inland Revenue.) This deals only with the matter of tax. It does not settle the question of employment. In one case it was held that there may be a status half way between employee and independent contractor. In *Ironmonger v. Movefield (1988)*[14] a skilled clerk of works was supplied by an employment agency to work for Bird's Eye Wall's. The terms of his arrangement with Movefield lacked certainty; in relation to his engagement he was issued with a P45 and Movefield completed form UB85 and confirmed to the Department of Employment that he had been in their employment. He was eventually found not to have been an employee either of Movefield or of Bird's Eye Wall's. The EAT held that it was not necessary to show that a person was an independent contractor, only that he was not an employee. It was possible to be neither. In practice, in order to avoid doubt, it is better to show that the individual is an independent contractor and thus cannot be an employee, and to draft the contract to that end.

Doubt has been thrown on the correctness of the Ironmonger decision by *Lee v. (1) Ching (2) Shun Shing Construction & Engineering (1990)*.[15] Lee, a self-employed mason working for a sub-contractor on a construction site, was injured. A Hong Kong ordinance similar to worker's compensation provided payments to employees, 'any person who has . . . entered into or works under a contract of service or apprenticeship with an employer in any employment'. Lee was found to be an employee because he did not provide his own equipment or hire his own staff, gave priority to Ching's work, made no investment in a business of his own, could not improve his position by management skills. He was not supervised in his work, but neither were skilled workmen. This was followed in *Lane v. Shire Roofing Ltd (1995)*[16] Lane operated a one-man business and was a schedule D taxpayer. Lane agreed to reroof a house for Shire for a fee of £200. Scaffolding would have made the job unprofitable. Lane used a ladder from which he fell, suffering severe injuries (brain damage). The CA held that he was an employee and was owed a duty of care by Shire. In deciding employment status the court should consider who controls the work, and the CA recommended the following questions:

1 Who lays down what is to be done?
2 Who lays down the way in which it is done?
3 Who lays down the means by which it is done?
4 Who lays down the time when it is done?

5 Who hires and fires the team?
6 Who provides materials and equipment?

Finally, even independent contractors are subject to some laws seen largely as protecting employees, such as the Sex Discrimination Act 1975, the Race Relations Act 1976 and the Employment Rights Act 1996 Part II on wages. They may not have conditions relating to their union membership included either in the contract or in the arrangements for selection under the Trade Union and Labour Relations (Consolidation) Act 1992. They are protected by the common law requirement to provide a safe system of work, and their health and safety are ensured under sections 3 and 4 of the Health and Safety at Work Act 1974. The Factories Act 1974 and the Offices Shops and Railway Premises Act 1963 cover persons on the premises – including independent contractors.

One way to avoid these difficulties is to deal with a person who has set up a company. The contract is then with the company and not with a person, and only persons can be employees. But the arrangement must clearly be with the company. If it is as follows:

Green Ltd
2 High Street
London W20

Dear Mary,

We are pleased to offer you the contract . . .

the deal has been made with Mary herself, contacting her at her company's address. It has not been clearly made with the company as was intended. It would have been better to have written 'to offer your company' or 'to offer Green Ltd' rather than 'you'.

Independent contractor contracts are generally used for buying in specialist skills on an irregular or short-term basis from persons who have established their own business supplying such services.

Key points

- Check the list of factors to ensure the contract is not a contract of employment.
- Use a contract for the supply of services as a model.
- Avoid employment terminology.
- Do not include employment procedures.
- Avoid payments such as sick pay and holiday pay.

References

1 2 All ER 345 HL.
2 1 All ER 574 CA.
3 1 All ER 433 QB.
4 IRLR 307 EAT.
5 EAT, noted in IRLIB 281.
6 IRLR 461 EAT.
7 IRLR 369 CA.
8 EAT, noted in IRLIB 232.
9 EAT, noted in IRLIB 292.
10 *The Times*, 11 November 1980, QB.
11 3 All ER 732 QB.
12 AC 12 HL.
13 IRLR 240 CA.
14 IRLR 461 EAT.
15 IRLR 236 PC.
16 IRLR 493 CA.

11
Open-ended or indefinite contracts

Flexibility

These are contracts which will last until the employee retires unless either party terminates it earlier. This type of contract is the 'typical' contract in EU terminology. Because it is likely to last a long time it must be flexible; it is unlikely that an organisation recruiting employees today will want them to be employed on the same terms in, say, five years' time. So, when drafting this type of contract, care must be taken to introduced flexibility. This may be done by using a wide term – 'Your place of employment is the United Kingdom' – or a changeable one – 'Your place of employment is 22 High Street, but we reserve the right to change this location to any other establishment, current or future, within the UK'. Consideration should also be given to including some mechanism for changing other terms. It could be done by incorporating future collective agreements or new staff handbooks (see above, 'Making contracts', p. 17).

It is also important to note terms which are too narrow or which limit powers that would otherwise be available. Examples of narrow terms are 'Your hours are 9.00 a.m.–5.00 p.m.' or 'You will work in the marketing department, in Chancery Lane.' When a need for change arises, unless there is machinery which will allow the change to be made, such terms as these will require renegotiation with each individual employee.

The employer has certain implicit powers at common law. For example, he may give new instructions as to the way in which work is to be performed and he may dismiss for serious breach of contract without giving any notice or wages in lieu. These powers can be restricted by the contract terms. If the job description is put into the contract, then new instructions may require a change in the terms to be negotiated. If a disciplinary procedure is incorporated, then it will restrict dismissal to the grounds specified in the procedure and a dismissal will be in breach of contract if the contractual procedure has not been followed. There is no reason why the employer should not include such terms in the contract, but he should be aware of the implications of doing so. These particular terms are discussed in more detail above, under 'Job descriptions', p. 41, and 'Procedures', p. 26.

Indefinite contracts are most suitable for permanent staff.

Contracts with break points

Indefinite contracts may include the option of, or discretion to grant, a break. Sabbaticals are common in education, and instances of provision for long maternity breaks are increasing in frequency. Other contracts give employees the chance to try a different occupation, or self-employment, etc., with the option of returning to the original employment. In such agreements the trigger point must be identified. It could be age, service, health or the result of a work appraisal. The length of the break must be clear and, most importantly, so must the position of the employee during the break. For example;

- Will employment end when the break begins?
- Will it continue during the break for some or all purposes? For example, will pension rights accrue? Will the car be retained?
- Will employment continue to run but with no contractual benefits available?
- Upon return does the old service employment plus or minus the break count for contractual rights?
- What is the position in relation to statutory continuity of employment?
- Must contact with the organisation be maintained during the break?
- Is the employee required to train or maintain skills during the break or undergo retraining on return?
- Does the employee return to the same or a different job?
- What are his rights if there is no job on his return?

These are just some of the questions which need to be answered before entering into a break contract.

Contracts of this type are often used for maternity, training and sabbatical breaks.

Key points

General

- Are the terms wide or flexible enough?
- Is there machinery to change the terms?

Break points

- What is the objective of the contract?
- Are the trigger points identified?
- Is the length determined?
- What is the position of the contract during the break?

- Do benefits continue during the break?
- Does continuity of service accrue for contractual or statutory rights?
- What is the employment position of the employee at the end of the break?

12
Fixed-term contracts

A fixed-term contract is one which runs for a certain period of time. It must, at the time of formation, include a fixed or calculable termination date such as 'This contract will run for three years from 1 January 1997' or 'This contract will terminate on 31 December 2000.' A notice clause enabling one or both parties to end it earlier will not prevent the contract from being fixed-term. This was decided in *Dixon v. British Broadcasting Corporation (1979)*,[1] despite the fact that it converts a contract which is to run for a fixed term into one which may run for a maximum period.

At common law fixed-term contracts terminate automatically on the predetermined date by operation of the contract term and no dismissal takes place and no notice need be given. But this advantage of contract termination without any procedure having to be followed or any rights arising does not apply in relation to the statutory rights of unfair dismissal and redundancy. The Employment Rights Act 1996, s. 197 provides that if a fixed-term contract expires without renewal it shall be treated as dismissal. It is possible to exclude redundancy and unfair dismissal rights upon expiry, but certain requirements must be fulfilled (see below). If they are not excluded, then, given sufficient continuity of employment, where there is still work for him to do the employee may succeed in an unfair dismissal claim, unless he has been warned about his performance, etc. If the work has been completed, then he will be redundant.

At common law, under a fixed-term contract the employer may have the advantage of automatic termination of the contract without any liability on his part. The employee also has an advantage. The contract must run for the fixed term. If it is terminated earlier (other than on a justified termination for serious breach of contract) the employer is in breach and will have to pay damages based on the contractual remuneration for the outstanding period of the contract. The employee must mitigate his loss, but although that may reduce the sum, the damages are often high. It is interesting to note that, even when the contract contains a notice term, damages are still based on the outstanding period of the contract and not on the period of notice. This is clearly seen in *Laverack v. Wood's of Colchester (1966)*.[2] Laverack had a five-year service agreement as European sales representative which was terminable by either party giving six months' notice. His contract was wrongly terminated with two years to run. His damages were based on the outstanding period of his contract, not on six months' notice. It would appear that if the employer wishes to take advantage of the notice termination provision he must actually give notice.

The statutory rights of employees on fixed-term contracts depend on the length of the contract.

Fixed-term contracts for one month or less

Once a person engaged under a contract for a fixed term of one month or less has been employed for three months or more the fixed-term contract becomes a contract of indefinite duration for the purposes of the Employment Rights Act 1996, s. 86, which sets out the entitlement to minimum statutory notice of the intention to terminate the contract.[3]

Fixed-term contracts for three months or less

An employee engaged under such a contract, or under one which has been made in contemplation of a task which is not expected to last for more than three months, is not entitled to guaranteed pay under the Employment Rights Act 1996, s. 28, or medical suspension pay under s. 64. The employer must prove that the employment is in that category, and it is not easy in the absence of written terms. Without written terms, although it may be possible to show that the expectation was that the contract would last only for up to three months, it may not be possible to show that it would not in fact last longer.

Even if the contract properly falls within the three months' exemption but in practice lasts for more than three months, then the advantages are lost.

There is one further benefit. Statutory Sick Pay is not payable to persons working under these contracts unless a further contract arises within eight weeks.

The benefit of these contracts is not clear. Rebates for Statutory Sick Pay may not be worth the cost of managing the contract and ensuring that there is no overrun.

Fixed-term contracts of one year or more

Generally an employee has no power to contract out of his statutory rights, but there is an exception in relation to the expiry of fixed-term contracts. The Employment Rights Act, 1996, s. 197, permits the insertion of an exclusion clause preventing the employee claiming unfair dismissal upon the expiry of the fixed term so long as the exclusion clause is in writing and signed by the employee, either when the contract was made or during the lifetime of the contract.

The exclusion is quite narrow in operation in that it applies only to the expiry of a fixed-term contract of one year or more. It does not apply to any termination of the contract, lawful or otherwise, during the term of the contract.

It therefore follows that any continued employment beyond the expiry date, other than for a further fixed-term contract of at least one year, is fatal to the exemption. Suppose an employee is engaged under a three-year fixed-term contract containing a valid exclusion clause but is asked to work a further seven days to complete the task. Had the employment ended with the expiry of the three-year contract the exclusion clause would have operated. But the employment terminated with the expiry of a seven-day contract in which there could be no valid exclusion clause. An extension for an indefinite period would have had the same effect. It is only the final contract and its termination to which the exemption in s. 142 applies.

In *McKee v. Tyne & Wear Passenger Transport Executive (1988)*[4] the EAT declared that a seven-day extension of a fixed-term contract defeated the exclusion defence. The exclusion clause in the contract had no effect. In this case the employer argued that while the exclusion clause operated the employee could not accrue continuity of employment for statutory rights. The argument was rejected. The exclusion clause applies only to a valid termination. So during a three-year contract containing an operative exclusion clause the employee accrues continuity, but has no claim he can bring when the contract expires. With a seven-day extension he can use his continuity to bring the unfair dismissal claim which is no longer barred by the exclusion clause. In *Mulrine v. University of Ulster (1993)*[5] the court interpreted a further period of employment expressed as an extension of her existing contract as a continuation of that contract and not as a second new contract on the same terms. They said that this was what the parties must have intended. It would be better to put it in writing and make it clear, eg '. . . It is agreed that the period of your contract shall be varied and will now be x years and x months with a new termination date of . . .'.

Fixed-term contracts are frequently renewed. When there is a simple renewal of such a contract, e.g. 'Your contract is renewed for a further two years,' the expiry clause may be renewed automatically, but it would be better to put it in writing again and get the employee to sign it. Renewed contracts must be at least one year long for the exclusion clause to be effective. If it is intended to renew the contract for less than one year it would be better to vary the original contract by extending the period for which it is to run, i.e. to substitute for the three-year period 'three years and six months', thus ensuring that there is no loss of protection as occurred in *McKee*.

Fixed-term contracts of two years or more

In fixed-term contracts for two years or more it is possible using the same procedure, to exclude redundancy rights upon expiry of the contract.[6] But when renewing the contract there must be a new written exclusion signed by the employee. A simple agreement to renew the contract on the same terms will not renew the exclusion. A new written term and a new signature are necessary. Renewed contracts will have to be of two years' duration.

The exclusion clause must be quite clear, e.g. 'It is agreed that upon the expiry of this contract you will have no rights in relation to unfair dismissal or redundancy.'

Fixed-term contracts for directors

The Companies Act 1985 provides that directors of public companies may not be given contracts exceeding five years in length without first obtaining the shareholders' approval.

Rolling fixed-term contracts

These are fixed-term contracts which automatically renew themselves on a set date. Thus it may be agreed that a three-year contract will automatically renew itself on 1 January every year. It is essential to include a clause enabling each party to give notice to prevent the roll-over, otherwise the contract will continue indefinitely. This type of contract is favoured by employees who see their employment at risk from management or company developments which are beyond their control. The benefit to them is that there is always a long period of the contract outstanding when it comes to assessing damages in the event of termination.

Often a person is engaged on sequential fixed-term contracts, with a gap between each contract, rather than under a series of continuous contracts. This raises some interesting questions in relation to the calculation of continuity of employment for statutory rights. If there is no break between the contracts then continuity of employment is the sum of all the contracts. A gap between two contracts may constitute a break in continuity, in which case the service prior to and during the break will not be taken into account. But not every gap between contracts will be a break. The complicated rules are to be found in the Employment Rights Act 1996 ss. 210–19, which set out additional rules for computing continuity of employment.

To constitute a break, the gap between employment contracts must last for seven days from Sunday to Saturday, and the gap must not count. The gap will count if it is caused by sickness or injury or wholly or partly by pregnancy or confinement so long as it does not last for more than 26 weeks. All of a period of statutory maternity leave is counted. It will count if, by arrangement or custom, the employee is regarded as remaining in employment for any purpose. Most important, it will count if it amounts to a temporary cessation of work. A temporary cessation of work is a period of temporary duration in which the reason why the employee is not working for the employer is because the employer had no work for him to do. There is no maximum period for this temporary cessation. In one early case a gap of 21 months out of a period of 15 years' employment was found to be a temporary cessation of work (*Bentley Engineering v. Crown and Miller (1976)*).[7] It must be doubted whether the same decision would be reached today.

Today the courts adopt two approaches to temporary cessation of work. The first is generally used in seasonal contracts and was enunciated by the House of Lords in *Ford v. Warwickshire County Council (1983)*.[8] Warwickshire gave a schoolteacher a series of annual nine-month fixed-term contracts. She was not employed during the summer holidays. The three-month period between the contracts was found to be a temporary gap and the reason for the gap to be the absence of work. So there were temporary cessations of work during the three-month gaps and her employment was continuous from the start of the first contract to the end of the last. The contract, being of nine months only, was too short for Warwickshire to use the exclusion clause.

In later cases there are examples of gaps which were too long to be temporary cessation of work. In *Sillars v. Charrington Fuel Oils (1989)*[9] a fuel oil delivery driver worked regularly for Charrington during the heating season, roughly from October to May. The periods varied from 21 to 32 weeks per year. The employment was described as temporary. It was held not to be continuous. Again, in *Berwick Salmon Fisheries v. Rutherford (1991)*,[10] it was held that continuity of employment may be preserved during gaps between contracts if that gap amounts to a 'temporary cessation of work'. The EAT explained that the mathematical test checks the period between seasonal contracts to ascertain whether it is sufficiently short as to be no more than a temporary cessation of work. The applicants were fishermen, normally employed for seven months each year, but two breaks in 1986 and 1987 of seven months each were held not to be temporary cessations of work.

Where the work pattern is irregular the courts and tribunals are more inclined to 'take a view' of the contract. So in *Flack v. Kodak (1986)*,[11] where employees worked as and when needed, the tribunal was instructed to consider each gap in relation to the employment as a whole and not use the mathematical test.

Of course, the gap must be due to lack of work; it it arises because the employee will not accept work or has gone on holiday (even with the employer's agreement), it is not a temporary cessation of work. This was the decision in *Letherby and Christopher v. Bond (1988)*.[12]

Finally, if an employee moves from one associated employer to another, the continuity of employment he has accrued with the first transfers with him to the second. And gaps between contracts with associated employers are dealt with in the same way as gaps between contracts with the same employer. Associate employers must be companies. They can be foreign companies if their form is similar to companies in Great Britain. They are associated if one controls the other or both are controlled by a third party. The third party need not be a company. Control is not defined but certainly includes voting control, so making subsidiaries associated companies both with each other and with the holding company (Employment Rights Act 1996 s. 231).

Fixed-term contracts have two main uses. The first is to provide the employer with a cost-free termination of employment when the contract terminates. The second is to provide the employee with security, at least in the financial sense. But in order for the contract to provide the benefits it has to be possible to identify the period of employment.

The employer benefits require careful management to obtain, both in ensuring that there is an operative exclusion clause and in preventing an overrun which will destroy the benefit. From a managerial point of view it may be more sensible to allow the overrun than to terminate the contract before the work is complete and either recruit someone else or re-engage the same employee after a gap to break continuity. The cost and risk attached to an overrun may be less. The main problems will be unfair dismissal and redundancy. If the employee is aware that his contract will end when the job is complete it will normally be fair to dismiss him for that reason. But if there is no more work he will inevitably be redundant. The cost of redundancy will depend on whether it is restricted to statutory redundancy pay or includes company benefit. It is not unusual to find fixed-term employees excluded from the company scheme. They are sometimes excluded from other company benefits. A shorter disciplinary or grievance procedure may be required where the normal procedure would not be exhausted during the length of the contract.

Fixed-term contracts and the EU

The EU regards fixed-term contracts as temporary contracts, regardless of their length. Thus the provision relating to information on the risks relating to the job and the qualifications required for the job must be notified to the employee in advance under the Directive on the Health and Safety of Temporary Workers 1991. See Chapter 16 below, on 'Temporary contracts' (pp. 105–7).

The draft directives on temporary workers would also apply. In particular they would restrict the renewal of fixed-term contracts of 12 months or less to a total period of 36 months, regardless of the holder of the job, and require *pro rata* terms and conditions as for persons on indefinite contracts.

Key points

Fixed-term contracts are generally used:

- when skills are needed for an identifiable period of time
- to obtain a cost free termination of the contract
- to give security to the employee.

Checklist

- Establish the reason for using a fixed-term contract.
- Ensure that a notice clause is included.
- Determine the availability of benefit packages.
- Consider application of procedures.
- Review mechanism needed to prevent extensions.
- Consider the insertion of clause excluding unfair dismissal and redundancy.

References

1 IRLR 114 CA.
2 3 All ER 683 CA.
3 *Brown v. DSS (1996)* applied this to a woman on a series of one-day fixed-term contracts. IRLB 558 CA.
4 Noted in *IDS Brief* 364 EAT.
5 IRLR 545 NICA.
6 Employment Protection (Consolidation) Act 1978, s. 142.
7 IRLR 146.

 8 IRLR 126 HL.
 9 IRLR 145 CA.
10 IRLR 203 EAT.
11 IRLR 255 CA.
12 Noted in *IDS Brief* 377 EAT.

13
Completion of a task

These are contracts which terminate not on a fixed date but on the occurrence of a pre-ordained event, commonly when the task is complete or when funding runs out. At common law they are dealt with in the same way as fixed-term contracts. But under the Employment Rights Act 1996 they receive different treatment. This is because they do not fall within the definition of dismissal set out in section 95. This is defined as:

- dismissal by the employer with or without proper notice
- expiry of a fixed-term contract
- constructive dismissal, i.e. a serious breach by the employer which would justify the employee's leaving without giving notice.

Task contracts have not been treated as fixed-term contracts. In several cases the courts have concluded that the termination of a task contract did not amount to dismissal and so neither the statutory right to claim unfair dismissal nor the right to claim redundancy arose, because these two rights were dependent on proof of dismissal within the definition of section 95. This was the effect of the decision in *Wiltshire County Council v. National Association of Teachers in Higher Education and Guy (1980).*[1] Mrs Guy was employed as a part-time teacher at the beginning of each year, and one of the conditions of her contract was that, if the principal decided that there were not enough students for her course, her employment would cease. There were not enough students for her course, so her contract terminated. The Court of Appeal upheld the tribunal's decision that there had been no dismissal, whilst doubting whether the facts would have been strong enough to convince them. (The tribunal's decision has to be unsupportable before it will be overturned.) This case was followed in *Brown v. Knowsley Borough Council (1986),* [2] where staff were employed on teaching contracts 'for as long as sufficient funds are provided by the Manpower Services Commission or by other firm/sponsors to fund it'. In *Cooper v. London Borough of Hounslow (1986)*[3] the EAT accepted the concept of the task contract but found that the contract in question did not fall into that category. Cooper had been employed until the double-glazing work around Heathrow Airport had been finished. The EAT decided that this was an indefinite contract, but the employer had indicated in advance an event which would cause him to terminate the contract. The tribunal decided that the burden of showing that there was an automatic termination clause, rather than the employer indicating one of the events which might cause him to give notice, was very heavy and in this case it had not been discharged. This case was in line with *Lee v. Nottinghamshire County Council (1979).*[4] Lee had been employed as a teacher trainer until the expected drop in demand when the baby boom was over. His contract was found to be of indefinite duration.

Clearly, this type of contract has advantages, but the wording must be absolutely clear, and there is a definite risk that the attempt may not succeed. 'It is agreed that the contract will end automatically upon . . .' or similar words may have the desired effect.

Even if the contract is not accepted as a task contract there are still advantages to the employer. As was pointed out in *Lee*, the employee had not been promised indefinite employment – quite the contrary: he had been told when he was offered the job that it might last only three years. So when he was dismissed because there was not enough work he was fairly dismissed. Today more emphasis is put on procedure, so in order to ensure a fair dismissal the employee should be warned of the impending termination (the equivalent of notice) and consulted about the availability of any other work.

But Lee was redundant. Redundancy was unavoidable. The cost of redundancy will depend on the employee's continuity of employment and whether he is entitled to organisation redundancy pay as well as the state benefit. Along with those employed on fixed-term contracts the organisation could exclude task contract employees from the redundancy scheme.

As task contracts are temporary contracts the EU Directive on Written Information will require the employee to be informed in writing of the expected length of the contract. The EU directives and proposals on temporary workers will cover these contracts as well as fixed-term contracts. See 'Fixed-term contracts' above, Chapter 12.

Task contracts tend to be used when no termination date can be identified but an event which will cause termination can be defined.

Key points

- Identify the event.
- Use unambiguous words.
- Consider whether organisation redundancy pay should be available.
- Consider which benefit packages should be available, e.g. redundancy.
- Length of contract could be taken into account.
- Inform the employee of the expected duration of the contract.

- Inform the employee of the qualifications needed for the job and the specific features of the job.

References

1 IRLR 198 CA.
2 IRLR 102 EAT.
3 EAT, noted in IRLIB 229.
4 IRLR 284 CA.

14
Probation and trial periods

Contracts for a probationary or trial period allow for a period of employment in which the employer assesses the suitability of the employee and the employee has an opportunity to prove his worth. They are common at the start of employment but may also occur on promotion.

There are no set legal rules applying to such contracts. It is a matter of interpreting the agreement. Alas, many do not even bother to specify the terms. The contract is simply stated to be subject to a period of probation.

The nature of probation is clear. In particular the employee has to prove himself. This makes it easier to justify a dismissal but the employer also has responsibilities. In *Hamblin v. London Borough of Ealing (1975)*[1] the industrial tribunal held that '. . . the employee knows he is on trial and must put his right foot forward and establish his suitability for the post. The employer on his side must give the employee an opportunity to prove himself . . .' The tribunal upheld a dismissal during a trial period for slow but efficient work. The employer's duty was spelt out further in *Post Office v. Mughal (1977)*,[2] a case involving a telephone sales trainee. The EAT said that the employer had to set a standard for the employees, and give them training and feedback. Then, if they did not meet the employer's standard they could be fairly dismissed. The EAT warned the tribunal against replacing the employer's standard with the tribunal's own. It is the employer's standard which is to be applied unless, of course, it is one no reasonable employer would adopt.

This easier power to dismiss will, of course, be more useful in relation to a probationary promotion than to a new-start probation, while unfair dismissal is restricted to employees with two years' continuity of employment. But the period has not always been so long (at one time it was as short as six months) and, if the dismissal procedure has been incorporated into the contract, the new-start probationer may be able to bring a complaint of breach of contract in the ordinary courts or the tribunal. Persons on probationary promotion contracts are likely to have qualified for unfair dismissal.

A person who has been promoted but has proved unsatisfactory may be dismissed, but the employer will have to justify the dismissal. Where he has failed to give the employee information as to the duties expected of him, other information relating to the job, feedback on his performance, and any necessary training, as in *Patey v. Taylor & Wishart (1988)*,[3] then the dismissal will be unfair. Rather than dismiss him the employer may prefer to transfer the employee to another position, demote him or return him to his previous post. Without an express term in the contract permitting this, or the agreement of the employee, it will be breach of contract and the employee can exercise his legal remedies. Such a provision had been made in *White v. London Transport Executive (1981)*,[4] allowing the transfer of a manager who had unduly favoured her husband as one of the employees who reported to her. Even when there is no power to transfer or demote when a probation proves unsatisfactory, the employer will be required to consider whether there is other suitable work before deciding to dismiss the employee, if unfair dismissal is to be avoided.

It should be clear to both parties what will happen when the probationary period ends. Will probation continue if nothing is said or done? Or is there automatic confirmation? Again, can the contract be terminated before the period is up? Or has the employer guaranteed the employee a period of time in which to prove his worth? It may be as well to provide for one week's notice on either side.

The length of the probation or trial period is usually specified. Care must be taken to ensure that this does not change the contract into a fixed-term one, preventing lawful termination during probation other than for a serious breach of the contract. The problem can largely be avoided by including an express notice clause. The period of notice will often need to be shorter than normal if it is to have any value. It might be provided that 'either party may terminate the contract by giving the other seven calendar days' notice in writing'.

When the probationary period expires the employee is automatically confirmed in his position unless the contract makes alternative provision. For example, the contract might provide that the employee will be on probation for a period of six months 'and thereafter remain on probation until such time as you receive written confirmation in your position'. Even without such a term it is possible to extend the period of probation where there is doubt as to the employee's suitability. Again the extension should be clear and preferably in writing.

The disciplinary procedure may also require adjustment. It may be too long to be completed during the period of probation. A shorter number of warnings may be desirable, especially if the procedure is contractual. Sick pay and other benefits may also be reduced during this period.

These contracts are used when the employer is uncertain of the suitability of the employee and wishes to give the employee an opportunity to prove himself.

Key points

- Define the period.
- Consider a short notice clause.
- Consider a shorter disciplinary procedure.
- Consider power to transfer or demote.
- Inform the probationer of his duties.
- Establish an assessment and feedback procedure.

References

1 IRLR 354 IT.
2 IRLR 178 EAT.
3 Noted in (1988) IRLIB 350.
4 IRLR 261 EAT.

15
Global contracts

This is a contractual arrangement whereby two or more apparently separate contracts with the same employer are linked in one global contract. The contracts may be simultaneous or sequential.

In *Lewis v. Surrey County Council (1987)*[1] Mrs Lewis was employed to teach photography part-time at Guildford School of Art. She held a series of separate contracts, each of one term only, then obtained two further part-time contracts for each term. She alleged that her contracts were all part of one overall global contract and could be aggregated to provide her with sufficient hours and service to give her a right to redundancy compensation.[2] The House of Lords accepted that such an arrangement could be made, but would not accept the aggregation without a total agreement. The Lords held that, where there are gaps in one series of contracts, then those may be continuous by virtue of the gaps being temporary cessations of work; but they could not find statutory authority for aggregating different series of contracts, nor for considering the gaps between contracts in different series as temporary cessations of work. So the concept of a global contract has been accepted by the courts, but they seem reluctant to infer them.

Obviously, if a global contract is desired, it is essential to make it an express term. This can be achieved by entering into an arrangement under which the employee makes a standing offer to be available to undertake work of a described kind. When the employer requires work done, he accepts that offer and a contract is concluded. It could be further provided that employment should be continuous, and that the hours worked each week under all contracts should be aggregated. It would be advisable to clarify who controlled the contract and where disciplinary powers lay.

On the other hand, if a global contract is to be avoided, then it might be better to make that express also. This could be achieved by inserting a provision to the effect that each contract is to be treated as complete and separate from any other contract entered into with the employer.

Global contracts may be useful to provide extra security for employees who will be undertaking different jobs for different parts of an organisation, at the same time providing a degree of flexibility for the employer.

Key points

- Identify the reason why the global arrangement is needed.
- Put it in writing.
- Establish who has overall control of the contract.

Reference

1 IRLR 509 HL.
2 The requirement for a minimum number of hours a week was removed by the Employment Protection (Part-time Employees) Regulations 1995.

16
Temporary contracts

There is no universal definition of a temporary contract. Whether a contract is temporary or not depends on the definition used by the employer, as do the rights available under the contract.

Statutory rights are a different matter. There are requirements on length of service for continuity of employment in the case of some statutory rights such as maternity leave, unfair dismissal and redundancy. Once the employee has accrued the necessary continuity he is entitled to those rights, whether or not his employment is described as 'temporary'.

As regards contractual rights, the employer can set his own qualifying service rules and benefit package. Temporary contracts frequently contain fewer benefits than the standard employees' package. Temporary employees may also top the list in redundancy selection. However, where temporary workers are predominantly female, equal pay claims and sex discrimination claims may arise unless the employer can justify withholding benefits for a good business reason. There will, no doubt, be just such a reason where the temporary employment is of short duration. The situation may be different when the worker has many years' continuous temporary service. In one instance a woman was found still to be on a temporary contract despite having received her long-service watch! However, it must be said that no equality claim has yet been brought in relation to temporary contracts. All such claims have related to part-time contracts.

Should the draft EU directives on part-time and temporary workers (COM(90)228 and COM(90) 533–SYN 280) be enacted in their current form, temporary workers would be entitled *pro rata* to the same benefits as full-time workers. This would create logistical differences in relation to some rights, such as the company pension scheme and mortgage benefits, when the duration of the temporary contract was short. The directives would also prevent the regular renewal of short fixed-term contracts of up to 12 months. Regardless of the holder, these could be renewed only for a total period of 36 months. The EU takes a very wide definition of 'temporary worker', including every contract other than one which is of indefinite duration. Thus five-year fixed-term contracts will, for EU purposes, be temporary.

One EU directive on temporary work has been enacted, and the Health and Safety Commission has already produced regulations to bring UK law into line.[1] The employer has to notify the employee, in advance, of the qualifications and experience necessary for the job, together with any increased specific risks relating to the job. The employee must receive sufficient safety training. The employment of temporary workers must be reported to a relevant authority. Finally, the member state may opt to exclude temporary workers from certain types of work and may require medical checks, even when the employment has ceased.

The Employment Rights Act 1996 requires employers to inform temporary employees of the likely duration of their contract and to give written particulars on short-term contracts.

Two types of temporary contracts are regulated by statute. These are the temporary contract for the replacement of a woman on maternity leave and for a temporary replacement for an employee on medical suspension under the Employment Rights Act 1996.

Employees in these two categories build up statutory and contractual rights in the same way as other employees. But section 106 of the Employment Rights Act 1996 provides that such a temporary employee who is dismissed so as to enable the absent employee to return to the job has been dismissed for a good reason.

Certain formalities are required. At the time of engagement the employee must be informed in writing that the contract will be terminated upon the return from maternity leave or medical suspension of the absent employee. And it has to be shown at the time of termination that dismissal is necessary to allow the other employee to resume work.

So it does not follow that the dismissal is automatically fair, only that the return of the absent employee is good reason for dismissal. The employer still has to show that it was fair to dismiss for that good reason. Thus section 106 is no help if the absent employee does not return, or seeks to return to different work which does not require the dismissal of the temporary employee. Moreover the need remains to look for available work for the employee and to follow a proper procedure during dismissal. In these situations the employer has to justify dismissal in the usual way. It is not impossible to do so. Ms Webster was taken on as a temporary maternity leave replacement secretary. Her speed was acceptable for a temporary worker but not for a permanent member of staff. The maternity leaver decided not to return, but Ms Webster was dismissed. It was found to be a fair dismissal.[2]

Where replacements are engaged it would be wise to ensure that they are informed in writing of the reason for their engagement and dismissal. But it is also essential to realise that not every dismissal is covered and that it is still necessary to follow a procedure and to show that the dismissal was fair. Notice will also have to be given. The term could be as follows:

> You have been engaged as a temporary replacement for ....
> who is on maternity/medical suspension leave. Your contract will be ter-
> minated when that employee returns to work.

Nor does it follow that dismissal of a temporary replacement is unfair because written notice was not given upon engagement. The employer is still able to follow the normal dismissal rules. But it is necessary to show that there was a valid reason for the dismissal without the benefit of the assumption in section 106.

Temporary contracts are used when there is a short-term need.

Key points

- Justify the use of a temporary contract.
- Identify the likely duration of the contract and inform the employee.
- Identify any special terms relating to temporary contracts.
- Give the employee health and safety information.
- Include temporary workers in the training programme.

References

1 EU Directive on the Health and Safety of Temporary Workers, 91/383/EEC.
2 *Webster v. Chester Health Authority*, COIT, 14 April 1985.

17
Casual contracts

These are contracts for staff who are employed only when work is available. It is easy, using contract terms, to limit their access to contractual benefits, such as pensions, sick pay, etc. It is more difficult to avoid employment protection rights based on length of service, because of the rules of continuity. *Flack v. Kodak* (see p. 94) highlights the problem. When the series of casual contracts is with the same employer or associated employer the employer has to show that a gap has broken the continuity, otherwise continuity is presumed. But if there has been a change of employer the burden is on the employee to prove continuity.

It might be sensible either to hold an exit interview, to see if the employee will remain available for work, or to keep a record of work offered. Non-availability or a refusal of work will be a break in continuity if it lasts for the prescribed period of seven days from Sunday to Saturday.

Casual contracts may be indefinite or for a fixed term, or even for a task. They may be part-time. But they are temporary contracts as far as the EU provisions are concerned. So the employer will be required to inform the employee, in advance, of the qualifications needed for the job, as well as the specific features of the job. Suitable training may be required.

The Employment Rights Act 1996 requires employees to be notified of the expected duration of their contract as part of their written particulars.

Key points

- Identify the reason for using a casual contract.
- Ascertain whether written information is required.
- Specify the duration of the contract.
- Notify the casual employee of the qualifications and features of the job.
- Identify the standard benefits that apply.
- Incorporate provision for training.
- Ensure there is a procedure for checking continuity of employment.

18
Nil hours

Under this type of contract the employee agrees to work and be paid only for the work done. The employer does not guarantee to provide work. It means that the employee has no guarantee of a wage. The prospect may not be attractive to the employee.

There are variants under which the employee is paid a retainer. Nil hours contracts differ from the casual contract in that the employment continues even when there is no work.

But, for the employer, these contracts did have distinct advantages. When continuity required an employee either to have normal hours of 16 per week (eight after five years' employment) or actually to work 16 (or eight after five years), it was virtually impossible for the nil hours worker to build up continuity. They have no normal hours and any week in which no work or too little was done broke continuity. But all this has changed with the removal of the hours thresholds for continuity. Once employment has commenced, every week will count, whether or not any work has been done. In *Colley v. Corkindale t/a Corkers Lounge Bar (1996)*[1] the EAT decided that continuity was not broken by a week in which the employee did no work.

This has considerable implications for organisations employing 'bank' staff whose hours vary, as well as those on standard nil hours contracts.

A further disadvantage will appear under the Working Time Directive. The maximum working hours – 48 – may be exceeded if the employee has another job, so it will be necessary to obtain written consent to work over 48 hours (it is assumed that the UK would adopt this option). There is also the problem of mandatory holidays – four weeks a year, but only three weeks during the initial transitional period of three years. Member states may attach conditions; we do not know what these might be. A qualifying period of employment would be unhelpful, and it may be difficult to introduce minimum hours, seeing that the Lords have already found them to be discriminatory.

This type of contract is useful when the employer wants to secure a workforce but has a very variable or uncertain amount of work to offer. In 1995 much publicity was given to Burgerking when they employed some staff on nil hours contracts, sending them home when work was slack, Burgerking withdrew that type of contract. However, in 1996 Daewoo, which provides a three-year service guarantee for their cars, offered nil hours contracts for collection, delivery and servicing. They hoped to attract persons who do not want full-time work.

Key points

- How variable is the work?
- No work is guaranteed.
- The employee guarantees availability.

Reference

1 IRLB 542 EAT.

19
Part-time contracts

There is no definition of a part-time contract. It may mean any contract under which the employee works for the organisation less than the normal hours per week, or less than the normal hours for the job, or less than a set number of hours such as 21 or 18.

There are no minimum protection rules for part-timers other than the standard entitlement of all employees to certain statutory rights. This position has partially been remedied by using the Equal Pay Act and article 119 of the Treaty of Rome. Where part-timers are predominantly female, and the provision has an adverse effect, a claim for equal pay can be made using a male full-time employee as a comparator to obtain *pro rata* remuneration.

In *Bilka Kaufhaus v. Webber von Hartz (1986)*[1] the European Court said part-timers were entitled to equal pay, on a *pro rata* basis, under article 119 of the Treaty of Rome. Pay is widely defined as covering all benefits, whether in cash or in kind, received directly or indirectly as a result of employment. In the *Bilka* case it included occupational pensions. Lesser rights can be accorded to part-timers only if the employer can discharge the heavy burden of showing a genuine business reason – for example, that part-timers are less satisfactory from a business point of view or that very few hours are worked. This equality rule has been applied, among other things, to pensions, redundancy pay, fringe benefits – including discretionary and *ex gratia* benefits – promotion and training. It also applies to selection for redundancy.

It had been decided in several cases that the imposition of an hours threshold for contractual or statutory rights could be discriminatory. (See *Rinner-Kuhn v. FWW Spezial-Gebäudereinigung (1989)*[2] and *Secretary of State for Scotland and the Greater Glasgow Health Board v. Wright and Hannah (1991)*.[3] But the Employment Protection (Part-time Employees) Regulations 1995 removed all the hours thresholds for statutory rights, following the decision of the Lords that they were discriminatory. The Lords would probably reach the same decision in respect of contractual rights, but such a case has not been before them. In *Vroege v. Insituut voor Volkshuisvesting BV and Stichting Pensionenfonds NCIV (1994)*[4] the European Court decided that it was discriminatory to bar part-timers from access to pension schemes but accepted that there could be a minimum hours requirement. Under the

Occupational Pension Schemes (Equal Access to Membership) Amendment Regulations 1995 employers must admit part-timers to pension schemes. The Finance Act 1995 s. 137 removed the statutory restrictions on the access of part-timers to share option schemes, share ownership trusts and profit-sharing schemes.

The EU draft directive on part-time and temporary workers would ensure that part-time workers obtained *pro rata* rights, health and safety coverage, and inclusion in the state insurance system, so long as they worked at least eight hours per week.

This type of contract obviously has economic appeal when there is insufficient work to justify full employment. Employers are also required to consider part-time work for a maternity returner if she so requests. This is the interpretation put upon the Sex Discrimination Act 1975, s.1, in *Home Office v. Holmes (1984)*.[5] After the birth of her second child, Ms Holmes requested part-time work because she was unable to obtain child care for five days per week. The Home Office turned her request down, despite several civil service reports recommending part-time work. The Home Office put forward no valid reason for the rejection. It was held that the Home Office had attached a condition or requirement to the job – that she should work full-time – with which, because of child care duties, fewer women than men would be able to comply, without being able to justify it. This amounted to indirect sex discrimination under the Sex Discrimination Act 1975, s.1.

A request from a maternity returner (regardless of her length of service) should not be turned down but should be given due consideration. Further details on maternity and equal pay issues are available in a companion volume in this series, *Discrimination*.

Part-time contracts are used when there is insufficient work to justify full-time working, to obtain flexibility in the workforce, to meet the needs of the available pool of workers and to cope with maternity returners.

Key points

• What is a part-time contract?
• Will the cut-off point cause discrimination problems?
• Are *pro rata* benefits available?
• Is there a procedure to deal with requests from maternity returners?

References

1 IRLR 317 ECJ.
2 IRLR 493 ECJ.
3 IRLR 283 EAT.
4 IRLR 651 ECJ.
5 IRLR 229 EAT.

20
Job-share

There are three common types of job-share:

- the married couple running a pub or residential accommodation
- joint managing directors
- (new on the scene) people with children.

The married couple are usually engaged jointly, i.e. two people agree to deliver one contract and have joint responsibility. The outcome is that, if one is in serious breach, both are liable to dismissal. Such dismissal will be fair so long as the duties of one spouse are not minimal. In *Great Mountain and Timber Rugby Club v. Howlett (1989).*[1] Mr Howlett was appointed club steward, with Mrs Howlett to assist him. Mrs Howlett left for domestic reasons, so Mr Howlett was dismissed. It was unfair because Mrs Howlett's duties were minimal.

The arrangement for joint managing directors will probably be more in the nature of a job split than the shared responsibility of the married couple. Certainly the contracts are less likely to be dependent on each other.

The child care/domestic duties job-share may fit into either category. It is obviously easier to deal with if it is devised as a job split, either on a time or on a functional basis, rather than as a job-share.

But if it is to be a true joint sharing of the job, and the position is at a decision-making level, some steps must be taken to avoid negative decision-making. It takes only one person to reach a 'no' decision but two to say 'yes'. There are other issues which must be dealt with. Are they to be jointly appraised? If pay is performance-related, is pay jointly or individually determined?

Job-share contracts are often used for residential care, for work in public houses, work in private households, for managing directors and for people with domestic duties. A contract of this type may be requested by maternity returners. See 'Part-time work', above, p. 111.

Key points

- What is the objective of the contract?

- Will the contracts be separate, interdependent or joint?
- How will strategic decision-making be dealt with?
- If there is budget control, how will disputes and responsibility be dealt with?
- Must the parties cover for each other during sickness and holidays?
- What happens if one resigns?
- How will promotion be dealt with?
- How will training be split?
- How will bonus and benefit packages be allocated?
- How will the scheduling of hours be arranged?

Reference

1 Noted in *IDS Brief* 401.

21
Workers supplied by agencies

If an organisation uses an employment agency to help in the recruitment of staff the individuals recruited will be employees of the organisation.

But in other situations the contract is with the agency which provides its own employees to work in the organisation. Whether they are employed by the agency or not is a matter of interpreting the contract. In *Harris v. Reed Employment (1985)*[1] the individual was self-employed, but in *McMeechan v. Secretary of State for Employment (1995)*[2] the use of terminology appropriate to an employment contract caused the EAT to decide he was an employee.

Nevertheless, the organisation has some duties towards the agency worker. It retains liability for health and safety risks arising from the work and the workplace, both at common law and under the Health and Safety at Work Act 1974. The EU Directive on the Health and Safety of Temporary Workers also applies to agency staff. The directive also makes the user organisation responsible for the health and safety of agency staff and requires the organisation to inform the agency of the qualifications needed for the job and the specific features of the job. Regulations have been produced by the Health and Safety Commission.

The organisation will also be responsible for the prevention of unlawful discrimination against agency workers while they are working under its control. The workers may not be selected on the basis of sex, race or union membership, unless there is a genuine occupational qualification under the Sex Discrimination Act 1975 or the Race Relations Act 1976, Disability Discrimination Act 1995, or unless some other legal justification exists.

In *BP Chemicals Ltd v. Gillick and Roevin Management Services Ltd (1995)*[3] the EAT had to grapple with the question whether an agency worker could claim sex discrimination when the user organisation, having said she could return after the birth of her baby, did not let her have her old job back, but instead provided a lower-grade one. The EAT held that the Sex Discrimination Act 1975 s. 9 applied to the offering of work as well as the terms and termination. It was remitted to a tribunal for a decision on the facts. The tribunal found on the facts that BP had not discriminated.

Key points

- Details of qualifications and the specific features of the job must be sent to the agency.
- The agency must be informed that there should be no discrimination.
- Agency workers must receive the same health and safety protection as the organisation's own staff.

References

1 EAT, noted in IRLIB 281.
2 IRLR 461 EAT.
3 IRLR 128 (1994) IDS 529 EAT.

22
Apprenticeships

Under an apprenticeship contract the master undertakes to teach the apprentice a profession or trade. The apprentice agrees to learn his trade and obey the master.

Apprenticeships must be in writing and signed by both parties. Often they are in the form of a deed. When the apprentice is under age his parent or guardian will complete the deed on his behalf, as minors cannot enter into deeds. Because minors (i.e. persons under the age of 18) can enter into contracts only for their own benefit, it is common for the master to require a guarantor. However, unless the terms are unfavourable to the apprentice, apprenticeships, like employment contracts, are viewed as being for the benefit of the minor and are therefore fully enforceable. When the minor reaches the age of 18 he has a reasonable time in which to repudiate the apprenticeship should he wish to do so.

Apprenticeships differ from employment contracts in several ways.

The apprenticeship contract may be with an individual or with the employer. There cannot be a change of master without the other party's consent. If the business changes, and the employer is thus unable to fulfil the teaching obligation, that is a breach by the employer. If the apprenticeship is with an individual, and he leaves the organisation, then that too is a breach. However, there should be no difficulty in obtaining consent to the transfer of the agreement to another master.

It is more difficult to dismiss an apprentice than an employee. Thus occasional drunkenness, illness and insubordination have failed to justify dismissal. But continual neglect of his duties and being a habitual thief were enough to permit dismissal. Wider powers of dismissal can be written into the contract.

An apprentice may not be suspended in the absence of a clear provision permitting it, because during the suspension the apprentice is not receiving training, and that would be a breach of the contract. An express power to suspend, plus power to extend the period of apprenticeship by a period equal to that of suspension, could overcome the problem.

Finally, if the apprenticeship is broken by the employer, the apprentice will not only receive the normal damages based on his remuneration to the end of the apprenticeship, he will also be compensated for his loss of training and his loss of a qualification. This was the clear decision of the

Court of Appeal in *Dunk v. George Waller & Son (1970)*.[1] Robert Dunk's apprenticeship as an engineering technician was wrongly terminated by the employer fifteen months before completion. The employer terminated it because Dunk was having difficulty passing his exams and the employer did not think he stood much of a chance of passing them in the future. The court said that apprentices get less pay than other workers because they receive the benefit of training, with the prospect of earning more in the future. Dunk was therefore entitled to damages for loss of his future wages in addition to the loss of wages during his apprenticeship. In this case, as the court considered that he was not very able, the sum was small – £2 per week for two years. In all, he obtained £500 damages.

Apprenticeship contracts are usually drafted by professionals.

One frequent question asked in relation to apprentices is whether they are entitled to redundancy benefit if, at the end of their apprenticeship, there is no work for them. The answer is no. An employee is entitled to redundancy benefit only if there is less work of the kind he was employed to do. An apprentice is employed to do the work of an apprentice. He is not employed to undertake the work of a qualified person. Lack of qualified work will therefore not make an apprentice redundant. He is no longer able to work as an apprentice, so lack of apprentice work will not make him redundant either! His dismissal is caused by the completion of his training and not by lack of work.[2] However, things would be different if an apprentice had been promised work after qualification. Also, an apprenticeship contract is a fixed-term contract, so its expiry amounts to dismissal and thus raises the question of fairness. It might be unfair to dismiss the apprentice if work was available which he was now qualified to do. It is probably for this reason that many apprenticeship contracts contain fixed-term contract exclusion clauses to prevent claims of unfair dismissal and redundancy upon expiry. (See 'Fixed term contracts', Chapter 12 above.)

Apprenticeships are mostly used in areas of employment where they are traditional or where they are required for entry into a professssion, as with solicitors and accountants. In other situations it may be preferable to enter into the more flexible training contract.

Key points

- Power to dismiss should be clear.
- If suspension is required, it must be express, and there should be power to extend the period of apprenticeship.
- Consider including exclusion clauses to avoid liability for unfair dismissal and redundancy on expiry.

References

1 2 All ER 630.
2 *North East Coast Ship Repairers v. Secretary of State for Employment (1978)* IRLR 149 EAT.

23
Training contracts

Training contracts are less stringent than apprenticeships. They are ordinary contracts in which the employer agrees to provide training. Failure to provide training will amount to breach and damages will be assessed in the same way as in *Dunk* (see the previous chapter).

Not infrequently employers want to recoup the training cost if the training is not completed or the employee leaves before the specified time. There should not only be a clause providing for the recoupment but also one permitting deductions from wages and/or repayment to avoid breach of the Employment Rights Act 1996 s. 15.

Training contracts are used where the employer is offering training and wishes to ensure that the employee will complete it.

Key points

- Training should be clearly specified.
- The circumstances that allow recoupment must be made clear.
- The power to make deductions and/or require repayment needs to be included in the contract.

24
Government-funded staff

From time to time the government produces schemes whereby training and work experience are available to the unemployed and the young. Many of these schemes involve subsidies to the participating employers. The key question is whether the participating individuals are employees. This is particularly important for the calculation of the continuity of employment of funded staff who are later taken into normal employment by the participating organisation. In all instances the organisation may choose to make the individuals employees. The choice may be deliberate, or may be inferred from the rights accorded to the individual or from the terminology used in relation to him. For example, if the individual were to be given the same rights, documentation, etc., as other staff, then he would probably be an employee.

Where this has not occurred the employment status will depend on the objective of the scheme. In *Dyson v. Pontefract and District Council CVS and CP Scheme (1988)*[1] the EAT held that workers on the then Youth Opportunities Programme were not employees because it was a training arrangement and a proper wage was not paid, only a training allowance. This set-up was to be distinguished from a work experience arrangement, where the workers were paid a wage, albeit a subsidised one. Dyson had been engaged on a Community Programme to obtain work experience. He had been paid a wage and was treated as an employee of the sponsoring organisation. He was an employee and had sufficient continuity of employment to qualify for redundancy benefit when the arrangement ended.

Key points

- Is the worker to be an employee?
- Should any special terms apply to this employment?

Reference

1 Noted in IRLIB 352 and *IDS Brief* 373.

25
Civil servants

There have been considerable changes in the legal status of civil servants over the past few years. Traditionally it has been presumed that, although civil servants may have an employment relationship with the Crown, and although they may be given employment rights under various statutes such as the Employment Rights Act 1996 and the anti-discrimination legislation they have no enforceable contract at common law. This assumption was based on the Crown's need to be able to dispense with unsatisfactory advisers without hindrance. It had an interesting side benefit for civil servants involved in matrimonial disputes. Because they were not entitled to their wage it could not be attached by the wife to obtain her maintenance!

Clearly, such a rule is inappropriate for the extensive civil service of today and recent cases have restricted its application. In 1989 the basic rule was restated in *R. v. Civil Service Appeal Board ex parte Bruce (1989)*.[1] The legal dispute in that and many subsequent cases was whether the employee was entitled to a judicial review of the actions taken against him or whether his claim lay in breach of contract. Judicial review provides a remedy in relation to the actions of inferior tribunals and administrative bodies. It is a discretionary remedy, not normally granted if there is another action available, and is restricted to actions involving some degree of public interest. Bruce claimed that the Civil Service Appeal Board, which had been established under royal prerogative to consider the fairness of dismissals, had failed to give sufficient reasons for its decision to dismiss him. The Court of Appeal based its decision on two grounds: (1) that he had no contract because he was employed by the Crown, (2) that he had another line of action, namely a claim for unfair dismissal, which he had brought and which had been settled. In the circumstances the court refused to exercise its power to grant a judicial review.

In *McLaren v. Home Office (1990)*[2] the court restricted the lack of intention to enter into a legally binding agreement to employment entered into under the prerogative powers of the Crown. McLaren was a prison officer engaged under regulations and not directly under the Crown prerogative. He was held to have an enforceable contract of employment. The presumed lack of intention to create a contractually binding relationship was restricted to appointments under prerogative powers. Even when the employment is directly under the Crown prerogative the implied presumption can be rebutted by showing an actual intention to create legal relations. The Lord Chancellor's department successfully alleged this in *R. v. Lord Chancellor's Department ex parte Nagle (1991)*,[3] relying on a detailed survey of the terms of Nagle's appointment, so depriving Nagle of the opportunity of a judicial review. The court was influenced by the existence of mutual rights and obligations, including terms relating to holidays, sick pay, pension, etc., which were normal in enforceable contracts. However, the court pointed out that, even when there was an enforceable contract a judicial review would be available in relation to matters concerning the exercise of public powers.

Special problems may arise in relation to office holders in the public sector. These are people appointed to a particular office. The method of appointment and the means of removing them from office is prescribed, but there is no person or body which controls their daily work. They are not employees. In *Miles v. Wakefield Metropolitan District Council (1987)*[4] the point came before the court in an unusual way. A superintendent registrar of births, marriages and deaths was refusing to work on Saturdays, so the local authority reduced his pay proportionately. Under the Registration Service Act 1953 the registrar was appointed by the authority, paid by the authority and held office at the will of the Registrar General. He was not an employee but an office holder, so the authority had no control over him and could not reduce his pay.

References

1 2 All ER 907 CA.
2 IRLR 203 CA.
3 IRLR 343 QB.
4 IRLR 193 HL.

Part III

The terms

26
Introduction

Part III is concerned with the terms which might be incorporated into the contract and how they may be expressed. The law is explained first, then examples are given to illustrate the problems and suggest solutions. But it must be emphasised that the examples should be used with care because the needs of organisations vary, the law may change and the term may interact badly with other terms in the contract.

The most difficult part of drafting any contract is deciding what terms will go into it and what they will contain. Once these decisions have been made, expressing those terms clearly and unambiguously can be far less difficult.

There are certain terms which are necessary in any contract. Where they have not been expressly agreed by the parties to the contract, the court or tribunal will imply a term to cover the point in question. This is discussed on p. 30. The court or tribunal will imply a term whenever there is a gap in the expressly agreed terms and a term on that topic is necessary in order to give the contract business efficacy. The basic question is 'Could the contract be operated without a term on that topic?' If the answer is 'yes', then no term will be implied. If it is 'no', then a reasonable provision will be implied. But the court or tribunal's decision may be quite different from the actual intention of either of the parties. The court will usually take guidance from the way the parties have acted, especially on topics such as hours and work. Some terms are so normal in contracts that the courts have accepted the presumption that they are to be implied unless an express term makes that impossible. For example, the duties of fidelity and mutual trust are automatically implied. Others have been implied so frequently that they have given rise to presumptions, such as the presumption that full pay will be paid when work is not available unless the provision of work is beyond the control of the employer. Otherwise the court or tribunal decides what would be a reasonable clause in the circumstances. In *Howman & Sons v. Blythe (1983)*[1] the court expressed the view that the provision of sick pay had become so common that it was difficult to imagine a contract without some such provision, and so maybe payment should now be presumed. The situation has, however, not yet reached that stage.

Terms may also be implied where it is obvious that the parties intended such a term to be part of the contract. In this respect it has to be remembered that conduct is ambiguous. It does not follow that conduct alone will be evidence that the parties intended a term to be included in the contract. For example, the fact that the employee has regularly worked overtime will not prove that the parties intended overtime to be contractual.

It should therefore not be assumed that because there is no express term there is no term at all. It is also vital to ascertain whether there are any automatically implied terms which may not suit the particular circumstances of the contract and which may necessitate an express term in substitution.

It is obviously better to aim for express rather than implied terms. Commonly the main terms, such as the work, pay, hours and holidays, are set out in the offer letter, while others, such as pensions, sick pay, compassionate leave, relocation allowances, etc., are incorporated into the contract from special schemes, collective agreements or staff handbooks. Where the terms are to be taken from collective agreements or staff handbooks the terms in the agreement or handbook must be drafted in the same way as contract terms if ambiguity and confusion are to be avoided.

The precise terms to be included are a matter for the parties themselves. In practice the proposal usually comes from management. But employees should not automatically accept proposals without checking them carefully. Repayment of training or relocation costs and restraint terms applying after termination can inhibit the employee's freedom to obtain new employment; location clauses may require more mobility than the employee realises. The final contract will probably be a compromise between the desires of both employer and employee.

The choice of terms and their content will vary from organisation to organisation, even within the same geographical area and industry. There are now so many different ways in which organisations and work are organised, and so many different ways of paying and motivating staff, that each contract has to be virtually tailor-made for each organisation.

So the first step is to identify the work to be done, the location, hours and other key requirements over a reasonable time scale. This information will obviously be taken from the financial and staff plans. The method of determining pay and benefits is also critical. At this stage most of the terms may be identified.

Next, the terms used by others in the industry and locality can be taken into account. Terms used by organisations in different industries should not be ignored; not only may the organisations be competitors for staff but they could have faced similar problems and have coped with them in their contract terms. They may also show the general expectations of the working population in the region. But these other terms should be adopted only if they meet the organisation's needs better than the original ones.

Finally, it can be decided whether the terms will be express or incorporated.

Key points

- Identify the work and other key requirements from the staff and financial plans.
- Determine the terms needed to meet those requirements.
- Check the terms used in other organisations.
- Decide whether terms will be express or incorporated.

Reference

1 IRLR 139 QB.

27
The parties

Written particulars in the Employment Rights Act 1996 requires the identification of the parties. This must be in the principal statement.

Special provision must be made if the organisation wishes to have the power to transfer the employee to another organisation. An employee cannot be transferred from one employer to another without his consent. To allow otherwise would be to permit something tantamount to slavery! The contract is a personal contract between the employer and the employee. This is illustrated by *Brace v. Calder (1895)*.[1] In that case a partnership was dissolved and the new firm offered employment on the same terms as the old one. But the contract did not transfer against the employee's wishes. In *Nokes v. Doncaster Collieries (1930)*[2] the amalgamation of two companies was insufficient to transfer the staffs' contracts to the new company. Today these two cases would be decided differently because the Transfer of Undertakings Regulations 1981, regulation 5, provide that, whenever an undertaking in the nature of a commercial venture transfers from one employer to another, all the staff employed by the transferring employer transfer across to the new employer on the same terms and conditions, whether the employees or the employers concerned like it or not. But the regulations apply to only a small number of transfers.

This can cause practical problems where there is a need to be able to transfer employment from one employer in a group of companies or associated organisations to another, or where there is a need to second staff to other organisations. The difficulty can be dealt with in two ways. In groups of companies, staff may be employed by a special service company and then assigned to other companies as required. Such a service company was set up by Barclay's Bank. The original employment contract with the holding company gave the holding company the right to transfer staff to any subsidiary, and this power was used to transfer them all to a service company which then supplied the staff under contract to other companies in the group. (*Barclay's Bank v. BIFU (1987)*.)[3] Or the contract may contain an express provision empowering the employer to transfer the contract to another organisation or to place the employee on secondment.

This power to transfer must be clear. If it is not in writing it will be very difficult to prove.

Once the transfer has been effected, the employee becomes employed by the new organisation. The effect on his contractual rights will depend on the terms in his contract permitting the transfer. If there is a simple transfer of the contract, then his contractual terms will transfer. Clearly, this can apply to matters such as organisation pensions only if both employers are in the same scheme, and there could be other benefits which may prove difficult to transfer. The contract terms do not automatically change on transfer. The work, location, hours, benefits will remain the same and can be changed only in accordance with the contract provisions. But the contract can provide that the payment package and/or other terms, etc., will be that of the new employer.

Transfers

In the original contract

The company (organisation) reserves the right to transfer this contract to any other company within the group (related organisation).

Upon such transfer you will cease to be entitled to participate in the company (organisation) pension scheme and benefits package but will be entitled to participate in those of the new company (organisation).

The new company (organisation) will include your continuity of employment with this company (organisation) when calculating continuity for the purposes of statutory and contractual benefits.

Upon transfer

As an employee of .... you will be subject to the standard terms and conditions as set out in ....

You will be entitled to participate in the company (organisation) pension scheme and benefit package, which are explained in .... and details of which can be obtained from ....

Your continuity of employment with this company (organisation) commenced on .... Your period of employment with .... is included in your total continuity of employment, which therefore commenced on ....

Continuity of statutory rights is preserved if the new employer is an associated employer. An associated employer must be a company. It can be a foreign company so long as the company resembles in form a company registered under the Companies Acts. In *Hancill v. Marcon Engineering (1990)*[4] the EAT decided that an American private company, Marcon Inc, met this requirement but a Dutch private company, Marcon BV, did not. Deciding whether the various forms of foreign companies qualify as associated companies could prove a difficult task. On the other hand employees are less likely to be encouraged to be mobile if it means loss of rights. If the employee will be returning to the employment of an associated company it is possible to preserve continuity of employment by agreement or arrangement before the transfer occurs.[5] It is advisable to put it in writing. But this provision cannot be used if the employee is transferred to an employer who is not an associated employer, and will not be returning later to the employment of another associated employer. All that can be done here is to give the employee an undertaking to provide him, via his contract, with benefits equivalent to statutory benefits based on both periods of employment. The employee would have to claim his equivalent benefits in the ordinary courts.

If the new employment is outside Great Britain there is an added problem. Employment abroad counts towards continuity for unfair dismissal and other rights under the Employment Rights Act 1996, except for redundancy benefit. If statutory redundancy entitlement is to be preserved it can be done only through a contractual guarantee enforceable in the ordinary courts. (In certain limited classes of transfer the statute does preserve continuity, but these are rare.)

Secondment needs to be treated in the same way. This is a temporary transfer to another organisation. Secondment will require an express clause; otherwise the agreement of the individual is needed.

Because the employee will eventually return, it is sensible to specify:

- *Whether the contract with the old employer is suspended, continues during the assignment or is extinguished.* This can be of considerable importance if the assignment is to an organisation other than to an associated employer. In such instances statutory continuity of employment will be lost unless there is prior agreement that it shall continue.
- *What will happen at the end of the assignment or transfer.* Will the employee return to the same position or to a different position? This was not clarified in *Doctus Management Consultancy v. Rostron (1989).*[6] Rostron started work for Doctus in 1984. In 1987 he agreed to work on six months' secondment with a subsidiary in South Africa. He was then told in June that the subsidiary was to be made independent of the group and he would be employed by this independent company. However, he would continue to be employed by Doctus until the new arrangements were made. Rostron did not receive a new contract from the new independent company. At all times during the secondment Rostron was paid by Doctus and a new contract was offered by the independent company. Rostron refused the offer and claimed unfair dismissal. It was decided that either the temporary six-month contract continued after its expiry date or it had terminated but Rostron had continued in the employment of Doctus, as evidenced by the payment of wages.

- *The powers and responsibilities of the respective employers in relation to discipline grievances etc.* It may be that the second employer's procedures will operate, save that the employee will be warned not that he will be dismissed but that the secondment will end and dismissal will be replaced by termination of the secondment. The original employer can then warn or dismiss under his own procedure.
- *That any procedures and policies of the second employer must be followed.* Thus the relevant safety policy will be that of the second employer. The employer with safety liability will be the second employer in so far as the second employer controls the work.

Secondments

In the original contract

The company (organisation) reserves the right to second you to any other company within the group (organisation).

During your secondment you will comply with any site terms and conditions prevailing at that time relating to hours, manner of work and [specify others].

Your pay and benefits will remain unchanged/be those of the new employer/will be as agreed with you/will be as follows.

You will also comply with any prevailing policies and procedures and will be subject to disciplinary action by (the company/organisation) while you are working with them.

During your period of secondment you will cease to be in the employment of this company (organisation)/your contract will be suspended/your contract will continue for the following purposes (specify).

When the secondment is completed you will return to your existing position or to another position of similar status upon the terms applying to that position upon your return.

Upon secondment

You will be seconded to .... for a period of ....

During this time the company (organisation) will remain responsible for your pay, pension and benefits package.

[or set out the new provisions]

You will comply with any prevailing site terms and conditions of .... and with any of the prevailing policies and procedures of that organisation, including the disciplinary procedure. Details of these will be available ....

The secondment is a triangular relationship. As well as the employment contract there must be an agreement between the two employers. This will cover the items above. It may also specify who will be vicariously liable for the seconded employee's negligence. Where the control is that of the second employer the second employer is vicariously liable, otherwise the liability is that of the first employer. However, an agreement between the two employers may provide otherwise. Such an agreement will not affect the rights of an injured party.

Closely allied to secondment is the temporary assignment of the benefit of an employee's services to another organisation. This is normally possible, unless prevented by restrictive work hours and location clauses, but again is better made express.

Employees should be aware of the transfer and secondment terms and, in particular, should check out the position on continuity of employment and their rights when the transfer or secondment ends.

Key points

- Decide whether the power to transfer is needed.
- Identify contractual benefits which will transfer.
- If the transfer is not to an associated employer, decide whether equivalent statutory rights should be provided in the contract.
- Decide whether secondment power is needed.
- Will the employer transfer absolutely to the new employer, will the old employment contract be suspended for the duration of the secondment, or will the old contract continue to apply for some, at least, of its purpose?
- Decide whether assignment of the benefit of services is needed.
- Check the mobility provisions.

References

1 2 QB 253.
2 2 KB 1.
3 ICR 495.
4 IRLR 51 EAT.
5 Employment Rights Act 1996, s. 212(3)(c).
6 EAT, noted in *IDS Brief* 404.

28
Continuity and commencement of employment

The employee must be informed of the date of the commencement of his employment and, if employment with a previous employer counts towards continuity of employment, the date when continuous employment began.[1] The commencement date must also be identified. These dates must be included in the principal statement.

When there is to be a gap in continuity, e.g. training or working abroad, which does not count for redundancy (it does for unfair dismissal) the employer may wish to make an agreement or arrangement stipulating that the gap will count. To be effective, the agreement must be in existence prior to the gap.

In the case of contractual rights, commencement date and calculation are determined by the employer. Some periods may not be counted towards contractual rights, for example initial periods of probation and earlier work for other companies in the group. But beware devising schemes which discriminate against part-timers and could lead to discrimination and equal pay claims, as in *Nimz v. Freie und Hansestadt Hamburg (1991)*.[2]

Mrs Nimz's employment was subject to a collective agreement which provided for severance payment after a qualifying period. Service in its entirety was counted if the employee worked at least three-quarters of the full hours, but only half the period of service was counted if an employee worked half to three-quarters of the full hours. More women than men worked part-time; thus they were disproportionately affected. The women part-timers should be entitled to severance payments *pro rata* to their hours unless the employer could produce a valid reason for requiring part-timers to work longer to qualify.

In *Barclay's Bank v. Kapur (1991)*[3] the calculation of service for pensions was racially discriminatory. Kapur was an African of Asian descent. He was employed by Barclay's in Kenya and Tanzania. During such employment there was no accrual of pension entitlement to a UK pension, although a UK national working in those countries would have accrued pension rights. Kapur came to work for Barclay's in the UK and claimed race discrimination. His claim was successful. His claim was not out of time because the discrimination was continuing to provide unfavourable pension rights. It was a continuing act of discrimination.

Key points

- Identify the method of calculating service for contractual rights.
- Identify start date for continuity of employment.
- Avoid discriminatory arrangements.
- Clarify continuity during contract breaks.

Continuity and commencement

Your employment with the company will commence on ....
    No previous employment will count as part of your continuity of employment OR
    Your previous employment with .... will count as part of your continuity of employment, which therefore commenced on
....

References

1 Employment Rights Act 1996, s. 1.
2 IRLR 223 ECJ.
3 IRLR 137 HL.

29
Work

Terms relating to the work an employee can be required to undertake are of the utmost importance. The employee may refuse to do work which is outside his contract. He may be disciplined for refusing to do contractual work. He is redundant if the employer needs fewer employees to do the work he is employed to do.[1] Many of the difficulties and cost associated with reorganisation are connected with the terms relating to work.

The employee must be notified of his job title as part of his written particulars, and will have to be given his title or grade, or a brief specification or description of his work in his written particulars of employment. Yet, despite its obvious importance, it is often not possible to identify with 100 per cent certainty the precise work which will fall within the ambit of the contract. For example a person employed as a sales manager may in some organisations be required to undertake strategic decision-making, but be restricted purely to sales work in others. And the exact work boundaries of a person in charge of administration will always be difficult to define.

There is certainty where the work is clearly and narrowly defined. If a person is employed to work on a particular type of machine he cannot be compelled to work on any other machine. Sometimes work for certain categories of employee is fully set out in an incorporated collective agreement.

The dangers of ambiguity in the collective agreement or of conflict with the contract terms are illustrated by *City Bakeries v. Guthrie (1986)*.[2] Guthrie received an offer letter engaging him as a 'Grade IV despatch worker' in a bakery. The national working agreement which was incorporated into his contract referred not to 'Grade IV despatch workers' but to 'Grade IV operatives'. The list of Grade IV operatives contained various other work, including machine cleaning. Different pay rates were set out for the various Grade IV operative jobs. Had Grist been employed as a 'Grade IV operative' he could have been required to do any of the work on the Grade IV operative list. But his offer letter terms were held to prevail, and so he was restricted to despatch work and could not be transferred to machine cleaning.

If the work is not defined, then the court or tribunal may look at the job title or grade for guidance. But the job title or grade is not conclusive evidence of contractual work. In *Speakman v. Northprint Manchester (1988)*[3] a man who had worked for 13 years as a newsprint controller was given and accepted the title of 'clerk'. For several more years he continued to control newsprint. But eventually his employer tried to transfer him to clerking duties. The EAT returned the case to the tribunal to decide whether accepting the title of 'clerk' but without any change in his work meant that Speakman had to undertake clerking duties.

In *Cresswell v. Board of Inland Revenue (1984)*[4] the court had to decide whether Inland Revenue employees could be required to use computers. The contracts were particularly unrevealing, the staff being employed as 'Clerical Assistants', 'Tax Officers' or 'Tax Officers, Higher Grade'. They were involved in the administration of PAYE. The problem arose when the board introduced computerisation. The staff refused to use the computers on the ground that it was outside their contract terms.

The court drew a distinction between the work the staff were employed to do and the manner or method of performing that work. The work was set out in the contract terms but, generally, the manner or method of performance was a decision for management, who were free to change it. Given the vague provisions of the contract on the work to be performed, the court looked at the work the staff were currently undertaking – PAYE administration – and decided that that was the work they could be required to do. The next question was whether doing the work by computer was different work. The court decided it was not. The use of computers was not difficult, and training was provided. This decision was followed in *McPherson v. London Borough of Lambeth (1988)*,[5] where the court refused staff an injunction to prevent their being required to use computers in the administration of housing benefit.

But in *Cresswell* the court warned against assuming that the employer had an absolute right to change the manner of work. The controlling (and restraining) factor is the contract term. If it includes the manner of work – and the court put forward the example of a person employed as an 'audio typist' – then no change could be made to the contract term, including the manner of performing the work. Also the change may affect the nature of the work itself. This can occur when new technology is introduced which requires entirely different skills. It is a question of degree – and a difficult question, at that.

But the distinction between the work and method of performance is a vital one. It leads to the question of job descriptions. These set out the areas of work on which the employee is to concentrate, how the work will be performed, to whom and for whom he is responsible etc. Quite simply, they are instructions and guidance as to how the contractual duties are to be fulfilled. In other words they are not about the work but about the manner of performance. Whenever a person is employed the employer is entitled to give lawful orders or instructions for the performance of the work, and these can be changed. So the employer, legally, is free to change the job description, so long as it has not been put into the contract. It will be in the contract if the employer has inserted a provision such as 'job duties: see attached job description' in the contract of employment. It might also, unwittingly, have become contractual as a result of a job evaluation scheme. Some schemes are based on agreed job evaluations. The format of the document may require the employee's and employer's signature on an agreement that this is the work required under the contract. It could make the job description contractual.

The fact that the job description is not in the contract does not mean that it is without effect, however, It is a lawful order, and in *UBAF Bank v. Davies (1978)*[6] the EAT held that breach of that lawful order would justify dismissal. In that case Davies had asked for and received a job description. He refused to accept it and was eventually dismissed. The dismissal would have been fair had the bank made it clear to him that, if he refused to accept the job description, he would be dismissed.

In many contracts flexibility in work provisions is desirable. This can be achieved in various ways. The work can be broadly described; it can be narrowly described, with the employer having power to change or add to the terms; or there can be some mechanism for change. The Disability Discrimination Act 1995 will require employers to review both the contractual work and the job description in order to avoid discrimination.

A very broad definition of the work can lead to problems when declaring redundancies. In *Nelson v. British Broadcasting Corporation (1977)*[7] Nelson was employed to perform such duties and exercise such authority as the BBC might vest in him. He was instructed to work in the Caribbean Service. For financial reasons the Caribbean Service was reduced, and the BBC said he was redundant. He was not. His work was not in the Caribbean Service but to undertake whatever work the BBC might require. There was other work available which he could have been asked to perform under his contract.

On the other hand, if the work is narrowly described, then additional or other work cannot be demanded. In *Milthorne Toleman v. Ford (1980)*[8] a sales manager who had resigned to work for a competitor was moved from sales work to sales estimating work during his period of notice. This was breach of contract. The employer could have protected his confidential information by giving him no work to do or by offering wages in lieu of notice, but he could not insist on Milthorne performing non-contractual work.

Even if the employee has undertaken the disputed work in the past, that will not make the work contractual. Past willingness to undertake non-contractual work does not change the contract terms.

There is no general duty to provide work. Normally the employee is entitled only to pay. But there are some exceptions to this rule. In two industries, entertainment and journalism, there is an implied duty to provide work. This is based on the fact that the employee is partially remunerated by publicity. Thus an actor, promised one of the three leading roles in *Hit the Deck*, successfully brought a claim for breach of contract when he was given a different part (*Herbert Clayton, etc. v. Waller (1930)*[9]), and in *Tolnay v. Criterion Film Productions (1936)*[10] the author of a screenplay succeeded in his claim for damages for loss of publicity. In *Collier v. Sunday Referee (1940)*[11] Collier, who was the sub-editor on a three-year contract, was given no work to do after the paper had been sold to new proprietors, and this amounted to breach of contract. In 1976 Phillips, J, who was then president of the EAT, thought this rule should be reconsidered and modernised, and in two cases, *Breach v. Epsylon Industries (1976)*[12] and *Bosworth v. Angus Jowett & Co. (1977)*,[13] it was held that the duty to provide work extended beyond entertainment and journalism. In Breach the employer was held to be under a duty to provide work to maintain his employer's skills and contacts, and in *Bosworth* it was held that, if there was work for an employee to do it was breach of contract not to give it to him. Since then no other tribunals have made similar decisions.

Defining the work

Defining the scope in broad terms

During the subsistence of this agreement the employee shall perform such duties and exercise such powers and authorities as may from time to time be vested in him . . . and the employee shall at all times obey and conform to the reasonable order and direction and restrictions given by the Board of Governors or the Director General for the time being of the corporation or such other person as aforesaid which shall include the right to direct the employee to serve wherever he may be required . . .

Broad powers to change the term

The company reserves the right when determined by the requirements of operational efficiency to transfer employees to alternative work and it is a condition of employment that they are willing to do so when requested.

Job title plus brief specification

You are employed as a lecturer in the Faculty of Economics. You may be required to lecture, undertake research and/or fulfil administrative duties.

An employer may choose to include an undertaking to provide work. This may be done when the employee is to be remunerated by commission. As long ago as 1901, in *Turner v. Sawdon (1901)*,[14] the court held that a salesman on commission might sue for pay but not for failure to provide work, and this would seem to be still the case. Of course, in entertainment and journalism the duty to provide work can always be excluded by an express term. This could be vital if a part may be reduced in editing or end up on the cutting-room floor. On the other hand, employees will seek further undertakings of publicity as well as retaining the part or the by-line.

The final option is to include machinery for change. This is discussed above in Chapter 8.

Key points

- Identify the work, using a job title or brief outline.
- Take due consideration before putting a job description in the contract.
- Ensure that the definition is broad enough or that there is power to change the terms.
- In entertainment and journalism review the duty to provide work.

References

1 Employment Rights Act 1996, s. 139.
2 Noted in *IDS Brief* 289.
3 EAT, noted in IRLIB 348.
4 IRLR 190 Ch.
5 IRLR 470 Ch.
6 IRLR 442 EAT.
7 IRLR 148 CA.
8 IRLR 30 CA.
9 AC 290 HL.
10 2 All ER 1625 KB.
11 2 KB 647, 4 All ER 234 KB.
12 IRLR 180 EAT.
13 IRLR 374 IT.
14 2 KB 653.

30
Location

This too is a vital term. If there is no express term the court or tribunal will imply one. Although there is no requirement under UK law to notify the employee of his place of work or if there is none, the fact that the employee is employed at various places and the registered place of business (or, where appropriate, the domicile of the employer) must be notified to the employee under the Employment Rights Act 1996.

This term may be vital in relocation or reorganisation, and is important for redundancy and unfair dismissal as well as breach of contract. Place of employment is especially critical in redundancy claims. The Employment Rights Act 1996, s. 139, which defines redundancy, refers to cessation of business 'in the place where the employee was so employed' or a diminution in the requirement for employees, again 'in the place where he is so employed'.

If there is an express term it will be applied, no matter how inconvenient it may be to either party. So in *Rank Xerox v. Churchill (1988)*[1] EAT decided Rank Xerox were not in breach of contract when they required clerical staff to relocate from Euston in central London to Marlow, Buckinghamshire, because there was a term in the contract to the effect that 'The company may require you to transfer to another location'. The tribunal had held otherwise because it did not think that such an open-ended mobility clause was reasonable. The tribunal considered it ambiguous, and so interpreted it against the employer, deciding that it permitted transfers only within reasonable daily travelling distance. The EAT reversed this decision. The words were unambiguous. So if the employees resigned they had not done so as a result of breach of a contract term and hence there was no constructive dismissal. If they had been dismissed by Rank Xerox their dismissal was not due to redundancy, because their place of employment was now Marlow and there was no diminution of staff requirements at Marlow.

If Mrs Churchill had been employed to work at the Euston Road headquarters of Rank Xerox without any right on the part of the employer to transfer, than any imposed transfer would have been breach of contract, and any resulting resignation would have been constructive dismissal. She would also have been redundant because the place of employment would have remained Euston Road and fewer staff were needed there.

But a slight softening of attitude is apparent in the case of *United Bank v. Akhtar (1989)*.[2] Akhtar was employed on terms which allowed him to be transferred to any of the bank's places of business in the UK on a temporary or permanent basis. On Tuesday 2 June he was told that he was being transferred, permanently, from Leeds to Birmingham, effective from the following Monday (8 June). He sought a postponement of three months because of his wife's health and the need to sell his home and find somewhere in Birmingham to live. The request was turned down, and so Akhtar resigned.

In order to bring a claim for unfair dismissal Akhtar had to show that his resignation was caused by a serious breach of contract on the bank's part. He could not complain about his transfer to Birmingham. The bank had every right to make him transfer, and the decision could not be questioned. But the EAT said that there was an implied term to the effect that the move must be possible in the time scale allowed. Otherwise the bank would be frustrating Akhtar in his attempt to comply with his duty and move to Birmingham. The tribunal and EAT noted that the bank had a discretionary relocation allowance scheme which they had not put into operation for Akhtar. The employer's conduct amounted to breach of mutual trust and confidence and thus to breach of contract.

It must be emphasised that this case did not apply any test of reasonableness to the decision to relocate Akhtar. The question of reasonableness – or, rather, whether the employer had behaved in such a way as to destroy trust and confidence – related only to the time given to him to effect his relocation.

If there is no express place of work clause, then one will be implied. There must be a term defining the place of work because a contract requires a clause on place of work in order to operate effectively. The Court of Appeal has stated that, where there is no express term, a term should be implied which the parties would probably have agreed had they turned their minds to it. The court added two caveats. The rule did not require the employer to justify a move for operational reasons. Nor did it permit the employee to refuse because, in the circumstances, the transfer was unreasonable.

The term implied is likely to be very narrow. In *O'Brien v. Associated Fire Alarms (1969)*[3] two electricians and their mate worked from home in the Liverpool area and their work was controlled by the company's Liverpool office. The company's business was the installation of fire and security alarms. Work in Liverpool was diminishing, so the new manager told them they would be working in Barrow in Furness. As they would not be able to work from home, they refused to go. The Court of Appeal held that their place of work was Liverpool. The trade might normally involve mobility, a mobility term might be reasonable from the employer's viewpoint, but that was not enough to imply mobility. So the men succeeded in their redundancy claim, because fewer staff were needed at Liverpool.

At one time even a move of a short distance was likely to be outside the implied term – for instance, a relocation of offices from Dover Street to Regent Street in central London, an easy walk (*Air Canada v. Lee (1979)*[4]). But more recently the courts have taken a different view of mobility. They held that a lorry driver who took his lorry out of one depot was not able to rely on an implied term that he should work only out of that depot, because the very nature of his work meant that he was mostly on the road – and his place of work was merely a starting and finishing point for his shifts. The move was to a site one mile away. (*Courtauld's Northern Spinning v. Sibson and TGWU (1988).*[5]) In *Prestwick Circuits v. McAndrew (1990)*[6] a term was implied permitting a location from Moss Hill Estate, Ayr, to Irvine, some 15 miles away. These cases seem to imply a term which might permit relocation within a reasonable distance of the employee's home.

In some special circumstances mobility may be implied. For example, a managing director could be required to relocate to a new headquarters building (*Little v. Charterhouse Magna Assurance (1980)*[7]). But it should not be assumed that, because an employee accepted a transfer in the past he is now impliedly mobile. His conduct may show only that the previous transfer was acceptable. Nor, for the same reason, can implied mobility be assumed from the fact that fellow employees have in the past accepted transfers.

Location clauses for different types of staff

Senior manager

Your place of employment is the Freeland Centre. You may be required to work on a permanent or temporary basis anywhere else in the United Kingdom.

Middle manager

Initially you will be based in the head office in Mayfair. You may be relocated to any other establishment within the boundaries of the M25.

Salesman

Your base will be the Baslow depot. You will work in the north-west region. Your base and sales area may be changed from time to time.

It *may* be possible to transfer staff outside their work or location where there is a short-term need. It is preferable to insert an express term. But the content of the term requires careful thought.

It may be tempting for an employer to include a broad mobility clause in every contract. The temptation should be resisted unless such a clause is needed. Too broad mobility clauses could amount to discrimination under the Sex Discrimination Act 1975, s. 1. This was the decision in *Meade-Hill and another v. British Council (1995)*[8]. Upon promotion to grade G all full-time staff were required to accept a variation of their contract by undertaking to work in any part of the UK. The CA decided that this was a requirement attached to the employment. Because a higher proportion of women than men were secondary wage earners, fewer women would be able to comply with the requirement; this would amount to discrimination under the Sex Discrimination Act 1975 s. 1(1)(b) and s 6(1), unless the employer could justify the clause irrespective of sex. They remitted the case to the County Court to see if such justification existed.

For an organisation with many sites one approach to the problem is to divide employment into bands of mobility. One band – say, senior staff, sales staff, etc. – will be required to be very mobile. The next band will be mobile on a more restricted regional basis, and the other band required to work only within a narrow area or within reasonable travelling distance of home.

The area chosen for mobility should therefore take into account the needs of the organisation and of the staff. Some of these needs will be obvious – for example, salesmen, service engineers and management trainees may be needed to work in a wide area, others will depend on impending organisation changes such as centralisation or decentralisation, lease expiries, etc. Management development may necessitate relocation. Others may be less obvious. A change in markets, customers, availability of materials or staff may also necessitate relocation.

Sometimes staff are employed not just to work in a particular location. In addition to working in a particular location they may have to work in a particular department. This prevents departmental mobility.

Some employees will be required to work or travel abroad. Again, the contract terms can be decisive. An employee with the job title 'Sales Engineer' who was required to undertake export sales and work abroad was later, for health reasons, transferred to a domestic post. He wished to remain abroad but the court held that his contract was such that he could be transferred back to the UK. (*Deeley v. British Rail Engineering (1980).*[9])

Although the employer is entitled to relocate any employee within the limits set out by the location clause, the employee may, in rare instances, be able to refuse. He can refuse if in the new location he would be subjected to risks not envisaged when the contract was made. The onus is on the employee to prove the risk. The risk must be a serious one. In *Bouzorou v. Ottoman Bank and Ottoman Bank v. Chakanian (1930)*[10], two Armenian Christians were relocated in accordance with their contract terms to parts of Turkey where Armenians were being persecuted. Both refused to go and were dismissed. Chakanian could show that he was likely to be physically mistreated and so his dismissal was wrongful. But Bouzorou could prove only that he would be unpopular, so he was rightfully dismissed. Even though the danger was apparent at the time of the contract, the employee could refuse if he could show that the danger had not been contemplated. So a sailor who after the commencement of the Spanish Civil War signed articles to sail to ports in the Mediterranean could refuse to sail to Spain because the belligerents considered the cargo to be contraband and might attack the ship (*Robson v. Sykes (1938)*.[11] It is not difficult to see how similar problems could arise today.

If the employee is to work outside the UK then he must be given additional written particulars before he leaves the country. These must cover:

- the duration of the employment abroad
- the currency to be used for the payment of remuneration
- where appropriate, the benefits in cash or in kind attendant on the employment abroad
- where appropriate, the conditions governing the employee's repatriation.

The written information must be in the employee's possession before his departure. It may consist of references to laws, regulations and administrative or statutory provisions or collective agreements on these points.

In fact many employers go further. They will set out:

- the nature of the transfer
- whether it is temporary or permanent
- if it is temporary, what will happen on the termination of the transfer
- whether employment will count towards contractual and statutory rights
- changes to hours of work, place of work and other terms.

One important point for employees is insurance. They may assume that the cover while abroad is the same as while they are employed in Great Britain. Many employees have found to their cost that such is not the case. Yet insurance cover is even more important, as the health and safety duties of the employer will be less while the employee is overseas.

When employees are required normally to work outside Great Britain they cannot, during their employment abroad, utilise their statutory rights under the Employment Rights Act 1996 and will lose accrued continuity of employment for redundancy. They may, of course, be able to benefit under protection laws in their country of work. 'Normally working abroad' does not always mean spending most of the time abroad. Service engineers, aircrew, etc., who spend much time abroad may nonetheless be normally working in Great Britain if their employment base is here. (*Todd v. British Midland Airways (1978)*.[12])

Relocation packages are an incentive to mobility. They are frequently discretionary, but any discretion should be used with care (see *Akhtar*, above). For recoupment of relocation costs see p. 206.

There is a growing move towards working at home. If the employee's place of work is his home and the employer wishes to relocate him to company premises or those of a client, this will be a contract change. It would be wise to incorporate the power to make the change. It must also be remembered that the employer owes the homeworker all the normal employment duties, including the duty to provide a safe system of work. So with those using display screen equipment the DSE Regulations must be met. These employees can presumably fix their own hours and so may come within one of the derogations under the Working Time Directive and be permitted to exceed 48 hours per week (see Chapter 33). Terms may be necessary to ensure that the employee is contactable during working hours.

Key points

- Identify events likely to result in relocation.
- Check the geographical area needed.
- Avoid sex and race discrimination.
- Consider a relocation package.
- If employees are to be transferred abroad, provide the additional information.
- Give time to relocate or use suitable relocation terms.
- Check that the relocation will not involve unforeseen physical risk.
- Before dismissal for refusal, follow a disciplinary or other suitable procedure to avoid unfair dismissal.
- Check insurance if transferring abroad.
- Consider the employment position on return if transferring abroad.

References

1 IRLR 280 EAT.
2 IRLR 505 EAT.
3 1 All ER 93 CA.

 4 IRLR 392 EAT.
 5 IRLR 305 CA.
 6 IRLR 191 Ct Sess.
 7 IRLR 19 EAT.
 8 IRLR 478 CA.
 9 IRLR 147 CA.
10 AC 271.
11 2 All ER 612.
12 IRLR 370 CA.

31
Competence

The employee implicitly promises that he is competent to perform the contractual work. One of the earliest cases on this point was *Harmer v. Cornelius (1858)*.[1] Harmer was employed to paint scenery but could not do so and was instantly dismissed. His claim for breach of contract failed. A more recent one was *Pinkerton v. Hollis Bros & ESA (1989)*,[2] in which the court decided that a managing director was required to have the requisite skills for the job. In this case the court pointed out that there was a difference between having the necessary skill and being negligent, and not possessing the necessary skill. In practice, however, the line could occasionally be difficult to draw.

Certain tasks and jobs can by law be undertaken only by persons possessing professional or specified qualification, e.g. pilots, ships' captains, heavy goods vehicle drivers, solicitors, managers of mines, etc. Loss of the qualification will mean either that the task cannot be performed or that the employee cannot work in that capacity. If only one task cannot be done, and that task represents only a small part of the work, or the loss is for a short time only, it will not amount to serious breach of contract. It is unlikely to justify dismissal without notice at common law, or to be a fair dismissal under the Employment Rights Act 1996. There are several cases of loss of an HGV licence which illustrate this. If driving is only a small part of the work, dismissal is not justified. But in *Tipper v. Roofdec (1989)*[3] the loss of a licence for twelve months meant that the employee could no longer be employed as a driver. In *Tarnesbury v. Kensington and Chelsea and Westminster Area Health Authority (1981)*[4] a doctor suspended by his professional body for 12 months was fairly dismissed.

If the professional qualification is not mandatory but is contractual then its loss will justify termination without notice at common law and will probably amount to grounds for fair dismissal, although the latter will depend on the importance of the relationship between the qualification and the work.

Although lack of competence and negligent performance are not the same, this is an appropriate point to consider the prospective liability of the employee for negligence. The employee who is negligent is personally liable to any person injured as a result of his actions. If he is acting in the course of his employment, then, in addition (not in substitution),

149

the employer is vicariously liable to the injured parties. The injured do not obtain double compensation. The employer and employee are jointly and severally liable and the court can apportion the damages between them in accordance with their respective fault and responsibility.[5]

Requirements of competence

Lorry driver

You are required to have a valid HGV licence.
   You will immediately report to the Distribution Manager any endorsement of your licence or loss of your licence.

Insurance salesman

It is a term of your employment that you are registered with LAUTRO.
   Loss of registration will result in termination of your employment without notice.

[For the insurance salesman there could be additional information, perhaps in the staff handbook, explaining that, under the Financial Services Act 1986, no person can carry on investment business unless he is an authorised person. It is not possible to be an authorised person without becoming a member of a regulatory organisation, of which LAUTRO is one. It can be further explained that registration is dependent upon being and continuing to be a person with aptitude and competence and of good character.]

The employee is also in breach of contract, and the employer can sue for damages, which will amount to the loss suffered, i.e. the money paid to the injured persons plus the inevitable legal costs. This happened in *Lister v. Romford Ice & Cold Storage (1957).*[6] An employee had negligently backed his lorry into his mate (who also happened to be his father) and seriously injured him. The father sued Romford and Romford claimed the money back from the son for breach of contract. In fact, although the claim was brought in the name of the employer, it was the employer's insurance company which was behind the claim. The case caused considerable disquiet, and as a result the major insurance companies gave an undertaking not to bring such claims against the wishes of the employer. From the employees' point of view this is not entirely satisfactory, because the undertaking cannot be enforced by them. Bearing in mind the increasing number of acts for which the employee might be personally liable the employee should check whether he is covered by the employer's insurance policy.

Key points

- Check the essential statutory qualifications.
- Include the qualifications where appropriate.
- Determine the appropriate insurance cover.

References

1 5 CBNS 236.
2 Noted in IRLIB 376 Ct Sess.
3 IRLR 418 EAT.
4 IRLR 369 HL.
5 Married Women and Joint Tortfeasors Act 1935.
6 1 All ER 125 HL.

32
Wages

It goes almost without saying that this is one of the most important contract terms. It is so important that, if an offer of employment is made without this term being fixed, either as a sum or a formula or by reference to some other document such as a collective agreement or the employer's standard terms, then there is in law no offer at all; even if the individual accepts the apparent offer there is no contract. This is because the key terms have to be identifiable when the contract is made.

The point is illustrated by *Loftus v. Roberts (1902)*, where the parties had agreed that the employee should be paid 'a West End salary to be mutually agreed'. The court decided that this was not a sum or a formula and that, in the absence of agreement, there was no way to determine what the wage was. Therefore Loftus had no contract.

But if an individual actually performs work on the basis of such an agreement he is entitled to be paid for the work he has done. The employer is not entitled to the benefit of his work without payment. The individual can seek payment – it is not his as of right – in equity by way of an action for *quantum meruit* (such as he deserves). Payment is usually ordered by the court where it is clear that both parties expected payment to be made. The actual amount will be decided by the court and will normally be based on the usual wage for such work. However, if the individual has been working and receiving payment under such an agreement, then the actions of payment and acceptance of the wage may well cure the defect and turn the agreement into an enforceable contract on the basis of the wage paid.

There is no universally applicable definition of 'wages'. There are different definitions for the purposes of the common law, redundancy, and deductions from wages under the Employment Rights Act 1996 Part II. It is worthwhile covering all aspects of pay in the contract to avoid problems of breach of contract or infringing any legislation affecting wages.

Wages are widely defined at common law and include the total contractual remuneration package. Commission, tips and bonuses may also be included where they are not discretionary. In *W P M Retail v. Lang (1978)*.[1] Lang's offer letter stipulated that he would have the 'opportunity to earn an additional £200 in a full financial year, based on your performance in the area'. He received one payment of £25 in the next month and was then told there would be no further payments. Just under three years later he was dismissed. The EAT confirmed the tribunal's finding that the promise was contractual and remained in force throughout his employment.

If payments are to be discretionary, this must be made very clear. Payments which commence as discretionary may also be converted into a contractual entitlement. This happened in *Powell v. Braun (1954)*.[2] Ms Powell sought a wage increase. Her employer said that, instead of increasing her wage, they would increase her annual bonus. Until this point the bonus had been discretionary, but the judge decided that by meeting a request for an increase to her contractual wage with a bonus increase they must have intended to make the bonus contractual. In other words, if a payment is to remain discretionary, it must always be referred to as discretionary. Braun would no doubt have been in a better position if they had offered to increase her *discretionary* annual bonus – and had put that in writing.

Terms relating to commission and bonus need to be precise. For commission the date when it accrues needs to be clear, although this date may be separate from the date of payment. It will normally be provided that, although commission may have accrued at the date when the sale is made, payment will not be due if the customer does not complete his side of the contract. If it is clear that the commission will form part of the pay, then the court may hold that damages are due if work is not provided (see Chapter 29, pp. 137–41).

A bonus scheme is often discretionary. It was decided in a recent case that 'discretionary' did not of itself have any particular meaning and the EAT had to decide what the employer meant. Some help was gleaned from the employer's explanation that 'it would not be paid where circumstances justified it – such as bankruptcy!' Non-payment was further stated to be 'unlikely'. The EAT concluded that the employer did not intend to pay other employees while withdrawing the bonus from an individual (*Kent Management Services v. Butterfield (1992)*).[3] Yet an employer might want to do just that. He may wish to reduce or remove a bonus where the employee has committed serious misconduct and may not wish to pay an accrued bonus after the employee has left. This must be made clear.

For the purpose of calculating statutory redundancy benefit, wages are restricted to cash payments and will not include benefits in kind. Overtime is not included unless it is not merely mandatory but forms part of normal working hours. Wages for calculating such redundancy benefit are subject to a statutory maximum, currently £210 (Employment Rights Act 1996, s. 227). On the other hand, when assessing loss for an unfair dismissal compensatory award, even non-contractual payments are taken into account. A very wide definition, not of wages but of pay, is taken under the Treaty of Rome article 119 (see below, p. 154).

The actual wage may be fixed in the contract, or there may be a formula or a procedure to determine the amount. Where unions are recognised it is common for the wage to be that agreed with the union. But it does not follow that the new wage agreed with the union is automatically incorporated into the contract. If the contract states that the wage is the subject of collective agreements, then a collective agreement will change the terms. Otherwise the union-agreed wage will be treated as an offer made by the employer to his employees which they may not accept. Employees have refused where it is too low, or where a new payment scheme reducing an aspect such as premium rates is unacceptable to them. If collectively agreed terms are to be incorporated automatically, complete clarity is needed.

The contract may provide for automatic increments, or for discretionary payments based on performance. In either case, the actual entitlement must be without ambiguity. An undertaking to review a salary does not mean that an increase will be granted.

Different pay for men and women performing the same work or work of equal value is a breach of the Equal Pay Act 1970, the Equal Pay (Amendment) Regulations 1982 and article 119 of the Treaty of Rome. Breach can arise in subtle ways via the wage payment system. Evidence suggests that individual performance-related pay can favour men. This was found to be the case in *Handels- og Kontorfunktionærernes Forbund i Danmark v. Dansk Arbejdsgiverforening*, often known as the Danfoss case (1989).[4] The union had found that women in the same wage band as men were, on average, receiving less wages than the men. The ECJ said the wage system was not transparent and could be operating in a discriminatory way, so they returned the case to the Danish arbitration court to see exactly how the wages were assessed. The system used by Danfoss was based on performance and took into account matters such as flexibility, responsibility, capacity, quality of work etc. In *Nimz v. Frei und Hansestadt Hamburg (1991)*,[5] the ECJ decided that employees should be paid for the work done and not for their length of service, so throwing doubt on service-based pay systems.

The actual amount of the wage is a matter for the parties themselves. In the United Kingdom there is no statutory minimum wage.

One of the most important changes in connection with wages in recent years has been the replacement of the Truck Acts, which were largely concerned with the pay of manual workers, with the Wages Act 1986 (now the Employment Rights Act 1996 Part II). This deals with two main issues: the manner of payment of wages, and deductions and repayments. Again the definition of wages is unique to the act. It covers any sums payable to the worker by his employer in connection with his employment, including:

(a) Any fee, bonus, commission, holiday pay (including accrued holiday pay) or other emolument referable to his employment, whether or not it is contractual.

(b) Any sum payable as a result of an order for reinstatement or re-engagement or for the continuation of a contract of employment or for guarantee payments and other statutory payments in lieu of wages under the Employment Protection (Consolidation) Act 1978.

(c) Statutory Sick Pay under Part I of the Social Security and Housing Benefits Act 1982 and maternity pay under Part III of the same statute.

(d) Payment by way of stamps, vouchers etc. of cash value which can be exchanged for goods or services.

On the other hand, wages *exclude*:

(a) Any advance (although deductions from wages in respect of such advance are covered).

(b) Any payment in respect of expenses.

(c) Any payment by way of a pension, allowance or gratuity in connection with the worker's retirement or as compensation for loss of office.

(d) Any payment referable to the worker's redundancy.

(e) Any payment to the worker otherwise than in his capacity as a worker.

(f) Payments in kind.

The provisions are extraordinarily complicated and have been the cause of much litigation. Where there is breach the employee has redress before an Industrial Tribunal. The claim must be brought within three months of the breach. Where the employer has a claim he must go to the ordinary court within 12 months of the breach. In 1995 21,912 wages claims were referred to ACAS Conciliation Officers. In many cases such claims stand or fall on whether the payment concerned falls within the definition of 'wage'.

It is now clear that commission, bonus and accrued holiday pay are wages. But in *Delaney v. Staples (1992)*[6] it was decided that wages or pay under the Employment Rights Act s. 13 referred only to remuneration for work done or to be done and not to any payment for loss of contract rights such as wages in lieu of notice.

As far as the manner of payment is concerned, the parties are free to decide that for themselves. Any change in the manner of payment will require negotiation. Any offers or inducements to change the manner of payment are likely to be binding. So an employer was unable to consolidate into basic pay an allowance he had agreed to pay employees who agreed to change from cash to direct transfer of wages to a bank account. (*McCree v. London Borough of Tower Hamlets (1992).*[7]

The main area of difficulty is that of deductions and repayments. With some exceptions, the employer may not make any deduction from the employee's wages nor demand any repayment from him in his capacity as an employee without complying with the provisions of the act.

Under s. 13 deductions and repayments must be (i) required or authorised by statute or (ii) required or authorised by a relevant term in the contract of employment. Alternatively, (iii) the employee must have consented in writing prior to the payment or deduction.

There are two kinds of relevant terms: written terms which have previously been shown to the employee (i.e. before the deduction) and other express or implied terms whose existence and effect has been notified to the worker in writing prior to the deduction (the notification procedure). It is difficult to prove the existence of an oral or implied term except in the instance of a loan, which by its very nature incorporates an implied undertaking to repay – but not an implied permission to make any deductions. The only safe term is a written one.

The cases show that the tribunals are interpreting the rules very strictly. In *Eaglesham v. Evets Computers (1988)*,[8] the employer had made a loan to the employee and included provision for repayment of any outstanding amount on termination of contract. Eaglesham than gave in his notice. The employer deducted the outstanding amount from the employee's wages. He had no right to do so because his entitlement was to repayment. The money had to be returned.

In order to make a lawful deduction the wording of the clause must be very clear, and it will be narrowly interpreted, as in *Fairfield Ltd v. Skinner (1993)*.[9] The contract provided that an employee's final wage was subject to deductions for damage to the company car during private use and provisional sums for van telephone calls and private mileage in excess of free allowance. As the actual amounts were not known at the time that the final salary was paid, the employer deducted provisional sums which were to be adjusted when the figures were available. There was power in the contract to make deductions of the actual sums due – but no power to deduct a provisional sum. So the deductions were unlawful.

There are certain exceptions to this wage protection and these deductions and repayments are subject to the pre-Wages Act rules. One of the most important of these exceptions concerns the over-and under-payment of wages. In relation to the overpayment of wages *Avon County Council v. Howlett CA (1983)*[10] still applies. The common law rule used in that case is based on the fact that the employee has innocently changed his position as a result of the employer's misrepresentation that the money was his. The employer can only recover the overpayment if the employee knew or ought to have known of the mistake (the employer must prove this) or if the employee has not acted on the representation. If the employee has in good faith acted on the representation then, even if some money is unspent, none can be recovered. If the employer makes a mistake of law (this is not common in employment cases) the money can never be recovered.

So the chances of recouping an overpayment are small, although they can be improved by an express term, preferably in writing. The term should always provide for the options of deduction and/or repayment because it is not always possible to predict which will be needed.

Other deductions and repayments which fall outside the act include those authorised by statutory disciplinary proceedings; deductions to public authorities which are authorised by statute; deductions and payments to third persons of sums requested by the worker, where the employee has signified his consent or agreement in writing or given his prior written consent; cases where the sum is due to the employer as a result of strike or other industrial action (the employer must show financial loss caused by the employee's breach); and deductions and payments with prior written consent or agreement, as a result of a court or tribunal order.

There is one final provision which is restricted to the retail trade. Following some instances of employers making deductions from employees' wages for stock losses and for the failure of customers to pay at petrol stations, the powers of the employer were restricted. The definition of 'retail employment' is very wide. Retail employment means employment involving the carrying out by the worker of retail transactions directly with members of the public (whether on a regular basis or otherwise). A retail transaction means the sale or supply of goods or the supply of services (including financial services) to members of the public or fellow workers or other individuals in their personal capacity. This covers banks, building societies, plumbers, builders, etc. The act restrains actions whereby the employee's wages are affected as a result of cash or stock losses. This includes formulae relating the wages to such losses, as well as deductions, fines and repayments. In addition to the above rules, the employee must be informed in advance of his indebtedness; and, except for the final wage payment, the employer is restricted to a maximum deduction of ten per cent of the gross wage. Consent must not only be freely given: it must also precede the event giving rise to the deduction. In *Discount Tobacco and Confectionery Ltd v. Williamson (1993)*[11] the employer found stock losses in one of their retail outlets. They met the manager and he agreed to deductions from his wages to cover the losses. The employer could not make deductions, even with the employee's agreement, in respect of losses occurring before he consented to the deduction. The purpose of this is to prevent pressure being put on the employee to agree to the deduction.

It is most sensible to collect together all the deductions or repayments which may be required and put an express term in the contract. A guide to the requirements can be found in the adjustments needed from the employee's final salary. Another is the adjustments made by payroll. The term can even cover overpayments, extending by agreement the right to recoup them.

Although there is little control over the amount of the wage, there are two laws requiring the employee to be notified of the amount. The contractual entitlement, including overtime payment, must be notified to the employee as part of his written particulars. The employee must also be told of the pay period and the manner of payment. In addition, the Employment Rights Act 1996 s. 8 provides that all employees are entitled to an itemised wage payment containing the purposes for which they are made, the net wage and, when different parts are paid in different ways, the amount and method of each part payment. This must be a clear statement so that the employee is aware of the cause of any deduction. The tribunal can award an employee a sum equivalent to any unnotified deductions.

Key points

- Set down the exact wages, whether fixed or paid by an agreed formula.
- Fix the manner and period of payment.
- Include details of deductions and repayment terms.
- Explain the methods of commission accrual and payment.
- Bonus – is it discretionary, and in what sense?
- Included in written particulars.
- Wage statements made.
- Avoid discrimination in payments.

Sample clauses

Simple salary term

You will be paid £x per annum monthly in arrears. Payment will be made on the last Wednesday of the month. Payment will be made by direct transfer into a bank account nominated by you. Your salary will be reviewed annually.

Commission

You will be paid a basic wage of £x per annum, monthly in arrears. Payment will be made into a bank or building society account nominated by you.

You will be paid a commission of x per cent on all sales made by you. Entitlement to commission will accrue when an order from the customer is accepted by the company. Payment will not be made to you until the customer has paid the company. Payment of commission will be made quarterly by direct transfer into your nominated bank or building society.

Bonus

The company operates a bonus scheme. The bonus is at the discretion of the Board of Directors. They will declare the amount of the bonus, if any, and the allocation to individual staff.

Any member of staff who has received a warning during the relevant year may lose his bonus or it may be reduced at the discretion of the Board.

To qualify for the bonus you must be employed on (date). You must still be in employment on (date), when payment will be made. Employees dismissed by the company between the date of entitlement and the date of payment other than for fault will be entitled to payment.

Deductions

A. The employee will be paid a salary of £x per year in 12 equal monthly instalments. The salary will normally be reviewed every 12 months.
B. Payment will be made by cheque on the last day of each month. If the employee so requests, payment will be made into a bank account or building society account nominated by him.
C. The Company may deduct from the employee's wages or require payment from the employee for any of the following:

   loans
   any monies due from the employee to the Company
   excess of holiday taken over entitlement
   excess of sick pay received over entitlement
   excess of expenditure claimed
   excess of any other payment made to him by the Company
   any money requested in writing to be deducted by the employee.

D. Should there be any underpayment of wages the Company will adjust the next available wage payment by the amount of the underpayment unless prior payment has been made.
E. Should there for any reason be an overpayment of the wages the Company reserves the right to adjust future wage payments until the overpayment has been recovered and/or to require repayment.

References

1 IRLR 243 EAT.
2 1 All ER 484 CA.
3 ICR 272.
4 IRLR 532 ECJ.
5 IRLR 222 ECJ.
6 IRLR 191 HL.
7 IRLR 56 EAT.
8 IRLIB 367 IT.
9 IRLR 4 EAT.
10 IRLR 171 CA.
11 IRLR 327 EAT, IRLB 475.

33
Hours

This too is an important term, particularly critical in relation to reorganisation and flexibility. In contracts of indefinite duration most employers try to include some power to vary this term. As part of his written particulars the employee must be notified of any terms and conditions relating to hours of work, including those relating to normal working hours. Where variable schedules or annualised hours make it impossible to be precise in setting out the normal hours, this should be made clear.

There are few restraints on the number of hours persons may work in the United Kingdom. There are restrictions on lorry drivers, pilots etc., but these are the exception rather than the rule. The EU has enacted a Directive on Working Time. It was due to come into effect on 23 November 1996. It was agreed under article 118a of the Treaty of Rome as a health and safety measure. At the time of writing, the European Court has rejected the UK's claim that the Directive is not a health and safety matter but one relating to employment rights, so requiring a unanimous vote. The Directive is now enforceable within the public sector. It will only be enforceable within the private sector when legislation is enacted.

The main provisions of the directive are:

- in every 24 hours each employee should have a break of at least 11 consecutive hours
- each employee working over six hours per day/shift should have a break during the course of their rostered hours
- each worker should have a minimum weekly break of on average 35 hours (i.e. one day plus the 11-hour daily rest period); this may be reduced to 24 consecutive hours where operational requirements dictate
- no worker should work more than 48 hours (including overtime) on average per week calculated over a reference period of four months. Employees may voluntarily agree to work over 48 hours (this will be reviewed in seven years). There would have to be records and medical checks on such employees
- night workers (including rotating shift workers who work night shifts regularly in the course of their rota) should have a maximum shift

length of eight hours on average, calculated over a jointly agreed reference period (excluding rest days)
- no overtime should be worked in association with a night shift involving 'hazardous work'
- free, regular health assessments must be provided for night workers; they may be allowed to transfer to day work in the event of health problems recognised as associated with night work
- night workers should enjoy equal health and safety protection and facilities with day workers.

Junior doctors, transport and sea fishing are excluded.

Some freedom from the strict provisions is available through derogations. These permit an adjustment of the rules, but require substitute safety arrangements to be made wherever possible. There are three categories in which derogations are possible:

1 Managers with autonomous decision-making powers and persons whose work time cannot be measured or who can determine their own hours; persons working in a family business; religious workers.
   Member states may allow derogations in respect of these workers from daily rest periods, breaks in six-hour working, weekly rest periods, a maximum of 48 weekly hours, length of night work and the reference periods.
2 Certain types of work:
   a where the workplace is some distance from the residence
   b security and surveillance
   c continuity of production and services required
   d *force majeure*, accidents etc
   e seasonal work
   f unusual and unforeseen circumstances, where national law so provides, and in cases of accident or imminent risk.
   Derogations can be made by national laws or collective agreements in relation to daily rest periods, breaks in six-hour working, weekly rest periods, night work and the reference periods, but not the maximum weekly hours.
3 The same derogations as in category 2 can be made via collective agreements.

Split shift-working can deviate from the 11- and 24-hour rest period so long as compensatory rest periods are given or other protection provided.
   Perhaps the most useful provision is the one under which employees can agree to work in excess of 48 hours. Employees working paid

overtime might be willing to enter into such an agreement. Whether those whose overtime is unpaid will do so is another matter. Employees may not suffer as a result of a refusal to work additional hours.

Although not affecting the number of hours worked, there are restrictions on shop workers and betting workers being made to work on Sundays (Employment Rights Act 1996 Part IV). These workers may not be compelled to work on Sundays, although they may 'opt in' to Sunday working. The opt-in must be in writing and the employee can opt out by giving three months' notice in writing. Although Sunday working can attract premium payments, the employee's wage and benefits must not be reduced because he refuses to work on Sundays. Claims for breach are heard by the tribunals.

Until such time as any EU restraints are introduced, there is considerable freedom to fix hours of work. The hours may even be unreasonable. This was the situation in *Johnstone v. Bloomsbury Health Authority (1991)*[1] (a case which went to the CA on a preliminary issue and is not a final decision). Johnstone was employed in a hospital as a senior house officer. His contract required him to work 40 hours and to be 'on call' for a further 48 hours on average. Thus he had contractually agreed to work for 88 hours per week. He alleged that these hours were unreasonable and, therefore, that the term could not be enforced. All three judges rejected this. The term was a clear express term and so was enforceable. He further alleged that the implied duty of the employer to provide him with a safe system of work overrode the express term. Again this was rejected. An implied term cannot override an express term. For one judge that was final, but the other two saw no conflict between the express and the implied term. The express term set the maximum hours he could be required to work and the implied term controlled the allocation of those hours. The allocation should not be such as to affect his health. It is hoped that this case will proceed to full trial, when a clearer decision should be made.

Provisions relating to hours should make it clear whether there are breaks such as meal breaks, and whether these are paid. Overtime raises two issues. Firstly, it must be clear whether it is compulsory; a phrase like 'You may be expected to work reasonable overtime' should be avoided and 'You will be required to work overtime as rostered' used instead. The second issue is whether overtime is to be paid, at what rate, and whether time may be taken off in lieu. If payment or time off is to be given, it is also normal to state that overtime requires prior approval.

If shift work or night work has to be done, this too must leave no scope for doubt. In *Westgate v. Mid Downs Health Authority*,[2] a midwifery sister had always worked days. Her contract provided that her hours were to be 'according to the needs of the service'. This contract allowed the Health Authority to require her to work night shifts. If weekend or bank holiday work is required, this should also be clear and it should be stated whether time off in lieu or extra pay is available if these days are worked.

Given the need for flexibility in working hours to meet operational requirements, many contracts contain clauses permitting the employer to change the allocation of hours, to introduce or remove shift working or even to alter the number of hours to be worked. Clearly the employee has to be notified of the change and a procedure may be set out in the contract. If so, it must be followed exactly or any change will be ineffective. In *Humphreys and Glasgow v. Broom and Holt,*[3] the employer had the power to change the terms relating to hours but had agreed to consult the staff first. He increased the weekly hours from 37 to 40 without consultation and so the change was ineffective.

There is no need for all staff to work the same number of hours per week. Some organisations have adopted part-time work while others allow staff to choose between, for example, 16, 20, 30 or 35 hours per week. Where some staff are working less than full hours there is the risk of a claim for equal pay under the Treaty of Rome (article 119) unless pay and benefits, cash or kind, received directly or indirectly as a result of the work are *pro rata* equal to those of full-time workers. Not only must the benefits themselves be checked but also any qualifying periods of service. Part-time workers who have to work longer to obtain organisation benefits are not receiving equal pay (see Chapter 19, pp. 111–13).

Annualised hours are becoming far more common. Under these arrangements the employee agrees to work a fixed number of hours per year and the employer is given a considerable degree of freedom in allocating those hours. Sometimes the work is seasonal and the hours may be concentrated in one part of the year.

Changing circumstances, however, may require these to be altered, so there should be power to make at least minor adjustments. When first introducing annual hours it may be better to do so on a trial basis, enabling a review to take place before the final scheme is in place. Otherwise adjustments may be very difficult to make.

There are certain decisions which have to be made in relation to annualised hours:

1. Are the contracted hours to exclude holidays, bank holidays etc.? In this case, will holiday pay be provided or accrue with service?
2. Similarly, will periods of sickness and other absence count towards contracted hours and, again, will payment be made?
3. Will overtime be worked and how will it be determined?
4. Will overtime be paid?

5. Can adjustments be made to the system, including extension and removal of the scheme?

When devising the scheme the employer will have regard to his current need, changes resulting or likely to result from growth or restriction of the organisation's activities, any possible re-organisation or introduction of new technology, the changing demands of clients and, last, but by no means least, the changing aspirations of employees.

Key points

- Set down clearly the number of hours to be worked.
- Include details of meal breaks.
- Is overtime, bank holiday or weekend work voluntary or obligatory? Is authorisation required? Is there payment or time off in lieu?
- Can shift work be introduced or removed? Is there a premium payment?
- Can night work be introduced or removed? Is there a premium payment?
- Ensure there is no inequality in remuneration for part-time workers. Do the staff cover for each other during holidays and absence?
- Are holidays, sickness and other absence dealt with in your annualised hours scheme? Is overtime required? Can the scheme be adjusted?
- In preparation for the EU directive, check the daily hours and overtime worked. Is there a weekly rest day? Are there any night-shift workers whose hours would be affected? Are there any health check provisions for night and shift workers?

Sample clauses

Manager

You are required to work such hours as are necessary for the needs and requirements of the business.

Production worker

You will work 35 hours per week. Your normal hours of work are 9.00 am to 5.00 pm, Monday to Friday inclusive. You are entitled to a lunch break of one hour.

Clerical worker

You may be required to work overtime. Authorised overtime will be paid at one and a third times your equivalent hourly rate, but no payment will be made unless 30 consecutive minutes have been worked. Overtime may be authorised by your supervisor.

Computer operator
(in an organisation operating 24 hours a day, 7 days a week)

You will be required to work 40 hours per week. You may be required to work day, shift or night work. Whenever possible, you will be given 28 days' notice of any change to your working pattern.

Shift work is paid at time and a third of the basic hourly rate. Night work is paid at time and a half the basic hourly rate.

You will be required to work overtime. Overtime payment will be the work, day, shift or night rate plus a further payment of half the basic hourly rate.

References

1 IRLR 118 CA.
2 IT (1988), noted in IRLIB 378.
3 Noted in (1989) IRLIB 369 EAT.

34
Sickness

Section 1 of the Employment Rights Act 1996 requires the employer to notify the employee of the existence of terms relating to sickness and injury payment as part of his written particulars of employment. It should these days be extremely unusual, therefore, to find a contract which does not have a clause relating to sick pay. Where such is the case, the matter will have to be determined by deciding what term can be implied into the contract. In *Howman & Sons v. Blythe (1983)*[1] the court said that it was essential as a last resort to imply some term relating to the payment of sick pay during absence caused by sickness. It is necessary to know the amount of payment, if any, which has to be made and for how long it should be. Past conduct is helpful, so, in *O'Grady v. Saper (1940)*[2] the doorman at a cinema had never previously received wages during his periods of illness and so was not entitled to sick pay. And in *Petrie v. MacFisheries (1939)*[3] there was a notice on the wall which said that payments during sickness were *ex gratia* payments and indicating the amount usually paid. This showed there was no clause in the contract entitling employees to sick pay. In *Mears v. Safecar Security (1982)*[4] the Court of Appeal decided that in that particular case a term could be implied from an industry agreement, and this included an implied term permitting deduction of state sickness benefits.

Although there is no presumption of an implied term that some wages must be paid, in *Howman & Sons v. Blythe* the tribunal was of the opinion that it must be unusual nowadays to conclude that no payment is due. The EAT considered that the issue was not whether wages were due but whether sick pay was due. This could be less than the full wage (in *Howman & Sons v. Blythe* sufficient to bring state sickness benefit up to the normal wage) and need not be of the same duration as wages, i.e. could last for only a limited time.

However, should the employee be dismissed, then the provisions of the Employment Rights Act 1996 ss. 87, 88 apply during the period of notice. During this period the employee is entitled to full pay at the current rate for the period of notice, less any deductions which the employer is legally entitled to make (*Notcutt v. Universal Equipment Company (London) (1986)*[5]. Oddly, this right is removed if the employee is entitled to contractual notice which exceeds the statutory notice by more than one week.

It is a mistaken belief that an employee cannot be dismissed before his sick pay entitlement has been exhausted. But the wording of sick pay arrangements is often vague. In *Smith's Industries Aerospace & Defence Systems v. Brookes (1986).*[6] the employment contract provided that:

(ii) Subject to the provisions of the Trade Union and Labour Relations Act 1974 . . .

(b) [If] for an aggregate period of not less than 225 working days in the period of twelve months ending with the date of notice you have been incapacitated by reason of ill health or injury from performing your duties under the contract, the company may terminate the contract by written notice of the minimum period to which you are entitled in accordance with the provisions of the Contracts of Employment Act 1972.

Not surprisingly, the employee thought this meant that he could not be dismissed so long as he was not absent for 225 days in 12 months. The EAT regarded that as 'palpably absurd' and held it to mean that only in those circumstances did the employer have to give statutory minimum notice. The employee could be dismissed earlier, but would have to be given reasonable notice. In *Hooper v. British Railways Board (1988)*[7] there was a collective agreement under which BRB agreed to pay, to staff who were declared fit by their own doctor but not accepted as fit by BRB's doctor, their basic pay until they returned to their job, were offered other suitable work or (implicitly) retired. Hooper suffered from a stress-related illness and was off sick after each return to work. BRB's doctor concluded that he was unlikely ever to be fit to work again and Hooper was dismissed. This was breach of contract and would have been unfair unless he had refused an offer of suitable work. The case was referred back to the industrial tribunal to see if suitable work had been offered. The Appeal Court held that BRB's actual intention was irrelevant. If the words were clear – and they were – then they must be applied, regardless of the unfortunate outcome.

This case was unusual. Normally the provision of sick pay means no more than that so long as the individual remains employed, he will be entitled to pay as set out. He can be dismissed before sick pay is exhausted so long as the employer can show the adverse impact of his absence.

One final point. If sick pay is to be discretionary or *ex gratia* rather than contractual, this should be made clear. During periods of probation or the first few months of employment some employers do make sick pay discretionary. The amount of pay as well as the entitlement may vary from one group of employees to another. If the employee has received more sick pay in the relevant period and the employer wishes to make a deduction from wages or demand repayment the wages protection provisions of the Employment Rights Act must be complied with, and an express clause will be needed.

Terms for a white-collar employee

After six months' employment, employees working more than eight hours per week will be entitled to the following sick benefit in any rolling period of 12 months.

Up to two years' service: eight weeks' pay.
From two to four years' service: 12 weeks' pay.
Over four years' service: 26 weeks' pay.

Benefit is dependent upon compliance with any reporting procedure which the company may publish from time to time.

Sick pay will be paid less any SSP or state benefit to which you may be entitled as a result of your sickness.

The company may, at any time, require you to undergo a medical examination by a practitioner of the company's choice. The cost of such examination will be the responsibility of the company.

Sick pay is pay for the purpose of the equal pay requirement set out in article 119 of the Treaty of Rome. In *Rinner-Kuhn v. FWW Spezial-Gebäudereinigung (1989)*[8] the European Court even went so far as to hold that German statutory sick pay was pay. It therefore follows that women are entitled to sick pay at the same rate as men, and that part-timers are entitled on a *pro rata* basis unless their hours are very low (not specified!) or part-timers cannot do the job as well as full-timers (*Bilka Kaufhaus v. Webber von Hartz (1986)*[9]). It should also be noted that it is discriminatory to refuse sick pay to women whose illness is connected with pregnancy or maternity (*Coyne v. Export Credit Guarantee Department (1981)*).[10]

In addition, under the Social Security and Housing Benefits Act 1982 employers are required to pay Statutory Sick Pay (SSP). In determining what terms relating to contractual sick pay should be included in the contract the SSP provisions should be borne in mind.

There are two levels of SSP, and depending on the wages earned by the employee, SSP is subject to tax and National Insurance payments. It is also wages for the purposes of the Wages Act 1986. The wording used is similar on the face of it, to that in the Employment Protection (Consolidation) Act, but SSP uses Department of Social Security terminology and words do not always have the same meaning as in Department of Employment statutes. It is not the purpose of this book to deal with SSP. However, it is worth pointing out that some of the reporting procedures and entitlements under the SSP provisions may be unsuitable for contractual sick pay. Table 2 shows some of the differences.

Table 2   Some differences between company sick pay and SSP

Common company terms	SSP
Early notification on day 1	Notification at any time on day 1
Self-certificate from day 1	Self-certificate from day 4
Medical note at any time	Medical certificate from day 8
Paid from first day of absence	Paid after absence of three qualifying days
May be a qualifying period of service	Entitled once he has started work

Sick notes are not conclusive evidence of illness, nor is the absence of one conclusive evidence of fitness; the employer may wish to obtain his own medical information. To this end, a clause providing that the employee must at any time undergo a medical examination by a practitioner of the organisation's choice, and with the cost borne by the employer, would be helpful. If the practitioner is a person who is or has previously been responsible for the employee's clinical care, then the employer must comply with the Access to Medical Reports Act 1988, which requires the employee's consent.

The contract is not totally suspended during the employee's absence. Even if the employee is genuinely ill and cannot perform some aspects of his job there may be some other parts of it he can do. In *Marshall v. Alexander Sloane (1981)*[11] a sick employee was held to be still under a duty to take care of her employer's property while it was in her possession. It may be possible to build on this and provide that the employee, with medical approval, may return to work part-time, or in a less strenuous or stressful position, on full pay until fully fit. Sick pay outstanding can then be conserved for a future occasion. This was the decision in *Aspden v. Webbs Poultry and Meat Group (Holdings) Ltd (1996).*[12] The EAT decided that, where there was a contractual entitlement to PHI, it would be unfair to dismiss an employee while he was sick, except for misconduct. Presumably the same would apply to a right to early retirement on medical grounds.

The employer may provide medical insurance to cover long-term ill health. This eases 'dismissal' and puts the employer in a caring role. Also the decision rests partly with the insurance company and so the burden on the employer is reduced. But there can be problems:

- It may be unfair to dismiss an employee who is about to qualify under the scheme.
- It may be unfair to dismiss on grounds of ill health without explaining the possibility that the scheme applies.
- The individual may remain an employee while receiving payment under the scheme. For this reason it may be appropriate to provide that

he remains an employee for the sole purpose of receiving benefit under the scheme.

The employer may also offer insurance against injuries at work. In *Rutherford v. Radio Rentals (1991)*,[13] Rutherford's contract incorporated provisions from the handbook which gave personal insurance cover in the event of an accident while on the company's business. This was subject to the terms of the insurance policy itself. Rutherford was injured while carrying a television set. His claim for negligence failed. The insurers refused a claim under the insurance policy. The court held that there was an implied term that the employer would pay in accordance with the terms of the contract, as otherwise the employer could take advantage of the insurers, wrongfully refusing to pay. The dispute would then be between the insurer and the employer, not the employee. This in effect makes the employer the insurer!

Private medical cover is also common. Both medical cover and permanent health insurance are suitable for the discretionary category. As *Baynham & ors v. Philips Electronics (UK) Ltd & ors (1995)*[14] shows, if there is no discretion the terms may be difficult to change. The organisation may wish to change the provider and the level of benefit, increasing or decreasing it.

Health insurance terms

Permanent health insurance

The company operates a permanent health insurance scheme. The scheme does not apply during the first six months of employment, nor does it apply to temporary staff or to staff on fixed-term contracts.
    The scheme is discretionary.
    Further details can be obtained from . . .

Private medical insurance

The company participates in a private medical insurance scheme. Subject to any eligibility requirements imposed by the scheme, you are entitled to benefit under the scheme. This is a discretionary benefit.

Key points

- The entitlement needs to be clear.
- The amount should be clear.

- Permanent health insurance? Check the employment position while the employee is in receipt of benefit.
- Private medical insurance? Consider making the benefit discretionary.
- The right to require medical examination.
- Entitlement is dependent upon complying with the reporting procedure. The procedure need not be put in the contract.
- Note the position during the period of notice.

References

1   IRLR 139 QB.
2   3 All ER 527 CA.
3   4 All ER 281 CA.
4   IRLR 183 CA.
5   IRLR 218 CA.
6   IRLR 434 EAT.
7   IRLR 517 CA.
8   IRLR 493 ECJ.
9   IRLR 317 ECJ.
10 IRLR 51 IT.
11 IRLR 264.
12 IRLR 521 EAT.
13 Ct Sess., noted in IRLIB 419.
14 *IDS Brief*, 551 2BD

35
Guarantee pay

A term is implied into employment contracts requiring the employer to pay wages in full during periods of work shortage unless the provision of work is beyond the control of the employer. This provision is related to the employee's undertaking that he will be ready and willing to work. To earn his wage, that is all that is required of him. He does not have to *do* any work. This was the decision in *Devonald v. Rosser & Sons (1906)*.[1] The employer was closing down because he had no orders. The employer paid his time-rate workers during the period of notice but not the piece-rate workers. It was decided that wages were due to piece-rate workers, either because piece rates were merely the method of calculating the pay or because when wages were dependent on work being provided the employer had undertaken to provide work, and so had to pay damages.

But payment need not be made when the provision of work is beyond management's control. It may be beyond management control if there is a strike at the works, if the electricity supply fails or if the works are unsafe, management not being at fault (*Browning v. Crumlin Valley Colliery (1926)*[2]. This exception is interpreted restrictively. So in *Jones v. Harry Sherman (1969)*[3] when there was less betting, owing to the cancellation of horse racing on account of foot-and-mouth disease, wages were still due.

This implied term will be rebutted by any term agreed by the parties. It is difficult to show such rebuttal unless there is an express term, and a written term is desirable. It will also enable the employer to clarify an area where the law is less than clear, namely industrial action at work. Those taking industrial action need not be paid; if they are taking industrial action short of a strike, they are in breach of their contract and can be sent home without pay. If they remain working they need be paid only for the work done, or the employer can offer a lower sum as the wage while the action continues. Continuance of the action will amount to acceptance of the lower wage. But the other staff are in a different position. In *Needs v. CAV (1983)*[4] the court decided that, once there was no work for the other staff, they could be laid off without pay, but not until then. A term could provide for earlier lay-offs and short-term working, and in return guarantee some payment for a period of lay-off during lack of work.

Provision for short time and lay-offs

The company reserves the right to put you on short time or lay you off work when for operational or other reasons it is in the opinion of management appropriate to do so. Management may instead require you to undertake any other available work, including work outside your contract and work at another site.

While undertaking other work your current wage will be maintained. Your wage during periods of short time working and lay-off will be at management's discretion but for the first four weeks will not be less than £x per week.

Any guarantee pay clauses incorporated in the contract will override the implied common law term, but failure to pay in accordance with the term will amount to constructive breach of contract, and redundancy claims will be difficult to avoid. The employee may also claim unpaid wages (under the wage protection provisions of the Employment Rights Act 1996), terminate the contract without notice and claim damages.

The provisions will need to address several consequential problems, for example:

- If the wage is reduced, is there any knock-on effect on other rights dependent on the actual or on the average wage, such as pension and holiday pay?
- If there is work available outside their contract, can employees be required to do it?
- Could they be transferred to another site or to an associated employer during this period?
- Will the guarantee pay be full pay or a lesser sum?
- For how long will payment be made?
- Has the employer the right to withdraw the guarantee payment?

The statutory provision for guarantee pay for five days in each rolling period of three months[5] does not exclude the above rights, but dual payments are not made; one is set against the other. The qualification criteria for statutory pay differ from the common law term in that the lack of work can be outside the employer's control. But no statutory payment is made if:

- There is no work because of industrial unrest at the establishment of the associated employer, or
- There is suitable alternative employment of a non-contractual variety (but it must be similar in status and wage to the contract work), or

- The employee fails to meet a reasonable condition imposed by management, as in *Purdy v. Willow Brook International (1977)*,[6] when employees who had been kept fully informed of the situation by management went home, refusing to wait at work for the delayed delivery of heating oil.

Except when the provision of work is beyond the employer's control, the common law is more generous. Of course, with good industrial relations, employees may be more accommodating.

Provision for short-time working

1 Subject to the provisions set out below, the company will guarantee the following payments in any week in which there is short-time working. Short time occurs when in any week the hours worked are less than the normal weekly hours.

Less than one year's service: 50 per cent of a week's pay.
Over two years' service: 75 per cent of a week's pay.

Actual pay will be based on full pay for the hours worked plus half the normal wage lost through short-time work.

[*Note* that the normal wage in this contract is the basic weekly wage and does not include overtime.]

2 The company reserves the right to withdraw the guarantee by giving notice in the following circumstances:

  (a) Without notice in the event of an unofficial dispute by employees of the company.
  (b) With five days' notice in the event of an official dispute by employees of the company.
  (c) With one week's notice in the event of industrial action, official or unofficial, by persons not employed by the company.
  (d) With two weeks' notice in the event of interruption or reduction of supplies or orders or in the event of any other circumstances outside the employer's control.

3 The guarantee will not apply:

  (a) To employees who refuse alternative work, including work at other sites.
  (b) To employees who have been absent from work without good reason or have received a disciplinary warning. These employees will not receive the guarantee during any week in which either of these events occurs.

Finally, as with sick pay above, under the Employment Rights Act 1996, ss. 87, 88, if the employee is under notice of termination he is entitled to the full wage. See p. 167.

Key points

- Is an express term needed?
- The amount of guarantee pay.
- The period for which the employee will be paid.
- Special inclusions and exclusions, e.g. industrial action at the employer's own plant.
- Whether the employee must be willing to undertake non-contractual work.
- Are lay-off or short-time provisions needed? Are they met by a basic weekly pay provision?
- The effect on entitlement to other benefits.

References

1 2 KB 728 CA.
2 1 KB 522.
3 ITR 63 IT.
4 IRLR 360 QB.
5 Employment Rights Act 1996, s. 28.
6 IRLR 388 IT.

36
Holidays

There is at the moment no general entitlement to a holiday. With a few special exceptions, entitlement to holidays and holiday pay is contractual. There is no general entitlement to bank holidays. The employer cannot insist that holidays have to be taken at a particular time, e.g. between the Christmas and new year breaks.

The written particulars require holiday entitlement to be specified, whether it is paid, and whether the employee is entitled to accrued holiday pay when his contract is terminated. There are several other points which need to be set out, either in the contract or in some other document such as the handbook. Some of them relate to:

- entitlement in an incomplete year
- the amount of holiday which can be taken at one time
- whether an additional day can be taken when a bank holiday falls during annual leave
- whether there are additional days if the employee is sick while on holiday
- who approves the timing of holidays
- whether holiday entitlement can be transferred to the following year.

If deductions are to be made because holiday taken has exceeded entitlement the wage protection provisions of the Employment Rights Act 1996 will apply and an express term will be needed.

The organisation may wish to make provision for extended leave, with or without pay. It is sensible to put any terms relating to this type of leave in writing and ensure that they are understood by the employee. It used to be common to provide that, if the employee did not return on the due date, for any reason at all, the contract would end. But the courts have decided that this is a term under which the employee contracts out of his right to claim unfair dismissal and that it is therefore void under the Employment Rights Act 1996, s. 203 as in *Igbo v. Johnson Matthey Chemicals (1986).*[1] The agreement is still a good idea, but before dismissing an employee the employer should check the facts to see whether the delay was unavoidable. Mrs Igbo had returned home with a genuine illness, so dismissal was not fair in her case.

Under ss. 87, 88 of the Employment Rights Act 1996, full wages must be paid if the employee is on holiday during the period of notice. See p. 167.

The Working Time Directive could introduce major changes to holiday terms. The Directive provides for a compulsory annual holiday of four weeks' paid leave, although in a transition period of the first three years this will be reduced to three weeks. Member states are permitted to apply qualifying conditions. This could be continuous employment (nil hours, casual and temporary workers can accumulate continuity and it includes employment with associated employers); hours per week (the Lords have decided that hours thresholds are discriminatory); or the actual length of the contract.

The holiday would be mandatory and so should be taken. It may not be transferred to the following year and there can be a cash substitute only in an incomplete year. Of course this will not apply to holiday in excess of the four (three) weeks. It is assumed that bank holidays (if paid) will be included.

There has been some doubt as to whether an entitlement to holidays or holiday pay can be implied. In *Morley v. Heritage plc (1993)*,[2] a claim for accrued holiday pay, the EAT decided that it depended on whether payment had been made in the past. In that case the written contract had stated that the only terms were those set out in the contract, and there were no other terms. This made it difficult to imply a term. The EAT was not so inhibited in *Janes Solicitors v. Lamb-Simpson (1995)*.[3] When Ms Lamb-Simpson left Janes she claimed accrued holiday pay. She had no written terms but said that an entitlement to holidays and accrued holiday pay had been agreed verbally. The tribunal and EAT accepted this. The EAT also said that in the absence of express terms they would have implied them.

Holiday entitlement

An assistant in an electrical shop

You will be entitled to twenty-three working days' paid leave per year.

The holiday year is 1 April to 31 March. All holiday must be taken in the year in which it accrues.

The timing of the holiday must be agreed with the store manager. More than ten consecutive days' leave may not be taken without the permission of the manager.

In addition staff are entitled to one day's leave for each statutory bank holiday. Except for Christmas Day, staff may be required to take this leave on a day other than the calendar day on which it falls.

Holiday pay is based on basic pay. If you are required to work on a bank holiday you will be entitled to be paid at time-and-a-half.

In any incomplete year your holiday entitlement will be *pro rata* your entitlement for a complete year.

On leaving the company you will be entitled to accrued pay for any outstanding paid leave.

Holiday entitlement

Factory manager

You will be entitled to twenty-five working days' paid leave per year. Five days must be taken during the annual closure and five days over Christmas and New Year. The remainder will be taken in consultation with your manager. In addition you will be entitled to paid leave on bank holidays.

[Plus terms relating to accrued pay and *pro rata* provision for an incomplete year.]

Key points

- Amount and time period.
- Pay, accrued pay, accrued pay if dismissed for misconduct.
- Timing, amount to be taken at one time, permission.
- Transfer to specific dates at management request.
- Bank/public/statutory holidays. Pay, time off in lieu. Bank holiday falling during holiday.
- Sickness during holiday.
- Entitlement in an incomplete holiday year.

References

1 IRLR 215 CA.
2 IRLR 400 CA.
3 *IDS Brief*, 549 EAT.

37
Maternity leave, paternity leave and other types of compassionate leave

Maternity rights in general and maternity leave in particular were extended by the EU Directive on Pregnancy. The provisions are now to be found in the Employment Rights Act 1996 Part VII. Briefly, women with two years' continuity of employment at the 11th week before the week of confinement are entitled to commence leave at that 11th week and return to their job up to 29 weeks after the actual week of childbirth. This may be extended by up to four weeks on medical grounds, on grounds of an industrial relations problem at the workplace, or where the employer has a good reason to delay it. For the first 14 weeks she remains an employee on full terms other than remuneration (see below), but after that date the question whether she is an employee depends on whether the employer has so decided or has treated her as an employee. The woman must comply with stringent notification requirements.

All women, regardless of service, are entitled to 14 weeks' maternity leave, during which they are employees entitled to full terms and conditions other than remuneration (undefined). Again, it can be extended by four weeks, but only for medical reasons, and again there are notification requirements. Statutory maternity pay is for 18 weeks (but an employee can probably extend her leave by four weeks on medical grounds), and to qualify she must have 26 weeks' continuity at the 15th week before the expected week of confinement. If she has less service she may be able to claim maternity benefit from the DSS. In addition a limited amount of maternity leave has been obtained for other women through a development of the Sex Discrimination Act 1975, s. 1. Under this Act it has been held to be discriminatory to treat women whose absence is related to pregnancy less favourably than men who are off sick. This, in general terms, entitles the woman to maternity leave equivalent to sick leave. It does not deal with pay or benefits during leave. Sex discrimination has been developed in many ways to obtain maternity rights, and the pivotal case is *Dekker v. Stichting Vormingcentrum voor Jonge Volwassenen (VJV) Centrum Plus (1991)*[1]. The ECJ held that because only women can be pregnant any detrimental decision based on pregnancy must be direct discrimination. In that particular case she was refused employment because she was pregnant and the employer could not afford two salaries for the period of her leave. The defence of justification does not apply to direct discrimination, only to indirect discrimination. Discrimination claims are extremely attractive because

180

there is no upper limit to damages, compensation can be obtained for injured feelings, and interest can be given on the award (Sex Discrimination and Equal Pay (Remedies) Regulations 1993). But an attempt to use discrimination to obtain full terms and conditions during maternity leave failed in *Gillespie v. Northern Health and Social Security Board (1996)*[2]. However, the court did decide that any wage increase occurring either during the reference period on which her maternity pay was based or during her maternity leave had to be taken into account in assessing her pay.

Given these complicated rules and the development of the Sex Discrimination Act to allow her request to return to adjusted working terms (see Chapter 19), as well as the growing recognition of the importance of women in the workforce, it is hardly surprising that many employers simplify the problem by producing more generous contractual terms. There is a wide variety of imaginative maternity packages. Many have extended the shorter maternity leave period to 18 weeks to allow her to utilise her full 18 weeks' maternity pay; others make it clear that she remains an employee during all maternity leave; yet others provide more pay and longer leave. For more detailed consideration of the law see the companion Law and Employment volume, *Discrimination*, by Linda Clarke.

But there are certain important points to consider when assembling the package. Some of them have been discussed earlier under 'Break points', p. 87. These cover the position of the woman while on leave, the continuance of certain contractual rights such as insurance, pension and the use of a car, training and contact during leave, and the position to which she will return. It is also vital to know whether her break will count for the purposes of statutory continuity and contractual service. Statutory maternity leave is part of continuity for statutory rights but other leave will be included only if there is agreement on it prior to the break or there is an established custom to that effect.

Paternity leave is entirely a matter for the parties, as is adoption leave. Organisations are increasingly providing both types of leave, but some have a qualification requirement, and others make leave discretionary. This type of leave is usually paid. Paternity leave is sometimes extended to the birth of the children of partners as well as spouses. Allied to this is leave for family purposes – weddings, funerals, change of residence, etc. Other compassionate leave is usually discretionary, both as to whether it is granted at all and as to pay. The EU has agreed a Directive on Parental Leave. The UK has opted out of this Directive under the Maastricht provisions. The Directive will provide each parent with up to three months' leave on birth or adoption. The leave may be unpaid and the contract may not continue during leave. But the parent would be entitled to return to his or her previous job. There would also be leave, which again might be unpaid, for occasions on which the individual's presence was essential – for example illness or funerals.

Maternity leave

Entitlement

All women employees are entitled to maternity leave. Leave may commence at the 11th week before the expected date of confinement, and the employee must return by the 29th week after the week of actual confinement. Leave will be with full pay for the first 18 weeks. Thereafter leave will be unpaid. The following benefits will continue to apply during maternity leave: pension, mortgage subsidy, private medical insurance and use of the car.

Notification

Medical proof of pregnancy and the date of confinement must be produced to the Personnel Department (for example, a form Mat. B1).

Three weeks' written notification of intention to take maternity leave must be given to Personnel, unless it is not reasonably practicable to do so.

Three weeks' written notification must be given of the date of return to work.

Extended leave

If the employee does not wish to return within the above period she may notify the Personnel Department in writing prior to the 29th week after confinement that she wishes to take extended leave. She may then give written notice of her wish to return at any time up to two years after the actual week of birth. She will be permitted to return if there is a suitable vacancy. If there is no such vacancy but one arises within the following six months that vacancy will be offered to her. Upon her return she will be entitled to count her previous period of employment and her period of leave as part of her continuity of employment for both contractual and statutory purposes. Her terms and conditions will be those applicable to the new post.

Paternity leave

The company provides 10 days' paid paternity leave for each child born. The child may be born to the spouse or the permanent partner. The leave is discretionary.

Adoption leave

The company will at its discretion allow up to ten working days for pre-placement meetings plus a period of adoption leave of up to 18 weeks for children up to five years, and up to 20 working days for children over that age. Where both parents work for the organisation they will both be entitled to the pre-placement leave but not the adoption leave; they may be split between them if they wish. The leave is with pay.

Family leave and personal leave

This leave is at the discretion of the company and may be granted with or without pay. The following are guidelines:

Serious illness of spouse, dependent or close family: five days.
Domestic difficulties caused by illness or any of the above: five days.
Death of any of the above where the employee has to make the funeral arrangements: five days.
Funeral of any of the above: one day. Further time may be allowed for travel.
Own wedding: one day.
Moving house: one day.

Key points

Maternity leave

- The employment qualification needs to be defined.
- Notification requirements should be specified.
- What will the period of leave be? Pay and benefits during leave should be considered.
- Notification of return should be required.
- The employment position on the mother's return must be clear.
- Any continuity of service for statutory and contractual rights should be specified.

Paternity leave

- Service qualification should be specified.
- The period and pay need to be defined.
- Discretionary?
- Is it to cover the child of a partner?

Adoption leave

- Service qualification.
- Period and pay.
- Discretionary?

Family leave

- Service qualification.
- Reasons.
- Period and pay.
- Discretionary?

Compassionate leave

- Is the granting of leave discretionary?
- Is pay discretionary?

All

- Who exercises the discretion in all these types of leave?

References

1 IRLR 27 ECJ.
2 IRLR 214 ECJ.

38
Public duties

The Employment Rights Act 1996, s. 50, provides that all employees are entitled to reasonable time off for public duties. The public duties concerned are as:

- a Justice of the Peace
- a member of a local authority
- a member of a statutory tribunal
- a member of a health authority
- a member of a relevant education body
- a member of the Environment Agency or the Scottish Environment Agency
- membership of a police authority
- a prison visitor or member of a prison visitors committee.

There is no provision for payment.

The needs of the employer are not ignored. The time off has to be reasonable, and, as well as taking into account any other time the employee may have off, the requirements of the business are also taken into consideration. In some cases it may be reasonable to expect the employee to use some of his own time to make up part of the lost work. An aggrieved employee can apply to the industrial tribunal, which has jurisdiction to make a decision on his rights and award compensation. But the tribunal has no power to draw up clauses to cover time off and incorporate them in the contract.

The best way to avoid problems and make certain that the arrangements are reasonable is to set out a contract term or a policy. It cannot override the statutory duty, but it goes a long way towards proving that no breach has occurred. At the same time other public duties may be added to the statutory list, which, among others, omits jury service, Territorial Army training and appearing in court as a witness. The arrangement may also specify the number of days which will be allowed off – identifying reasonableness – and provide for pay. Where the employee obtains some payment for his service he can be required to bring this into account. As the ability of the organisation to accommodate time off may change, it may be sensible to make any arrangements discretionary, or at least subject to change by the employer.

The right of members of recognised unions to unpaid time off for union activities and of union officials to paid time off for union duties under the Trade Union and Labour Relations (Consolidation) Act 1992 s. 168 and s. 170 can be dealt with in the same way. But these rights are more properly dealt with under the recognition agreement with the union and kept outside the contract.

Provision for public duties

Employees who are called upon to perform jury service should inform their manager. The employee will be encouraged to serve on the jury, although the organisation may request the employee to seek a postponement of service if service at that particular time would unduly interfere with the activities of the organisation.

The employee will receive full pay while on jury service, less any allowances received from the court.

Employees who undertake public duties as a Justice of the Peace, member of a local authority, member of a statutory tribunal, member of a health authority, governor of a school (local or state) or of a river purification board will be granted twenty days' leave on full pay (less any allowances received) each year for the performance of these duties, provided that the leave is not to the detriment of the organisation.

Key points

- Which duties will be covered?
- Will there be a limit upon time off?
- Will any payment be made?
- Will the employee have to bring into account any payment he receives?
- Will the arrangement be discretionary?

39
Expenses

In a recent case the EAT decided that there was an implied term in an employee's contract that he would be reimbursed 'all expenses, losses and liabilities incurred by the employee in the execution of his employer's instructions . . . or during the reasonable performance of his employment' (*Cosslett Contractors v. Quinn (1990)*[1]). The employer had agreed to pay £12.12 per night as 'away pay' for a category of mobile workers. Quinn did not fall into that category. The EAT refused to imply the £12.12 arrangement for Quinn, giving him instead full reimbursement of his overnight expenses.

A better agreement would be one which required prior authorisation for expenses and perhaps put an upper limit on certain types of payment such as meals, accommodation, class of travel, and set a precise amount for others, such as mileage.

Control of expenses

The company will reimburse all authorised expenses properly incurred in the execution of the employee's duties. Wherever possible, expenses must be supported by receipts or other proof of payment. Claims must be submitted monthly. Payment will be made with the following month's salary.

Authorisation for expenses may be obtained from the section director.

Guidance as to the amounts which may be incurred for accommodation, travel and meals will be found in the leaflet available from the Personnel Department.

Key points

- What expenses will be reimbursed?
- Who will authorise them?
- Is supporting documentation required?
- Are maxima to be set?

Reference

1 EAT, noted in IRLIB 413.

40
Company car

Viewed by many employees as one of the most important perks, this is a fertile area for disputes. There is also a considerable amount of misunderstanding about the status of the terms dealing with the car. Many employers mistakenly thought that the term was discretionary, and so they could change the size of the car and the period of renewal. They found to their cost that it was not so. The terms were often expressed in clear, contractual language. Even where there is ambiguity it seems that courts and tribunals readily find that anything to do with transport is contractual. So in *Chapman v. Goonvean & Rostowrack China Clay (1972)*[1] it was concluded that an arrangement whereby an employer hired a mini-van to bring staff into work was contractual: therefore its withdrawal amounted to a serious breach of contract and constructive dismissal. There were no express terms in relation to the van.

In *Keir and Williams v. County Council of Hereford and Worcestershire (1985)*[2] Mrs Keir was employed by the authority as a social worker and Mrs Williams as a home help organiser. Under the conditions incorporated into their contracts, there were two types of car user: casual users, for whom a car was desirable, and essential users, for whom a car was necessary. Different allowances were paid to the two categories, with essential users obtaining the higher sum. Essential car users were defined in the agreement. Mrs Williams fell within that definition, and Mrs Keir had been expressly informed in her offer letter that the job attracted an essential car user allowance. Unless they ceased to be essential car users they were contractually entitled to the higher allowance. The authority could not transfer them to the casual category.

But car provisions are terms which may require changes. They are dependent on tax rules and may cease to be viable if the rules change. A degree of flexibility or discretion would appear vital. It could be obtained by a com-bination of a contractual promise to provide a car, linked with a discretionary policy which determined which car and when it would be renewed. Employees would then be promised provision of a car within the scope of any car policy which the organisation might issue from time to time. A new policy could introduce change. Or employees could be promised a car which the company considers suitable to their position. Or employees could be provided with a car only when it is considered necessary for them to do their job, the 'essential' car user rather than the recipient of the perk.

Provision when a car is supplied

All employees of grade X and above will be provided with the use of a car by the company. Other employees will be provided with a car only when the car is necessary for the performance of the job. (The offer letter will inform the employee of the category into which he falls.)

The type of car and conditions of use are set out in the company car policy, which may be changed from time to time. A list of approved models is available from the Personnel Office. Wherever possible the company will utilise existing cars should such cars be available rather than acquiring new ones. The company reserves the right to reallocate, replace or recall cars.

The cost of maintaining and insuring the car will be met by the company. Employees with a company car are responsible for their own private mileage. Mileage incurred on company business will be reimbursed by the company at the standard business mileage rate.

Provision for a mileage allowance

Authority for an employee to use his or her own car for work must be obtained from the departmental manager. The employee must ensure that the car is in good condition and that his or her insurance covers this use.

Upon proof of mileage, employees using the car for the performance of their work will be entitled to a mileage allowance of xp per mile.

Employees travelling more than 1,000 miles per year may choose to join the company car scheme (car provided by the company). If the employee travels more than 10,000 miles per year the company can require him to join the company car scheme.

As well as the type of car there are many subsidiary points which must be clear. These may be included in the policy. The list is lengthy. It includes:

- insurance
- maintenance
- permitted drivers
- fines
- taking the car abroad
- driving licence
- reporting accidents.

- whether essential car users have to return the car during long periods of absence for use by the replacement.

If the employee is permitted to use his own car for work, then a car allowance may be paid. In addition to questions such as setting the allowance, proof of mileage, etc., there will again be a need to require that the car should be maintained in good condition, insured, and that the employee should hold a valid driving licence.

Key points

- Is the car a perk or essential for work?
- Is provision of a car contractual or discretionary?
- Is there discretion as to the capacity or cost of the car and its renewal?
- Are all the subsidiary points dealt with in the policy or some other changeable document?
- Do essential car users return the car during long periods of absence?
- Where the employee provides his own car is an allowance payable?

References

1 IRLR 124 EAT.
2 IRLR 505 CA.

41
Share options

These schemes are best drawn up by experts, as they have tax and company law implications. But one or two points must be considered from the personnel angle.

The first question is whether the share option agreement should be part of the contract or a separate binding agreement. The latter would seem preferable. If the scheme is part of the employment contract, then, on a transfer under the Transfer of Undertakings Regulations 1981, that term would transfer to the new employer. In *Chapman and Elkins v. CPS Computer Group (1987)*[1] the Court of Appeal could not see how that could work. The court decided that the particular employee share option agreement was not part of the employment contract but a separate contract which continued to operate after the employment contract had ended, so Chapman could exercise his option to buy shares even though he was no longer an employee. The company in which Chapman sought to buy shares had ceased to exist because it had merged with another company. That indeed was why Chapman's contract had ended. Because the shares were no longer available he obtained damages for his lost profit. In *Thompson v. Asda-MFI Group (1988)*[2] the scheme contained a provision that the employee's participation would end should the subsidiary which employed him move out of the group. This avoided the *Chapman* problem.

A further development has occurred in Scotland, in *Chapman v. Aberdeen Construction Group (1991)*.[3] Under a share option scheme, in the event of dismissal the employee was not entitled to damages or compensation as a result of any right or expectations under the scheme. Section 23 of the Unfair Contract Terms Act 1977 renders void any term excluding or restricting rights or remedies arising under another contract which would not be lawful under that other contract. Section 23 was held to apply, and Chapman was entitled to damages for the loss of his option rights. An attempt to apply the Act in England failed because in England shares are excluded from its operation whereas in Scotland they are not. (*Micklefield v. SAC Technology (1990)*.[4])

Key points

- Should the agreement be outside the contract of employment?
- Do the employee's rights end on termination of employment?

References

1 Noted in IRLIB 336 CA.
2 IRLR 340 Ch.
3 IRLR 505 Ct Sess.
4 IRLR 218 Ch.

42
Intellectual property

Intellectual property falls into three main categories:

- ideas
- copyright material
- patents.

No legislation deals with ideas, and it may be said that there is no 'ownership' of an idea. If an idea is disclosed in confidence, then the rules preventing disclosure and the use of confidential information will give some protection.

Some employees are actually employed to produce ideas. Where an employee is employed to invent or give advice it may be a breach of his duty of fidelity to refuse to disclose them. This was part of the decision in *British Soda Syphon v. Homewood (1956)*.[1] In that case the employee had an idea for a new product. He failed to disclose it to the employer, but left his employment and set about manufacturing on his own behalf. It was decided that, if the employer had asked him a technical question connected with his work he would not have answered because he wanted to keep the idea for himself. That would put him in breach of contract. It is better to provide that ideas shall be offered to the organisation, as in *Bauman v. Hulton Press (1952)*.[2]

The Copyright Act 1988, ss. 11 and 219, makes similar provisions. Any copyright in material related to the employment belongs to the employer, whether the material was requested or not. The employee who writes about his work, the systems used by his employer, tasks undertaken for clients, etc., may well be breaching the employer's or the client's copyright as well as being in breach of his own fidelity. In such cases an injunction can be obtained to prevent publication. The copyright in work connected with employment belongs to the employer, whether or not the work was done at the employer's cost or request.

Although under the Copyright Act the copyright in works relating to his employment belong to the employer, where the writing is based on the employee's own skill and knowledge it belongs to the employee. This leads to problems when the work is a combination of both. In *Stevenson, Jordan and Harrison v. MacDonald and Evans (1952)*[3] the book consisted of descriptions of work undertaken for the employer and of material taken from outside lectures given by the employee with the encouragement of the employer. The latter material was in the copyright of the employee, but the case descriptions were the employer's copyright and the employer could prevent publication of that part of the book. It is always possible to prevent an employee publishing any material on topics relating to employment without first obtaining written permission.

The ownership of design copyright and copyright in computer programs is similar.

More than one person may have produced the copyright work, in which case they share the ownership rights. If the work is for a third party he may wish the copyright to be transferred to him. In instances such as these an express copyright provision, stating ownership, is the only solution.

The law concerning the ownership of employees' inventions has been altered by the Patents Act 1977. Now, despite anything to the contrary, an invention will belong to an employer only if it could have been expected as a result of his employee's work. This has been restrictively interpreted, and so only the inventions of employees who are employed specifically to invent and research belong to their employer (*Reiss Engineering v. Harris (1985)*.[4] In *Reiss* the employee was a salesman who was expected to advise customers on the use of the company's products. He invented a new version of the company's valve. The invention belonged to the employee.

Protection of intellectual property

It will be part of your duties to consider how the products, services, processes, equipment or systems of the company might be improved promoted and marketed.

Any patent rights expected as a result of work undertaken by you as part of your work are the property of the company.

The copyright in any material produced by you relating to your employment with the company shall rest with the company.

You undertake to provide the company with every assistance in protecting the company's intellectual property rights.

If the employee whose invention belongs to the employer, because it arose from his work, feels that his employer is getting outstanding benefit from the invention he can apply to the Comptroller General of Patents for an award of compensation.

Where the employee owns the invention but transfers ownership to his employer the employee can apply for further compensation if he feels that the amount he has received is inadequate.

Key points

- Provide for the disclosure of ideas relating to the work of the employer.
- Specify the ownership of copyright.
- Consider placing a restriction on unauthorised publication of material relating to the employment.
- Include a patent ownership provision.

References

1 RPC 27.
2 2 All ER 1121 QB.
3 1 TLR 101.
4 32 Ch.

43
Confidentiality and related provisions

In all organisations there is much information of a confidential nature which cannot be protected by the intellectual property rules. It may range from technical information on production methods to strategic plans, from price and discount lists to the identity of customers and suppliers. In addition, the employee may acquire information about customers or suppliers or others which is private and confidential. For example, an employee in a hospital could have access to confidential information about patients and their visitors. Such information needs protection.

The law restrains the publication or use of any information of a confidential nature by the person receiving it. This applies to all confidential information, whether it is obtained within the employment contract or not. In *Fraser v. Thames Television (1983)*[1] three out-of-work actresses put an idea for a television series to Thames's staff, who turned it down. Later the staff produced a Thames series based on the same idea, *Rock Follies*. This was a breach of confidence. The actresses were entitled to damages.

It can be difficult to identify confidential information. Information usually has a far wider circulation than is realised. And in the technical area confidential information has to be separated from the skill and knowledge of the employee. It can be a monumental task.

The confidential nature of the information does not terminate with employment. This has encouraged employers to try to use confidentiality as a means of restricting the employee's activities after the employment has ceased. It is possible but not easy. The employer must in any case show that misuse or disclosure of confidential information is likely, and after employment has ceased the burden is heavier. Misuse could not be shown in relation to pricing policy and salesmen's routes in *Faccenda Chicken v. Fowler (1986)*,[2] where the employee had set up a similar business selling chilled chickens from travelling vans. The routes, etc., would be different, though some ground covered would be the same. In *Roger Bullivant v. Ellis (1987)*[3] an employee was prevented from using a card index of contacts and in *Johnson & Bloy (Holdings) v. Wolstenholme Rink and Fallon (1987)*[4] a chemical formula was protected.

But during employment the employer can put quite a heavy embargo on the disclosure of information. He may even prevent the employee disclosing information which is available rather than confidential. He may forbid the employee to give information to the media.

Terms governing confidentiality

The employee will not, either during or after the termination of his employ-ment, use or disclose to any person, firm or corporation any information relating to the company and the group, their business, customers or third parties which shall come into his possession in the course of his employ-ment, without first obtaining the permission of the company or the party concerned, except in the course of his duties under the contract or unless ordered to do so by a court of competent jurisdiction.

A public statements clause

The employee will not make any public statement or any statement to a per-son employed or associated with the media concerning the company, the group, customers, suppliers or any aspects of the activities of the company or the group without first obtaining the written consent of the chairman.

Conflict of interest

The employee will not place himself in a position in which his interest conflicts with that of the company.

Working for others

During the existence of this contract the employee will not work for any other organisation without first obtaining the written consent of the chair-man. Such consent will not be unreasonably withheld.

Conflicting financial interest

The employee will declare the ownership of any shares or interests in any business held by himself, his partner or any minor children in any compet-ing organisation. If required to do so by the company he will take steps specified by the company to ensure that there is no conflict of interest.

Allied to this is the need to prevent conflict arising between the duty owed to the employer and the employee's other interests. Again there is an implied duty – this time, the duty to give faithful service; the duty of fidelity. It even covers situations in which the employee is not at fault. In *D. C. Foot v. Eastern Counties Timber (1972)*[5] it was found to have been fair to dismiss a confidential secretary when her husband set up in competition. She had access to confidential sales information and there was a risk that she might disclose it, because she could not be expected to forget in the evening what she had been doing during the day. The duty of fidelity can prevent the employee working for competitors and so putting confidential information at risk (*Hivac v. Park Royal Scientific Instruments (1946)*[6]). To avoid the heavy burden of proof, a clause preventing the employee undertaking other work, a 'no moonlighting' clause, is often used.

Finally it may be desirable to require the employee to disclose his shareholdings and interests in other businesses, and those of the spouse and any minor children. In addition, he may be prevented from having an interest in competing companies (*Bell v. Lever Bros* above, p. 11).

The duty of confidentiality is not one-sided. The employer is also under a duty to maintain the confidentiality of information supplied by the employee and not to disclose it without his consent. In *Dalgleish v. Lothian and Borders Police Board (1991)*[7] policemen used this to prevent the employer disclosing their addresses to the local authority who were checking on the payment of community charge. The duty to maintain adquate records and maintain confidentiality will be increased with the advent of the Data Protection Directive in October 1998. The Directive will apply to manual as well as computerised filing systems.

Key points

- Consider inserting a confidentiality clause in all contracts.
- Identify situations where disclosure of the occupation of the partner is needed.
- Give thought to whether a 'no moonlighting' clause should be included.
- Ensure that disclosure of interests is required.

References

1 2 All ER 101 QB.
2 IRLR 69 CA.
3 IRLR 491 CA.
4 IRLR 499 CA.
5 IRLR 83 IT.
6 1 All ER 350 CA.
7 IRLR 422 CS.

44
Restraints

Clauses restraining the types of occupation the employee may pursue after the termination of his employment have come back into vogue in the past few years. However, successful clauses are difficult to draft. Their enforcement is not easy and can be costly. Careful consideration needs to be given to these terms, and they are best drafted by an expert. As the terms have to be reasonable, they need to be tailor-made to the exact needs of the organisation. There are many different types of terms.

All terms that restrict the employee in his ability to earn a living after his employment has ceased are viewed with suspicion by the courts and are initially deemed to be void and unenforceable. They will become enforceable only if they can be shown by the employer to be no more than is necessary to protect his legitimate interests and to be reasonable. It is, then, possible for the employee to show that the term is contrary to the public interest, whereupon the term becomes void once more.

Before planning any type of restraint clause it is essential to identify these legitimate interests. They may be production know-how, lists of clients and suppliers, marketing and strategic plans, pricing and discount rates, etc. If there is a geographical limitation, e.g. a sales area, it must be identified. It is also vital to know how long the information remains valid – when is it out of date or when does it become public knowledge? The clause may restrain the employee only where he has access to the information, and for as long as the information remains vital and private. The term may not be designed simply to prevent competition, nor may it prevent the employee using his skills, including those obtained in his employment. If there is no information belonging to the employer at risk there can be no enforceable restraint clause, as in *Cantor Fitzgerald (UK) Ltd v. Wallace (1992)*[1]. A firm of inter-dealer brokers in fixed-income bonds and warrants and brokers of Eurobonds put restrictive covenants into employment contracts which prevented employees from working in a competitive business for six months after the contract had terminated. The job involved few technical or financial skills – just speed, accuracy and trust. The employer feared loss of business because of the trust and integrity built by staff with the traders. It was decided that the clause was void because no proprietary right or interest existed to require protection. The 'customer connection' was based on the personal qualities of the employees.

The need for protection can arise even before the contract ends – when the employee gives notice to leave. The employer may wish to ensure than the employee leaves without up-to-date confidential information. This can be done if there is a long period of notice and the employee may not work for another organisation during his employment. The employer then insists (taking out an injunction or interdict if necessary) that the employee should serve his full notice – but that he should not come into work. This is known as 'garden leave'. If the employee has been guaranteed work, it may not be feasible. The combination of a 'no moon-lighting' clause and a long period of notice ensures that any information the employee may take with him is out of date.

In the *Evening Standard v. Henderson (1987)*[2] the employer was held to be entitled to insist that a production manager who had accepted employment with a rival paper should give full notice. This prevented him from working for a competitor until the notice was exhausted. But the courts have subjected 'garden leave' to the reasonableness test in *Provident Financial Group and Whitegates Estate Agency v. Hayward (1989)*.[3] Hayward was the financial director of an estate agency but gave one year's notice to leave. After six months the employer decided to tell him to remain at home on 'garden leave'. Hayward wanted to start work for Asda as financial controller of the supermarket chain's agency. The contract contained the term that he would not 'undertake any other business or profession or become an employee or agent of any other person or persons or assist or have any financial interest in any other business or profession'. The court refused an injunction to stop him working for Asda, on the ground that he was only an administrator and would not possess any confidential information of use to Asda. A surprising decision. Injunctions will be given only when the business is at risk. Many employers exaggerate the risk. If the employer has insisted on garden leave this may be taken into account when deciding whether the post employment restraint is reasonable. The employee on garden leave may not be restrained for the full period of notice. Restraint will be limited to the period of time needed to protect the employer's interests. Although not strictly necessary, employers are beginning to put express garden leave clauses in the contract, under which they have the discretion not to provide work and to exclude the employee from the premises. The employer can transfer him to non-confidential work during notice only if there is a clause to that effect.[4]

It is quite common to insert clauses which prevent the employee from accepting similar work for similar employers within a defined area and for a defined time after the contract has ended. This is the covenant in restraint of trade. In these clauses the employer must identify the work, duration and geographical area of the restraint. It is vital to ensure that all the elements of the clause are necessary and no more than is required to protect the employer's interests. A clause can be void because it is too narrow, as in *Office Angels v. Rainer-Thomas and O'Connor (1991)*.[5] The covenant must protect some business advantage or asset which it would be unjust to allow the employee to appropriate. The employment agency in this case was entitled to protect its connections with clients and workers. But a restraint covering the City of London (1.2 square miles) was too narrow. It did not protect interests, because business was conducted by phone, and the geographical area was not only incorrect as far as business clients were concerned, it was irrelevant. It would have been relevant for staff clients, but there was no restraint term in relation to them. A non-solicitation or non-dealing clause would have been better. In *Lansing Linde v. Kerr (1991)*[6] the restraint was too broad because, although the director concerned attended meetings at which international strategy was discussed, his information was meagre and so a restraint covering any region in which the group operated would have been too wide. The restraint clause may protect the group if the employee's activities require it. The success of this clause is dependent on defining correctly the geographical area, the work and the time scale on the basis of the turnover of clients, technology or information. The clause will need updating whenever the employment changes.

Even when this hurdle has been overcome, it is open to the employee to show that the clause is contrary to the public interest, e.g. because it deprives the country of the services of an efficient researcher, manager, etc., as in *Bull v. Pitney Bowes (1966)*,[7] in which case the clause becomes void again.

Occasionally the courts will cut down clauses which have been drafted too broadly by striking out the part that is excessive – the 'blue pencil' rule. There is no guarantee that the rule will be used. But, to give it a chance to operate, the restraints must be set out in as small units as possible. For example they might cite the UK not as a whole but county by county.

Today employers are more likely to use other restraint terms, such as non-solicitation, non-dealing, loyalty, confidentiality and 'no poaching' clauses either in addition to, or in substitution for, the traditional covenant in restraint of trade. One such clause is the non-solicitation clause, under which the employee agrees not to solicit clients or contacts for a defined period after the termination of employment. Another is the non-dealing clause when the employee agrees not to deal with clients or contacts for a defined period after the termination of employment. In *John Michael Design v. Cooke and Foley (1987)*[8] a non-dealing covenant was upheld and the ex-employees were forced to break contracts they had entered into in breach of that term. The clients must be identifiable and the employee must have had direct or indirect contact with them. It is common to restrict clients to those with whom he had contact during the previous two years. The period of post-employment restraint should reflect the waning influence the individual will have over clients, and also client turnover over time.

Another clause is the confidentiality clause, which is an extension of the employee's general agreement not to disclose confidential information. In addition, the employee agrees not to enter into any employment or to be involved directly or indirectly in any business where, in the faithful performance of his duties, he or she might be expected to disclose information of a confidential nature relating to the previous employer's business. In *Norbrook Laboratories v. Smyth (1987)*[9] this enabled Norbrook to prevent one of their production staff from accepting employment with another pharmaceutical company, Pfizer. This is a useful clause for back-room staff contracts.

Finally there are 'loyalty' clauses. Such clauses are used largely in the public sector. They prevent an employee working for or being interested in any organisation with which he may have had contact during the final period of his employment.

Terms for a sales executive

The employee will not for a period of 12 months following the termination of his employment be engaged or concerned directly or indirectly in any company or business which is involved wholly or partly in the design, manufacture or sale of fitted furniture for kitchens, domestic premises or offices in Scotland, Cumbria or Northumberland.

The employee will not for a period of 12 months solicit or deal, directly or indirectly, on his own behalf or on that of any other company, business organisation or person, with any person, company, business or organisation with whom he has had contact in the course of his employment in the 12 months prior to the termination of his employment.

During the 12 months following the termination of his employment the employee shall not induce, solicit or endeavour to entice away any person who is an employee of a company with whom the employee had direct contact in the 12 months preceding the termination of his employment.

These clauses shall apply to any termination of the employee's employment howsoever caused.

Each of the above covenants shall constitute a separate and independent covenant and shall be construed independently of the other covenants.

A different problem is dealt with by 'no poaching' clauses. These prevent the ex-employee poaching his ex-colleagues. It will operate only if it is restricted to those he knew worked for the company, and perhaps only in relation to those he actually met.

All these clauses will fail if they are shown to be unreasonable, i.e. if they are broader than is necessary to protect the legitimate interests of the employer. The latter include trade secrets, know-how, pricing strategy and customer lists. The employee must have had access to such data for the protection to be necessary. The information must still be 'live', and so the period of employment to be covered may have to be stated, e.g. the last two years of employment, or the information must still be confidential. The period of restraint must also be covered, e.g. one year after the termination of employment. And all the provisos must be reasonable. The employer cannot prevent the employee using his skill, nor prevent competition as such. Only his legitimate interests can be protected.

One final example of this sort of clause in operation is *London & Solent and Carritt & Partners v. Brooks (1989)*.[10] The founders of a firm of Lloyd's marine underwriters entered into identical employment contracts providing for a one-year non-solicitation clause, a clause that prohibited dealing with the clients of the past two years and a prohibition of the use of confidential information. Brooks' five-year contract ended after two years. All the clauses were upheld by an interlocutory injunction, despite Brooks' claims that the employer was in breach; that the clauses were too wide, because in a small market clients would gravitate to the individual, so he would be unable to work in his specialism of the past 20 years; and that, in addition the ban would be contrary to public policy. The court held that the prohibition was reasonable, because it left him with the greater part of the market to exploit and the interests that were protected were legitimate ones.

Restraint clauses cease to apply if the employer wrongfully terminates the contract. In *Briggs v. Oates (1990)*[11] Oates was a salaried partner in a firm of solicitors. The EAT decided that he was in fact an employee. He had a five-year fixed-term contract. The senior partner terminated the partnership and set up on his own. It was held that Oates was employed by the partnership and had no contract with the senior partner. As his fixed-term contract had been broken when the partnership ended, the restraint clause in it could not be enforced. To overcome this, contracts often provide that the restraint shall apply however the contract may end. If the clause specifically mentions 'including breach by the employer', the clause will be unreasonable and void, as in *Living Design (Home Improvements) Ltd v. Davidson (1994)*.[12] If the term merely specifies 'howsoever the contract may end', there are conflicting cases. In *D v. M (1996)*[13] covenants in a contract were expressed to apply on termination 'for any reason whatsoever' and 'irrespective of the cause or manner of termination'. The contract terminated through the breach of the employer. The court held that 'a covenant drafted so as to take effect even where termination arises because of breach of contract by the employer is necessarily unreasonable.' They refused to sever the unreasonable part.

But a different decision was reached in *PR Consultants Scotland Ltd v. Mann (1996)*.[14] In this case Mann's contract with PR provided that for 12 months after 'termination howsoever caused' he would not seek employment, work on an account, etc. of any PR client with whom he had direct contact in the previous 12 months. The court decided that 'howsoever' caused' covered only lawful terminations and not termination caused by breach, and so was not too wide on that point. This has now been followed in *Rock Refrigeration v. Jones (1996)*.[15]

Agreements made between employers not to employ each other's ex-employees are treated in the same way, and individual employees can bring the matter before the courts.

If the covenant is too broad the employer can still rely on the implied duty of confidentiality (see Chapter 43).

Key points

- Identify protectable information.
- Specify how long information is to remain confidential.
- Define the geographical area, if appropriate.
- Change terms on transfer or promotion.
- Will you enforce it?
- Choose the most appropriate term.

References

1 IRLR 215 QBD.
2 IRLR 64 CA.
3 IRLR 84 CA.
4 *Milthorne Toleman v. Ford (1980)* IRLR 30 CA.
5 IRLR 214 CA.
6 IRLR 80 CA.
7 3 All ER 384 CA.
8 ICR 445.
9 Noted in *IDS Brief* 350.
10 CA, noted in *IDS Brief* 389 and IRLIB 373.
11 ICR 473 QB.
12 IRLR 69 CS(OH).
13 IRLR 192 IDS 559 ChD.
14 IRLR 188 IDS 564 CS(OH).
15 IRLR 675 CA.

45
Search

There is no implied right to search an employee, or indeed to search any other person, on or off the employer's premises. The only way an employer can obtain the right to search is to put an express clause in the contract. Even when there is a clause, great care must be taken in exercising the power. Excessive use of force will amount to assault and battery, and trespass to the person; if the individual is detained against his will, that will amount, in addition, to false imprisonment. All these are civil wrongs for which high damages can be obtained. A search clause should be included only were really necessary. Other methods of ensuring security may be more successful.

The right to search an employee

The company reserves the right to search the employee, his belongings and his vehicle at any time. The exercise of this right will be authorised by the departmental director.

When there is no right to search, the employer can still *ask* to search and, where circumstances justify it, refuse access to premises, or discipline the employee who refuses. This would apply during security alerts caused by bomb scares.

Care is essential when the right to search is being exercised. A witness should be present, and there should be no enforced search. A refusal should be used as grounds for discipline, not for an enforced search.

Key points

- Is the power necessary?
- When will it be used?
- Is there a procedure, ensuring witnesses and, where appropriate, a chaperone, etc.?

46
Recoupment of training and relocation costs

When the employer undertakes to provide training, either as part of the original contract or by a separate agreement at a later date, he will want to ensure that the employee completes the training successfully and will take steps to protect the organisation in the event of the employee failing to do so. Inevitably this entails express terms.

Failure to complete the course successfully, without just cause, could be made grounds for termination and, perhaps, for repayment of some of the cost. If the employee leaves soon after the completion of the training, depriving the employer of the full benefit of his investment, the employer may want to recoup some of his loss.

The employer may also provide a relocation package which meets some or all of the costs of relocation. It may cover estate agents' fees, legal fees, removal costs, a bridging loan, temporary accommodation, etc. It is frequently a discretionary benefit. Again, if the employee leaves shortly after relocation, some recoupment of the expenses may be sought by the employer.

The law on recoupment is unclear. One approach is to treat the terms as liquidated damages. These are sums of money identified by the parties to the contract in advance as the loss likely to arise on breach. If the sum is a genuine pre-estimate of the likely loss, the innocent party can claim that precise sum and does not have to prove his exact loss. But if the sum is too high it is not liquidated damages but a penalty: a sum held *in terrorem* over the head of the other party to force him to comply. Penalties are unenforceable, and the actual loss has to be proved. Where the sum is too high the recoupment would be a penalty and the employer would be able to recover only actual loss, which might be difficult to prove. For example, if an employee left three years after the completion of his training and his contract required him to repay the full training cost, that would be likely to be regarded as a penalty. The employer would have had three year's benefit of the training, and that would have to be taken into account.

Another approach is to see whether the clause is a restraint on future employment because, before he can work for anyone else, the employee will have to pay money to his current employer. Restraint clauses have to be shown to be reasonable, so the relationship of the sum to the actual loss is again relevant.

Recoupment terms for a trainee personnel officer

The company will pay your fees for the postgraduate diploma course in personnel management to be taken at the polytechnic, and allow you to take the necessary day release.

The fee for any year will be repaid by you should you fail to complete that year's course other than for ill health or other good cause.

Should you leave the company's employment without completing the year's study you will pay the part of the fee *pro rata* to the outstanding period of the year's course.

Recoupment terms for a junior manager

The organisation will agree to pay the cost of a two-year part-time MBA at the Business School and will permit you paid time off to attend the course and for study leave.

If you fail to complete the course other than for good cause you will be required to repay the course fees for that academic year. If the first year has already been completed you will repay in addition 25 per cent of the fees for the first year.

If you leave the employment of the organisation within one year of completion of the course you will repay 50 per cent of the course fees, and if you leave between one and two years after the completion of the course you will repay 25 per cent of the course fees.

In *Hubble v. Electronic Data Systems (1988)*[1] a computer company claimed back some of the training costs it had incurred in providing extensive training for a new employee. The court decided in a preliminary hearing that Hubble had an arguable defence to the employer's claim on both the above grounds. The employer appealed to the Lords, but the case was withdrawn, so no actual decision was reached. But at least the Court of Appeal did indicate that in its view a reasonable term would succeed. An earlier case had reached a similar conclusion. In *Strathclyde Regional Council v. Neil (1984)*[2] it was decided that the money was recoverable so long as the arrangement was reasonable. This is the rule on which most companies are basing their terms.

As a general rule it is better not to recoup all the cost, as some benefit must have been obtained by the employer. Also the percentage to be repaid should be smaller the longer the termination is from the training or relocation.

Any form of recoupment, whether by deduction, repayment or post-dated cheque, will fall within the ambit of s. 13 of the Employment Rights Act 1996. The employer needs to ensure that he has, firstly, the right to the precise sum involved; secondly, that the employee agreed to recoupment before the event causing the recoupment; thirdly, that the employee had been notified personally, in writing, of the term, and finally that he uses only the method of recoupment specified in the agreement.

Key points

- What is the training requirement?
- Will failure to complete the training result in the employee's dismissal?
- How long will it take the employer to benefit fully from the training?
- Set a repayment schedule which diminishes through time.
- Identify any relocation costs to be recouped.
- Produce a repayment schedule, as for training.
- Put all repayment provisions in writing.

References

1 CA, noted in IRLIB 348.
2 IRLR 11 Sheriff's Ct.

47

Retirement

The age of retirement is used for various purposes. It is the age at which employment will cease and also the age at which the right to claim unfair dismissal and redundancy is lost.

The contractual age is used for retirement. It may be defined in the contract itself or there may be an implied term. If there is no term at all, then either party may give notice to end the contract. Different retirement ages for men and women were removed under amendments introduced by the Sex Discrimination Act 1986. If an employer allows a member of one sex to retire at a later age than a member of the opposite sex in a comparable position, then the member of the disadvantaged sex can work to the later retirement age if he or she so wishes. This does not make different retirement ages unlawful, but it does render them unenforceable. So if the contract provides that women retire at 60 and men at 65, the women can choose to work to any age up to 65. It was not felt necessary to provide that men could retire at sixty, because anyone can retire early simply by giving notice and leaving. Pension entitlement is a separate issue, but some degree of equality in pensions has been introduced by *Barber* (Chapter 48).

Any unilateral attempt by the employer to change the contractual retirement age will constitute breach of contract. The amount of damages to be paid by the employer if he terminates the contract before the retirement date is unclear. The normal rule for assessing damages is to calculate the remuneration package for the period it would have taken to terminate the contract properly, i.e. any relevant procedure plus the period of notice. It has been argued, but not before a court, in an early retirement dismissal, that the period for compensation should be based on the period to retirement, unless dismissal was likely to occur earlier – for example, because of redundancy. In *McClelland v. Northern Ireland General Health Services Board (1957)*[1] it was decided that if a woman had been appointed until retirement it was possible to dismiss her earlier only for a reason specified in the contract or for breach. The case was a public-sector one, and the inability to dismiss may have been based on status.

The right to claim unfair dismissal is lost when the normal age of retirement is reached. The normal age of retirement was defined by the House of Lords as the age at which an employee in that particular group of employees would expect to be retired (*Waite v. Government Communications Headquarters (1983)²*). It may not be the contractual age, although that will be the starting point of any enquiry into the normal age of retirement. If the contractual age is 65, but in practice the employer retires staff at 60, then 60 will be the normal retirement age, even though enforced retirement at 60 is a breach of contract. So the employer may, for unfair dismissal or redundancy (below), alter the age by diktat. He may also decide the boundaries of the group. It is the normal age for the group which applies and not the agreed or expected age for the individual. This permits the employer to make special arrangements with some individuals, allowing them to retire earlier or later without destroying the normal age of retirement for the group. But these special agreements will not grant the individuals a different normal retirement age from the group. If the normal retirement age is 60 but an employee has a contractual agreement to work to 62 he will lose unfair dismissal and redundancy rights at the same age as the other members of his group – 60.

Specifying retirement age

Your retirement age is 65. You may continue in employment after your retirement age at the discretion of the company.

If there is no normal age of retirement, or there are different retirement ages for either sex, then, under the Sex Discrimination Act 1986, the fall-back age of 65 applies. There may be no normal age of retirement if employees are allowed to choose their retirement age, even if that choice has to be within a particular band. So if the employee may choose to retire at any age between 57 and 60 there is no normal retirement age and the fall-back age of 65 will apply.

Redundancy rights are lost at 65 or at the normal age of retirement if it is less than 65. Entitlement reduces during the employee's 64th year, reaching an entitlement of nil at the age of 65 (Employment Rights Act 1996). Whenever the age of retirement differs for the sexes the age of 65 will apply.

A clear retirement age, or band of ages, the same for both sexes, is needed and has practical advantages.

Key points

- Is there a contractual retirement age?
- Is there a normal age of retirement? Is it the same as the contractual one?
- Is the age the same for both sexes?

References

1 2 All ER 129 HL.
2 IRLR 341 HL.

48
Pensions

The written particulars must include information on pensions, and where the scheme is contracted out of the state scheme the employee must be informed of the contracting-out certificate.

It is no longer possible to make it compulsory for an employee to join the organisation's pension scheme. Employees may choose their own pension arrangements if they so wish.

Entitlement to a company pension is usually based on the contract and on the terms of the pension scheme itself. The terms of the scheme will normally be incorporated in the contract. The scheme will also define the way in which pensionable service is to be calculated.

Employers may change the pension scheme. The freedom to do so will be affected by the contract terms and the terms of the scheme itself. It may be possible to change one but not the other. Change outside the contract and scheme provisions will require the employee's consent. It must be properly informed consent if the change is to be effective (*BP v. Joseph (1980)*[1]). If the employee is wrongly advised of the implications of the change, it is the terms as advised to him that he is deemed to have accepted and not the real change. In the *BP* case Joseph had received incorrect advice on the new pension terms from his manager but had later obtained correct advice from the pension department. He chose to believe his manager. It was decided that, as the last advice was the correct advice, he could not rely on his manager's version. Had he not been so persistent, and had not approached the pension department, the decision would have been different.

Pension provision

You are eligible to join the organisation's pension scheme. The scheme is a non-contributory scheme, and full details of the scheme, which includes life insurance cover, are available from the Personnel Department. If you do not wish to participate in the scheme you must inform the Personnel Manager.

The organisation has contracted out of the state pension scheme and a contracting-out certificate is in force.

Changes in the scheme are often restricted to changes which will not place the employee in a 'worse position'. This type of term almost needs a health warning, since they are very difficult to interpret. Is the measurement to be a general one for all persons covered, so that a minority might be worse off? Must the scheme be looked at as a whole, including all the available benefits? Is it an item-by-item comparison? And what is 'worse off', anyway?

Pension provision is in a complete state of confusion as a result of EU law. In *Barber v. Guardian Royal Exchange Assurance Group (1990)*[2] the European Court decided that pensions were pay and so brought in equality for men and women as from 18 May 1990. In *Vroege v. Insituut voor Volkshuisvesting BV and Stichting Pensionenfonds NCIV (1994)*[3] the European Court decided that it was discriminatory to bar part-timers from access to pension schemes, but accepted that there could be a minimum hours requirement. If the scheme was a contributory one the employee would have to pay the contributions she would have made had she been a member of the scheme. Under the Occupational Pension Schemes (Equal Access to Membership) Amendment Regulations 1995 employers must now admit part-timers to pension schemes. Employers who fail to do so must meet the full cost of their failure without any contribution from the employee.

Future pension entitlement seems clear, but claims based on refusal of access before the Regulations changed the law are the subject of much litigation. Part-timer claims are being restricted by a strict application of the equal pay procedural rules. Claims must be brought within six months of the termination of employment, and compensation is restricted to two years' loss.

Provision for introducing equality into pension schemes was made in the Pensions Act 1995. s. 62 automatically incorporates an equality rule into every pension scheme and s. 65 gives trustees or managers the power to alter the scheme to comply with the equality rule.

Women on paid maternity leave accrue full pension rights but any contribution they are required to make is in proportion to the pay they receive. Persons on paid family leave also accrue pension rights, but in this case both accrual and contribution are in proportion to the pay received (Social Security Act 1989 s. 23 and Schedule 5).

Pension schemes containing beneficial terms of which the employee is unaware may need to be communicated to the employee (*Scally* above, pp. 22–3).

Key points

• Refer to the organisation in the written particulars.

- Ensure that the terms of the contract and of the scheme are identical.
- Comply with the Equality Rule.

References

1 IRLR 55 EAT.
2 IRLR 240 ECJ.
3 IRLR 651 ECJ.

49
Redundancy

Many organisations have a redundancy scheme of their own which is more generous than the state scheme. It may require a shorter service qualification and provide larger payments. Frequently such schemes have been negotiated with the unions. The key question in relation to redundancy schemes, whether they have been negotiated with the union or simply devised by the employer, is 'Are they in the contract?' If they are, then any adjustment to the scheme will require renegotiation of the contract in order to change the terms, and the employee can enforce his contractual rights even when he has no right to claim statutory redundancy benefit.

Where a collective agreement is incorporated only those parts which give rise to individual rights will be in the employment contract. They will include any procedure in relation to the individual, such as consultation with him, selection criteria and the benefits package. Although a redundancy dismissal is no longer automatically unfair if the employer has failed to follow an established redundancy procedure and can produce a good reason for departing from it[1] the employer is still bound contractually to follow any procedure which has been included in the contract. So if the contract incorporates collective agreements made with the union, and the redundancy procedure is in a collective agreement, then it is contractual.

It is not so easy to imply a redundancy term from a company policy even when it is has been applied consistently. In *Quinn v. Calder Industrial Materials Ltd (1996)*[2] the EAT refused to hold that a redundancy policy which had been applied on the occasions of the four redundancies occurring between 1987 and 1994 had become a contractual term. Policies will stand a chance of becoming terms only if they have been drawn to the attention of employees by management, or have been followed for a substantial period, and all the other circumstances of the case are taken into account. In this case the payment of the enhanced redundancy payment followed a decision to make the payment on each occasion.

The problems which can arise can be seen in *Alexander v. Standard Telephones & Cables* Nos. 1 and 2 (above, pp. 19–20), when an employee sought damages for selection in breach of the procedure which he alleged was written into his contract.

215

It must be questionable whether the redundancy agreement is suitable for incorporation into the contract. There is a tendency for the scheme to be devised with a particular event in mind. The criteria to be used next time and the money available for benefits may change. Organisations which chose to select on the basis of 'last in, first out' (LIFO) and put this in the contract could find themselves in a difficult position if they wish to move to selection on the basis of the skills and criteria possessed by the staff to be retained. The move to selection for retention rather than selection for dismissal is much in favour at the moment. Obviously any

---

Redundancy term

Should it be necessary to declare staff redundant the company will follow the principles set out in the redundancy policy, copies of which are available in the Personnel Manager's office.

Redundancy policy (not in the contract)

It is the policy of the company, should a redundancy situation arise, to seek to retain those staff with the skills and experience necessary to enable the company to remain profitable.

Selection for redundancy will be based on the skills and experience required, performance, work record, reliability, conduct, appraisals, health and attendance. If these criteria are insufficient to produce the required number to be made redundant, seniority and length of service will be taken into account.

---

redundancy scheme should not be devised just for the single occasion but should be suitable for use in the future. If the term is to be contractual it must be flexible, possibly with a discretionary element in the benefits package itself.

Finally, discrimination must be avoided. *Barber* also applies to redundancy benefits. These must be equal for men and women. There will also be discrimination if part-timers are excluded.

Redundancy is dealt with in greater detail in the companion volume *Redundancy* in this series.

Key points

- Should the scheme be in the contract?

- Are the selection criteria broad enough to provide flexibility?
- Is there a discretionary element in the package?

References

1 This provision in the Employment Protection (Consolidation) Act 1978 s. 159 was repealed by the Deregulation Act 1995.
2 IRLR 126 EAT.

50
Discipline and grievance procedures

In *WA Goold (Pearmark) Ltd v. McConnell (1995)*[1] it was decided that it was an implied term in every contract that the employee should be provided with a grievance procedure. Their decision was based on the fact that Parliament considered the procedure so important that they require its inclusion in written particulars.[2] The same would apply to disciplinary procedures.[3] The EAT did not decide that the procedure provided had to be contractual, but merely that there was a duty to provide these procedures. Procedures must be provided for all staff with one month's service regardless of hours worked. If the contract is for a short period or is subject to a probationary period it may be necessary to adjust the procedure so that it can be completed within the time of the contract. Although employees with less than two years' service cannot claim unfair dismissal if they have not been provided with a procedure, they can bring a breach of contract claim.

The facts of *Goold* were that the new MD had introduced a new pay system for sales staff, which reduced their pay. They raised it with the MD, who said he would look into it but not in the immediate future. When they sought to bring their grievance to the chairman they had to make an appointment through the MD, who said it was for him to decide, not the chairman. So they resigned and successfully claimed unfair dismissal because there was no grievance procedure.

If they are incorporated into the contract, any failure to follow the procedure will be a breach of contract. In *Elder v. Clydesdale Co-operative Society (1988)*[4] the EAT returned a case to the tribunal for it to decide whether a grievance procedure had been incorporated into the contract. Mrs Elder had wanted to raise a grievance relating to her employer's decision to select her, rather than employees with less service, for transfer to another site, but she had not been allowed to use the grievance procedure. So she left, claiming that she had been constructively dismissed. The EAT told the tribunal to decide whether the grievance procedure was in the contract. If it was, then refusing to let her follow the procedure should result in constructive dismissal.

If the disciplinary procedure is incorporated in the contract then all employees, regardless of length of continuity of employment, will be able to bring a breach of contract claim if the procedure has not been followed. They may now bring such claims before the tribunal, which can award up to £25,000 damages. Although this can be seen as allowing the employee with less than two years' continuity a claim akin to unfair dismissal, it is not an unfair dismissal but a breach of contract claim. Damages are calculated as for breach of contract and not as for unfair dismissal. In *Boyo v. London Borough of Lambeth (1995)*[5] the council had incorporated the disciplinary procedure in the employment contract. They failed to follow the procedure when terminating Boyo's contract. This was breach of contract, allowing the employee to claim damages. Damages for breach of contract consist of the contractual remuneration package for the period of notice and for the period of time it would have taken to terminate the contract in accordance with the procedure. He would not have been able to claim compensation for the period he was without work, or for any future loss.

One further disadvantage to the employer is that, once incorporated, the procedure is difficult to change. From the employee's angle an incorporated procedure is definitely desirable.

Disciplinary procedure

The details of the disciplinary procedure will be found in such staff handbooks as may be issued from time to time.

A procedure which is in a collective agreement and restricts the right to strike is not incorporated in the contract unless the provisions of section 180 of the Trade Union and Labour Relations (Consolidation) Act 1992 are complied with. This means that the collective agreement must:

- be in writing
- expressly provide for incorporation into the employment contract
- be reasonably accessible at the place of work
- available for reading during working hours
- actually incorporated in the contract.

Further information on disciplinary procedures will be found in the companion volume in this series on *Discipline*.

Key points

- Have these procedures been supplied?

- Should the procedure be incorporated?
- Has the employer power to update the procedure?

Reference

1 IRLR 516 EAT.
2 Employment Rights Act 1996 s. 3 (1)(b)(ii).
3 S. 3(1)(a) and (b)(i).
4 EAT, noted in *IDS Brief* 366.
5 IRLR 50 (1994) 530 *IDS Brief* CA.

51
Other policies and procedures

Generally these are not appropriate for inclusion in the contract. It is the duty and the responsibility of management to ensure that policies and procedures are adequate. If the health and safety policy is inadequate, or does not exist, then the employer and the manager concerned are committing a criminal offence (Health and Safety at Work Act 1974). Failure to follow a proper equality policy can result in breach of the sex and race discrimination provisions. So management must be free to change policies and procedures. If these are outside the contract they are still not totally devoid of legal effect. They take the form of lawful instructions, and appropriate disciplinary action can be taken against employees who do not follow them.

However, if they are included in the contract, that will make it more difficult to change the terms if they prove inadequate. If they are included there must be power to change the terms, perhaps by referring to 'policies issued from time to time'.

Other policies and procedures

You are required to comply with policies and procedures issued by the company from time to time.

This does not mean that unions and employees have no role to play. It must be obvious that they should be consulted in the formulation of any policy and procedure if the operation of that policy or procedure is to be smooth.

Key points

- Is it appropriate to include the procedure or policy?
- Would general flexible incorporation do?

52
Notice

The Employment Rights Act 1996 s. 1 requires the employer to inform the employee of the period of notice that both he and the employer must give to terminate the contract.

Fixed-term and task contracts do not need to contain notice clauses because they end automatically when the termination date arrives or the event occurs. However, if the contract is to be terminable prior to that date or event, then a notice clause is needed. One will not be implied. It must be express.

On the other hand, if the contract is of indefinite duration, then it must contain a term relating to notice, otherwise it would be impossible to end it except for serious breach. There may be an express notice term in the contract. If there is no express term, it is implied that the contract may be terminated by reasonable notice. Ultimately this will be determined by the judge. It has been decided that a cinema controller (*Adams v. Union Cinemas (1939)*[1]) and a colour photographer working on Picture Post (*Bauman v. Hulton Press (1952)*[2]) were both entitled to six months' notice, an estate agency manager (*Mullholland v. Bexwell Estates (1950)*[3]) to three months', a senior clerical worker (*Phillips v. M. J. Alkam*[4]) to one month's and a chorus girl (*Thomas v. Gatti*[5]) to two weeks'.

The contractual period, express or implied, must then be compared with the statutory minima set out in the Employment Rights Act 1996, s. 86. These are based on the employee's continuity of employment as follows:

- Four weeks' continuity up to two years: one week's notice.
- Two years' to 12 years' continuity: one week's notice for each year of continuity of employment.
- The maximum period is 12 weeks.

The minimum period to be given by employees is one week's notice after they have completed four weeks' continuity of employment.

No notice need be given if the other party is in serious breach of contract, and the parties are free to agree to accept lesser notice or wages in lieu in the actual event of dismissal. It is regularly assumed that the employer can substitute wages in lieu for the period of notice. He has no legal right to do so unless the contract provides for it: what has been promised is a period of time, not a sum of money. However, if the employee is offered the wages in lieu and refuses them it will not usually be worth the employee's while to bring a legal action. The employer is in breach, but so long as he has offered the employee the sum which the court would have awarded as damages the latter will get no more money from the court and could end up paying the employer's costs. Damages would be based on the employee's remuneration package for the period of notice and would be assessed net of tax for the first £30,000, and grossed up to include tax for any sum in excess of £30,000. However, many employers pay wages in lieu gross.

Provision for giving notice

In a manager's contract

Either party may terminate the contract by giving the other ninety calendar days' written notice.

Upon termination the employee will promptly return to the company any company property or any property belonging to any third party held by the employee on behalf of the company, including equipment, papers, disks, computer programs and copies of the same.

In a shop assistant's contract

During your first four years of employment you will be entitled to four weeks' notice. After four years' employment you will be entitled to one further week's notice for each year of continuous employment, up to a maximum of 12 weeks' notice after 12 years' service.

You are required to give four weeks' notice.

Notice must be in writing and notice given to the company must be handed to the store manager.

Under contract law the employee can insist on notice rather than wages in lieu unless the employee has acted in a way that makes this impossible, but again it is rarely worth his while to do so. But where a valuable contractual right might accrue during the period of notice, such as the right to an early pension, it may be worth taking notice instead and forgoing any possible tax advantage which might accompany wages in lieu. But the courts have decided that, although the employee may contractually continue his employment, he cannot extend his statutory continuity of employment in this way. The effective date of termination will remain the date the employer said the contract ended.

If the contract provides for the payment of wages in lieu at the option of the employer, the money is subject to PAYE, because it is paid as a result of a contract term.

Because wages in lieu are damages, they are subject to the duty to mitigate. So an employee with one year's notice may not be entitled to one year's wages in lieu if he could obtain suitable gainful employment during that period. The longer the period of notice the less likely the employee will receive damages or wages in lieu for the full period, unless of course the employer decides to pay the full amount. This reduction was avoided in *Abrahams v. Performing Rights Society (1995)*[6]. Abrahams had originally been given a five-year fixed-term contract with the Society. This provided that if at any time during the last two years of the contract the Society terminated his contract, or at the end of his five-year period, he would be entitled to two years' notice or an equivalent payment in lieu. At the end of his five-year period he agreed to remain in post for a further two years 'under the terms of his existing contract'. It was held that this included the wages in lieu term. The CA then went on to hold that the claim for two years' wages in lieu was not a general claim for unliquidated damages. The parties had fixed a sum to be paid under the contract. Abrahams was entitled to that sum and he was not required to mitigate his loss or give credit for actual earnings. Even if the claim were for liquidated damages there would be no duty to mitigate, Employees seeking the security of a guaranteed payment on termination should bear this in mind.

For the sake of certainty it may be worth requiring the notice to be in writing and specifying the person to whom it should be given.

There is a curious provision in the Employment Rights Act s. 87(4). This provides that during the period of notice the employee who is not entitled to all or part of his wages because he is off sick, or because there is no work, or because he is on holiday, is entitled to the current wage for the job for the period of notice. Any sick pay, etc., paid by the employer is taken into account. The curiosity is that this does not apply if the notice which the employer must give the employee under the contract exceeds the statutory period by one week or more. It is difficult to understand why such employees should not also benefit for a period equivalent to the mimimum period of notice.

Key points

- Is a notice clause needed in fixed-term and task contracts?
- Insert an express term into all other contacts.
- Check the express term against the statutory minimum term.
- Consider requiring notice to be given in writing to a particular person.

References

1 3 All ER 136 CA.
2 2 All ER 1121 QB.
3 94 *Sol. Jo*. 671 KB.
4 1969; case unreported.
5 *Times*, 22 June 1906, KB.
6 IRLR 486 CA.

53
Miscellaneous terms

The list of possible terms covered in Part III is by no means complete and there are some obvious omissions: mortgage subsidies, luncheon vouchers, loans, insurance and other fringe benefits have not been considered. There are also special allowances and care provisions for children and dependants, and time off to participate in sporting events. But a line has to be drawn somewhere, and the approach in dealing with these clauses hardly varies from the approach used in other terms. The benefit has to be clearly defined, those entitled to it identified, there must be a check for possible discrimination, and it must be decided whether the benefit should be discretionary. But, to finish, there are three miscellaneous terms which deserve consideration.

The conflicting terms provision

Where there is more than one document the prospect of a conflict between their terms arises. This can be avoided by stating which one is to prevail, e.g. 'If there is any conflict between the terms set out in your offer letter and the terms in this document, the terms in your offer letter and any later agreements relating thereto shall prevail.'

The superseding provision

This is used where there may be an earlier agreement between the parties. It makes certain that the new terms override the old agreement. Example: 'This agreement shall supersede all previous agreements and arrangements between the parties.'

The law of the contract

The Enforcement of Foreign Judgements Convention, introduced into the law of the United Kingdom in 1990, changes some of the rules for deciding which law is to govern a contract if more than one country is involved. It is now better to make a choice of the law governing the

contract, especially if there is a possibility that the contract may be performed abroad. The choice should have a connection with the contract,
the place of performance or the parties. Example: 'This contract shall be
subject to English law.' However, it is not possible to guarantee that the
jurisdiction chosen will be applied by the courts. In *Mulox IBC Ltd v.
Geels (1994)*[1] Geels' contract specified English law. The employer was
English, Geels Dutch but living in France and using his home as a base
from which he travelled all over Europe. Under the Convention claims
can be brought in another state if that is the place for performance. In
employment cases this will be based on the employee's residence and
where he carries out his duties. The Court concluded that this was
France, and so French law applied.

Reference

1 IRLR 222 ECJ.

Appendix
Examples of contracts

Manager

The parties to this contract are ....
..................................of ....
.... and ....
.... of...

This contract supersedes any other contract or arrangement which may have been entered into by the parties.

Definitions

(a) The *employer* ....,
hereinafter referred to as the company.
(b) The *board*, the board of directors of the company.
(c) The *chairman*, the chairman of the board of directors of the company.

1 Position

1.1 The employee is appointed to the position of Deputy Marketing Director

1.2 As Deputy Marketing Director he will undertake such duties as the board or the chairman may determine from time to time.

2 Period

2.1 The contract will last for a period of three years from 1 January 1996. That date will also be the date from which continuity of employment for statutory rights will be calculated.

2.2 During that period either party may terminate the contract without notice if the other party is in serious breach of the contract.

2.3 The first six months of the contract will be a period of probation. The position will be reviewed on or before that date. If the board are satisfied with the performance of the employee he will be confirmed in his position.

2.4 The company may terminate the contract without notice if the employee is in serious breach of contract. This includes but is not restricted to:

2.4.1 Any material dishonesty, gross misconduct or neglect of duty.

2.4.2 Deliberate failure to follow the company's policies and procedures.

2.4.3 Breach of the duty of fidelity.

2.4.4 Any conduct likely to bring the employee or the company into disrepute, including any conduct which renders him unsuitable to perform the duties of a Deputy Marketing Director.

2.5 The company may also terminate the contract without notice if the employee:

2.5.1 Is made the subject of a bankruptcy order or of an application for an interim order under section 253 of the Insolvency Act 1986 or has an interim receiver of his property appointed under section 288 of the said Act or enters into any voluntary arrangement or composition with his creditors.

2.5.2 Is incapacitated by ill health or accident from performing his duties under the contract for a period of six months or periods aggregating 180 days in the preceding twelve months.

2.5.3 Is rendered permanently incapable of performing his duties or is unlikely to be able to perform them in the foreseeable future.

2.5.4 Has become of unsound mind or is admitted to hospital in pursuance of an application for admission for treatment under the Mental Health Act 1983 or if an order is made by a court having jurisdiction (whether in the United Kingdom or elsewhere) in matters concerning mental disorder for his detention or the appointment of a receiver or *curator bonis* or other person to exercise powers in respect of his property or affairs.

2.6 The provisions set out in 2.5 shall not affect any right which the company may have to terminate the contract with notice.

2.7 The employee agrees to the exclusion of any rights relating to unfair dismissal or redundancy which may arise upon the expiry of this contract.

3 *Salary*

3.1 The employee will be paid a salary of £25,000 per year in twelve equal monthly instalments. The salary will normally be reviewed every twelve months.

3.2 Payment will be made on the last Friday of each month into a bank account or building society account nominated by the employee.

3.3 The company may deduct from the employee's salary or require payment from the employee for any of the following:

    3.3.1 Loans.

    3.3.2 Any money due from the employee to the company.

    3.3.3 Excess of holiday pay over entitlement.

    3.3.4 Excess of sick pay over entitlement.

    3.3.5 Excess of expenditure claimed.

    3.3.6 Excess of any other payment made to the employee by the company.

    3.3.7 Any money requested in writing by the employee to be deducted.

3.4 Should there be any underpayment of wages the company will adjust the next available wage payment by the amount of the underpayment, unless prior payment has been made.

3.5 Should there for any reason be any overpayment of the wages the company reserves the right to adjust future wage payments until the overpayment has been recovered and/or to require repayment.

4 *Hours*

4.1 The normal hours of work are 9.00 a.m. to 5.00 p.m. Monday to Friday, inclusive of an hour each day for lunch. But different hours may be worked with the agreement of the chairman.

4.2 In addition the employee will be required to work such further hours as are needed to fulfil the requirements of his position as Deputy Marketing Director.

5 *Location*

5.1 The employee will work at the offices of the company at
....
or such other office of the company as may be designated by the board from time to time wheresoever those offices may be situated.

5.2 With the permission of the chairman of the board the employee may, when appropriate, be authorised to work from home.

5.3 The employee may be required to work on any other site of the company or on that of any other party on a temporary basis.

5.4 The employee may be required to travel both within the UK and outside the UK for the purpose of his work.

6 *Paid holidays*

6.1 The holiday year runs from 1 January to 31 December.
6.2 The employee will be entitled to thirty working days' paid holiday in each year of employment and *pro rata* in an incomplete year.
6.3 The holidays must be taken at a time to be agreed with the chairman. Permission will not normally be given for more than ten consecutive working days' holiday to be taken at any one time.
6.4 Holiday entitlement not used in one year may not be held over into the following year except with the written consent of the chairman.
6.5 The employee will be entitled to paid statutory holidays.
6.6 Upon termination of employment other than by expiry of the contract the employee shall be entitled to accrued holiday pay.

7 *Sick and injury pay*

7.1 The employee will be entitled to 180 working days' sick pay in any rolling period of twelve months.
7.2 Receipt of sick pay does not affect any right which the company may have to dismiss on grounds of ill health.
7.3 If the employee qualifies for statutory sick pay or state sickness benefit or any other payment for sickness or injury which may be provided by the state, an equivalent sum will be deducted from any sickness payment made by the company.
7.4 The employee is required to comply with any reporting requirements and procedures which the company may issue from time to time. Failure to do so will affect entitlement to sick pay.
7.5 The company reserves the right to consult the employee's doctor with the employee's consent and/or to require the employee to be examined by a medical practitioner of the company's choice. All costs occasioned by such a requirement will be met by the company.
7.6 The company may at its discretion provide private medical insurance and permanent health insurance. These benefits may be changed or withdrawn by the company on 30 days' written notice.

8 *Pension*

The employee is entitled to participate in the company's non-contributory pension scheme, details of which are available from the Personnel Department. This scheme is contracted out of the earnings-related section of the state pension scheme. If the employee chooses not to participate in the company's scheme a sum equivalent to 5 per cent of gross basic salary will be paid into a pension scheme nominated by the employee.

9 *Compassionate leave*

Compassionate leave, which may be with pay, is granted at the discretion of the company. A request should be made to the chairman.

10 *Intellectual property*

10.1 Patent or design rights arising from work the employee is employed to undertake for the company or expected to arise from such work shall belong to the company.

10.2 The copyright in any material relating to or arising from this employment rests with the company.

11 *Expenses*

11.1 The company will reimburse authorised expenses properly incurred in the course of employment.

11.2 Payment will be made only against receipts or other proof of expenditure.

12 *Notice*

12.1 Either party may terminate the contract by giving the other ninety calendar days' written notice.

12.2 Upon termination the employee will promptly return to the company any company property or any property belonging to any third party held by the employee on behalf of the company, including but not limited to equipment, papers, disks, computer programs and all copies of the same.

13 *Confidentiality and conflict of interest*

13.1 The employee will not disclose, either during or after the termination of his employment, any information of a confidential nature relating to the company, its customers or suppliers or any third party which may have been obtained in the course of this employment without first obtaining the written permission of the company or the party concerned.

13.2 The employee will not make any public statement or any statement to a person employed by or associated with the media concerning the company, its suppliers or customers or their activiites without first obtaining the written consent of the Director of Marketing or a member of the board.

13.3 The employee will not place himself in a position in which his interest conflicts with that of the company.

13.4 The employee will declare the ownership of any shares or interests in any business in competition with the company held by the employee or the employee's spouse or children under the age of eighteen. The employee will take such steps as may be notified to him or her by the company to ensure that there is no conflict of interest.

14 *Working for other organisations*

The employee will not, during this employment, work for any other organisation without obtaining the written consent of the chairman. Such consent will not be unreasonably withheld.

15 *Restrictions*

15.1 For a period of two years following the termination of the employment, howsoever that employment may end, the employee will not directly or indirectly on his or her own behalf or on behalf of any other organisation, business or person solicit any organisation, company, business or person who was a customer of the company in the three years prior to the termination of the employment.

15.2 For a period of two years following the termination of this employment, howsoever that employment may end, the employee will not directly or indirectly on his or her own behalf or on behalf of any other organisation, business or person deal with any organisation, company, business or person who was a customer of the company in the three years prior to the termination of the employment.

15.3 The employee shall not for a period of twelve months after the termination of his employment directly or indirectly on his own behalf or on behalf of any third party induce, solicit, or endeavour to entice away any employee with whom he had direct contact in the twelve months prior to the termination of his contract.

15.4 Each of the restrictions in this clause 15 shall be a separate covenant.

16 *Policies*

The employee is required to comply with any policies which the company may issue from time to time. These will be found in the company handbooks which may be issued from time to time.

17 *Further details*

Further details of the contract may be found in any staff handbook which may be issued from time to time, with which the employee should make him or herself familiar. Should there be any conflict between the provisions of this agreement and those in any staff handbook the provisions of this agreement and any variation thereto will prevail.

18 *Variation*

The company reserves the right to change any of these terms but will not do so without first consulting the employee.

19 *Interpretation*

The headings of these paragraphs do not form part of the contract and shall not be used to interpret the contract.

20 *Replacement*

This contract supersedes any agreement or arrangement which may have been made between the parties.

21 *Law of the contract*

The contract shall be subject to English law.

Signed by .... on behalf of the company.
Date ....

Signed by the employee ....
Date ....

Production worker

This contract is entered into between .... (the company) of .... and .... (the employee) of ....
....

    Employment will commence on .... The date of commencement of continuity of employment is ....

1 *Job title*

Production operative.

2 *Remuneration*

(a) Your pay is £x per year. Your pay will be such as may be agreed from time to time with the trade union. You will be notified of any changes on your pay slip.

(b) Payment will be made monthly in arrears on the last Wednesday of the month. Payment will be made directly into a bank account or building society account nominated by you.

(c) Premium payments will be made of time and a half for shift work and time and three-quarters for authorised overtime. Further details of these payments will be found in the substantive agreement with the trade union.

(d) The company reserves the right to make deductions from your wages or to require you to repay money to the company in relation to:

    (i)   Loans made to you by the company.
    (ii) Any money due to the company from you.
    (iii) Excess of holiday pay over entitlement.
    (iv) Excess of sick pay over entitlement.
    (v)   Excess of expenses claimed by you.
    (vi) Excess of any other payment made to you by the company.
    (vii) Any money requested by you in writing to be deducted.

(e) If there is for any reason an overpayment of your wages the company reserves the right to make deductions from your future wages or to require you to repay the overpayment. If your wages have been underpaid the company, once notified, will adjust your wage payment accordingly.

3 *Place of work*

Your place of work is ....
.... the company may require you to work at any other site within
....

4 *Normal hours of work*

(a) Your normal hours of work will be those of the location at which you are working. The hours for the location at which you are initially working are ....

(b) You may be required to work shifts.

(c) You may also be required to work overtime.

5 *Holidays*

(a) You are entitled to .... working days' paid leave per year. You are also entitled to statutory bank holidays.
(b) In an incomplete year of service you will be entitled to paid leave in proportion to your period of service. If you leave the employment of the company you will be entitled to accrued holiday pay in respect of any outstanding holiday entitlement.

6 *Sickness and injury benefit*

The company operates a sickness and injury benefit scheme, details of which are set out in the handbook.

7 *Pension*

You are eligible to join the company pension scheme. This scheme is contracted out of the earnings-related part of the state pension scheme. Details of the scheme can be obtained from ....

8 *Confidential information*

You shall not disclose, either during or after the termination of your employment, any information of a confidential nature referring to the company, its customers or suppliers or any third party which you may have obtained in the course of your employment without first obtaining the written permission of the company or the party concerned.

9 *Notice*

Either the company or you may terminate the contract by giving the following periods of written notice:

(a) Up to two years' continuous service: one week.
(b) Two years' to twelve years' service: one week for each year of continuity of employment up to a maximum of twelve weeks.
(c) Thereafter the period of notice shall be twelve weeks.

10 *Handbook*

The handbooks contain further terms and conditions of employment. Handbooks are issued from time to time, and any reference to a handbook refers to the latest issued handbook. If there is a conflict between the terms of this contract and any variation made to it and the terms in the handbook then the terms of this contract shall prevail.

11 *Union agreements*

Your employment is subject to such collective agreements as the company may enter into from time to time with the trade union.

12 *Cancellation*

This contract cancels any other contract or arrangement which the company may have entered into with you.

13 *Law of the contract*

This contract shall be subject to the law of Scotland.

Signed

....
            For the company   *Employee*

Date ....   Date ....

Clerical worker

The Company of ....
agrees to employ .... of ....
as a Senior Clerk.

1 *Commencement*

The employment will commence on ....
Continuity of employment will commence on the same date.
This contract replaces any earlier contract which the parties may have made.

2 *Salary*

You will be paid £x per annum four weekly in arrears. Payment will be made into a bank or building society account nominated by you.

The Company reserves the right to make deductions from your salary or to require you to make a payment to the Company in any of the following circumstances:

> loans made to you
> any monies due to the Company from you
> when you have received more holiday or sick pay than your entitlement

when your salary or expenses or any other payment to you from the Company has been overpaid

whenever you have requested in writing that the Company should make a deduction or be entitled to a repayment.

3 *Hours of work*

You will be required to work such hours as are necessary for the fulfilment of your duties. Normal hours of work are 9.30 a.m. to 5.00 p.m. with one hour for lunch.

4 *Place of work*

You will work in the Headquarters building in High Holborn. You may be transferred on a permanent or temporary basis to any other establishment within the boundaries of the M25.

5 *Holidays*

The Company's holiday year is from 1 March to 28 (29) February. You are entitled to twenty working days paid holiday per year. The timing of your holiday must be agreed with your manager. For each incomplete year of service you will be entitled to 1.66 days holiday for each completed month of service. On termination of employment you will be entitled to pay for any outstanding accrued holiday. Should you be dismissed for just cause or terminate your employment in breach of contract you will forfeit your entitlement to accrued holiday pay.

You will also be entitled to statutory holidays.

6 *Absence sickness and injury*

Whenever you are unable to attend work you must inform your manager by 11.00 a.m. You will be required to complete an absence form after three days absence and complete an absence form on your return to work. After seven days absence due to ill health you will be required to produce a doctor's certificate.

Once you have completed six months' employment you will be entitled to paid sick leave for a period of thirteen weeks in any one period of twelve months.

Any benefits due to you from the State as a result of your ill health will be deducted from your wages. If you are a married woman who has elected to pay reduced National Insurance contributions deductions will be equal to the sum you would have received but for your election.

The Company participates in a permanent health insurance scheme. Subject to your meeting any eligibility requirements imposed by the insurers this will apply to you after the completion of six months' service. This benefit is discretionary and may be varied or withdrawn at any time on 30 days' written notice.

7 *Retirement age*

The Company retirement age is sixty-five.

8 *Pension*

You are contracted into the state pension scheme.

9 *Confidentiality*

You may not disclose to any person nor use for your own benefit any information of a confidential nature which you may obtain in the course of your employment about the Company, the Group or third parties without first obtaining the written consent of the Company or the party concerned.

You may not make any statement to the media and any request for information from the media should be referred to your manager.

10 *Notice*

During the first six months of this contract either party may terminate the contract by giving two weeks notice in writing. After six months' service the period of notice to be given by either party will be one calendar month. This period will increase to two months after six years' service and three months after ten years' service.

11 *Policies and procedures*

You must comply with any policies and procedures which the Company may issue.

12 *Other terms and conditions*

More details on these terms and conditions and additional terms will be found in the Company Handbook which the Company may issue from time to time. Reference should always be made to the latest Handbook. Copies of the Handbook are kept in the Personnel department and in your manager's office, where you may consult them.

13 *Law*

This contract will be governed by the Law of England.

Signed by and on behalf of the Company ....

Date ....

Signed by ....

Date ....

List of cases

241

List of statutes and regulations

Regulations